"Herbert Bateman's latest contribution on the book of Hebrews is truly excellent. I appreciate the effort he put into it. Anyone willing to dig into the treasures of this book of charts will not be disappointed."
—David Alan Black, Professor of New Testament and Greek,
Southeastern Baptist Theological Seminary

"Professor Bateman has managed to distill and organize an astonishing variety of perspectives, problems, and data into charts that provide almost immediate visual access to a wide range of issues and problems that must be faced by all interpreters of Hebrews. His survey of contemporary views provides a judicious cross section of English scholarship on contested areas of Hebrews. The perennial questions of authorship, manuscript support, canon, background, structure, Old Testament citations, and much more are well represented. The range, reliability, and clarity of the charts will make this a gold mine for both beginning and advanced students of this challenging but vital New Testament discourse."

—Jon Laansma,
Associate Professor of Ancient Languages and New Testament,
Wheaton College

"Contemporary commentaries and monographs offer rich help for navigating the book, but most students find digging for their treasures overwhelming. Bateman has pulled together a phenomenal amount of useful information in a way that is clear and easily accessible. What a helpful, substantive resource! This will be a standard tool in my classes on Hebrews from this point on."
George H. Guthrie,
Benjamin W. Perry Professor of Bible,
Union University

This will be a godsend to students and pastors working their way through this sometimes enigmatic book. The charts deal with all of the obvious questions and many not so obvious ones. The charts are clear, thorough, and easy to use. Anyone who is studying this wonderful book of the New Testament will find these charts exceptionally helpful."

Samuel Lamerson,
Professor of New Testament,
Knox Seminary

"This is one of those now-why-didn't-I-think-of-that books! Herb Bateman is eminently qualified to write on Hebrews. This collection of charts arranges in easy format information ranging from background, genre and structure, canonicity, influences from second temple Judaism, theological themes, and crucial exegetical issues. Laymen, students, pastors, and scholars will constantly refer to this work whenever they read, study, teach, or preach Hebrews. An indispensable resource."

—David L. Allen,
Dean, School of Theology,
Southwestern Baptist Theological Seminary

KREGEL
CHARTS OF THE
BIBLE

Charts on the
Book of Hebrews

Herbert W. Bateman IV

Kregel
Academic

Charts on the Book of Hebrews

© 2012 by Herbert W. Bateman IV

Published by Kregel Publications, a division of Kregel, Inc., P.O. Box 2607, Grand Rapids, MI 49501.

The Greek font GraecaU and the Hebrew font NewJerusalemCU are both available from www.linguistsoftware.com/lgku.htm, +1-425-775-1130

The drawing of the tabernacle used in chart 35 is from the *Kregel Bible Atlas* and is used by permission.

Library of Congress Cataloging-in-Publication Data
Bateman, Herbert W., 1955-
    Charts on the Book of Hebrews / Herbert W. Bateman IV.
      p. cm
  1. Bible. N.T. Hebrews—Charts, diagrams, etc. 2. Bible. N.T. Hebrews—Criticism, interpretation, etc.—Miscellanea. I. Title.
    BS2775.55.B38 2012
    227'.8700223—dc23
                                                    2012036244

ISBN 978–0–8254–2466–3

Printed in the United States of America
12 13 14 15 16 / 5 4 3 2 1

Contents

PART ONE: INTRODUCTORY CONSIDERATIONS IN HEBREWS

Authorship of Hebrews

Destination, Recipients, and Dating of Hebrews

Genre and Structure of Hebrews

PART 2: OLD TESTAMENT AND SECOND TEMPLE INFLUENCES IN HEBREWS

PART 3: THEOLOGY IN HEBREWS

The Godhead in Hebrews

Theological Themes in Hebrews

Words of Exhortation in Hebrews

PART 4: EXEGETICAL MATTERS IN HEBREWS

Interpretive Issues in Hebrews

Text Critical Issues in Hebrews

Figures of Speech in Hebrews

Important Words in Hebrews

Preface

Charts on the Book of Hebrews provides information about Hebrews succinctly in visual format for today's student and congregant. It is very user-friendly so that the charts may be used as both a foundational tool for study as well as a visual pedagogical and preaching tool. Ultimately it will benefit pastors, teachers, students and anyone wanting to study as well as teach the Book of Hebrews. Naturally, I am greatly thankful for the "great cloud of scholars," who went before me and presented most of this charted material in commentary format. People like David Allen, Harold W. Attridge, F. F. Bruce, Gareth L. Cockerill, Paul Ellingworth, George H. Guthrie, Donald A. Hagner, Luke Timothy Johnson, Simon K. Kistemaker, Craig R. Koester, William L. Lane, Peter T. O'Brien, and many others who published the books from which this set of charts has emerged. In essence, this work is built upon their faithful study of and publications on the book of Hebrews.

I am also indebted to my very dear friends at Morgan Library in Winona Lake, Indiana. For three consecutive summers, Bill Darr (director), Rhoda Palmer, Jody Hopper, and Steve Robbins extended library privileges and provided valuable assistance that enabled my tracking the information needed to complete this project. In addition to the Morgan Library staff, I am grateful to three graduate assistants who helped me in various ways and at numerous times: Phillip Andrew Davis Jr., Charles T. Martin Jr., and Patricia Jean Schwerdtfeger. In fact, Charles Martin and Patricia Schwerdtfeger contributed a few charts of their own to this collection.

I am, however, most indebted to Jim Weaver, the former Director of Academic Books for Kregel Publications. Our relationship spans fifteen years. It was in 1995, while Jim was working at Baker Books, that I first approached him about publishing my dissertation and later a book on dispensationalism. He turned me down for both since Baker did not publish those types of works. Yet, he provided extremely helpful advice that eventually led to the publication of *Early Jewish Hermeneutics and Hebrews 1:5-13* (Lang, 1997) and *Three Central Issues in Contemporary Dispensationalism* (Kregel, 1999). After leaving Baker, Jim meandered his way over to Kregel Publications, which has led to my ever-growing relationship with him. Moving beyond the fact that he has been instrumental in the publication of *Four Views on the Warning Passages in Hebrews* (Kregel, 2007), *A Workbook for Intermediate Greek: Grammar, Exegesis, and Commentary on 1-3 John* (Kregel, 2008), *Jesus the Messiah: Tracing the Promises, Expectation, and Coming of Israel's King* (Kregel, 2012), and now *Charts on the Book of Hebrews*, Jim has been a very good friend over the years. Therefore it is to my good friend, Jim Weaver, that I dedicate this *Charts on the Book of Hebrews*. It is my hope that as Jim has been a valuable guide in directing my publishing career, these charts will help direct your studies in this magnificent New Testament book known to us as Hebrews.

Herbert W. Bateman IV

Abbreviations

ESV	English Standard Version	NLT	New Living Translation
KJV	King James Version	NRSV	New Revised Standard Version
NASB	New American Standard Bible	RSV	Revised Standard Version
NET	New English Translation	TNIV	Today's New International Version
NIV	The New International Version		

GENERAL

b.	born	MT	Masoretic Text
B.C.E.	Before the Common Era (B.C.)	n.p.	no publisher
ca.	circa	NT	New Testament
C.E.	Common Era (A.D.)	OT	Old Testament
cf.	confer	ref.	reference
ch(s).	chapter(s)	§	section
cp.	compare	s.v.	*sub verbo* (under the word)
d.	died	txt	text
esp.	especially	var	variant
idem	the same	v(v).	verse(s)
LXX	Septuagint		

APOCRYPHA & OT PSEUDEPIGRAPHA

Apocrypha:

Bar	Baruch
1–2 Esd	1–2 Esdras
1–4 Macc	1–4 Maccabees
Sir	Wisdom of Jesus the Son of Sirach (Ecclesiasticus)
Wis	Wisdom of Solomon

Old Testament Pseudepigrapha:

Apoc. Ab.	*Apocalypse of Abraham*	*Sib. Or.*	*Sibylline Oracles*
2 Bar.	*2 Baruch*	*T. Dan*	*Testament of Dan*
1–3 En.	*1–3 Enoch*	*T. Jud.*	*Testament of Judah*
Jos. Asen.	*Joseph and Aseneth*	*T. Levi*	*Testament of Levi*
Jub.	*Jubilees*	*T. Mos.*	*Testament of Moses*
Pss. Sol.	*Psalms of Solomon*		

OTHER ANCIENT TEXTS

Abr.	*On Abraham (De Abrahamo)*; Philo
Ad. Nat.	*ad Nationes*; Tertullian
Agr.	*On Husbandry (De agricultura)*; Philo
Ag. Ap.	*Against Apion*; Josephus
Ann.	*The Annals*; Tacitus
Ant.	*Jewish Antiquities*; Josephus
Apol.	*Apologeticus pro Christianis*; Tertullian
Congr.	*On the Preliminary Studies (De Congressu quaerendae)*; Philo
Ebr.	*On Drunkenness (De Ebrietate)*; Philo
Ep.	*Epistulae*; Pliny the Younger
Flacc.	*Pro Flacco*; Cicero
Hist. eccl.	*Ecclesiastical History*; Eusebius
J. W.	*Jewish War*; Josephus
Leg.	*Allegorical Interpretation (Legum allegoriae)*; Philo
Legat.	*On the Embassy to Gaius (Legatio ad Gaium)*; Philo
m. Yoma	*Mishnah Yoma*
Mos.	*Life of Moses (De Vita Moses)*; Philo
Mut.	*On the Change of Names (De Mutation Nominum)*; Philo
Somn.	*On Dreams (De Somniis)*; Philo
Spec. Leg.	*On the Special Laws (De Specialibus Legibus)*; Philo
t. Yoma	*Tosefta Yoma*

QUMRAN SOURCES

Number	Abbreviation	Name
	CD	*Damascus Document (Cairo Genizah copy)*
	1QM	*War Scroll*
	1QpHab	*Pesher Habakkuk*
1Q20	1QapGen	*Genesis Apocryphon*
1Q28	1QS	*Rule of the Community*
1Q28a	1QSa	*Rule of the Congregation*
1Q28b	1QSb	*Rule of Blessings*
1Q34bis	1QLitPr	*Festival Prayers*
4Q161	4QpIsa[a]	*Pesher Isaiah[a]*
4Q171	4QpPs[a]	*Pesher Psalms[a]*
4Q174	4QFlor	*4QFlorilegium*
4Q177	4QCatena[a]	*Catena[a]*
4Q180	4QAgesCreat	*Ages of Creation*
4Q182	4QCatena[b]	*Catena[b]*
4Q246	4QapocrDan ar	*Apocryphon of Daniel*
4Q252	4QCommGen A	*Commentary on Genesis A*
4Q258	4QS[d]	*Rule of the Community[d]*

4Q270	4QD[e]	*Damascus Document[e]*
4Q280	4QCurses	*Curses*
4Q285	4QSM	*Sefer Hamilhamah*
4Q286	4QBer[a]	*Blessings[a]*
4Q369	4QPEnosh	*Prayer of Enosh*
4Q375	4QapocrMoses[a]	*Apocryphon of Moses[a]*
4Q376	4QapocrMoses[b]	*Apocryphon of Moses[b]*
4Q377	4QapocrPent B	*Apocryphon on Pentateuch B*
4Q382		*Paraphrase of the Kings*
4Q400–407	4QShirShabb[a–h]	*Songs of the Sabbath Sacrifice[a–h]*
4Q423		*Instruction[g]*
4Q427	1QH[a]	*Thanksgiving Hymns[a]*
4Q444		*Incantation*
4Q458		*Narrative A*
4Q491	4QM[a]	*War Scroll[a]*
4Q504	4QDibHam[a]	*Words of the Luminaries[a]*
4Q521		*Messianic Apocalypse*
4Q544	4QAmram[b]	*Visions of Amram[b] ar*
11Q13	11QMelch	*Melchizedek*
11Q17	11QShirShabb	*Songs of the Sabbath Sacrifice*
11Q19	11QT[a]	*Temple[a]*

PERIODICAL, REFERENCE, AND SERIAL

AB	Anchor Bible
ACW	Ancient Christian Wrtiers
BAGD	Bauer, Arndt, Gingrich, Danker, *A Greek–English Lexicon of the NT*
BDAG	Bauer, Danker, Arndt, Gingrich, *A Greek–English Lexicon of the NT*
BDF	Blass, F. A. Debrunner, and R. W. Funk. *A Greek Grammar of the New Testament and Other Early Christian Literature*
BibSac	*Bibliotheca Sacra*
CBQ	*Catholic Biblical Quarterly*
CGC	*Cambridge Greek New Testament Commentary*
DSS	Dead Sea Scrolls
EDNT	*Exegetical Dictionary of the New Testament*
EDSS	*Encyclopedia of the Dead Sea Scrolls*
EvQ	*Evangelical Quarterly*
Exp	*The Expositor*
ExpTim	*Expository Times*
FRLANT	*Forschungen zur Religion und Literatur des Alten und Neun Testaments*
GOTR	*Greek Orthodox Theological Review*
HTR	*Harvard Theological Review*
JBL	*Journal of Biblical Literature*
JETS	*Journal of the Evangelical Theological Society*
JSOT	*Journal for the Study of the Old Testament*

KEK	*Kritisch-exegetischer Kommenter über das Neue Testament*
LW	*Luther's Works*
NICNT	New International Commentary on the New Testament
NIGTC	New International Greek Testament Commentary
NovT	*Novum Testamentum*
NPNF	Nicene and Post-Nicene Fathers of the Christian Church
NTS	*New Testament Studies*
PNTC	The Pillar New Testament Series
SNTSMS	*Society for New Testament Studies Monograph Series*
RB	*Revue biblique*
RBén	*Revue bénédictine*
RS	*Studies in Religion*
SBT	Studies in Biblical Theology
SwTJ	*Southwest Journal of Theology*
TBT	*The Bible Today*
TDNT	*Theological Dictionary of the New Testament*
TDOT	*Theological Dictionary of the Old Testament*
TJ	*Trinity Journal*
TLNT	*Theological Lexicon of the New Testament*
WTJ	*Westminster Theological Journal*
WUNT	Wissenschaftliche Untersuchungen zum Neuen Testament
ZNTW	*Zeitschrift für die Neutestamentliche Wissenschaft und Kunde der älteren Kirche*

Part One

INTRODUCTORY CONSIDERATIONS
IN HEBREWS

Potential Author of Hebrews First Proposed

CHART 1

Suggested Author	Proponent	Date	Source
Barnabas	Tertullian	ca.150–220	*De pudicitia, 20:2; On Purity* in ACW, Vol. 28, pp. 115, 277.
Paul	Pantaenus	ca. 190	Eusebius, *Ecclesiastical History*, 6.14.1-4, cf. 6.13.1-2.
Paul (translated by Luke)	Clement of Alexandria	ca. 155–220	Eusebius, *Ecclesiastical History*, 6.14.1-4, cf. 3.38.2, 6.13.1-2.
Unknown	Origen	ca. 185–254	Eusebius, *Ecclesiastical History*, 6.25.11-14, cf. 6.23.1.
Clement of Rome	Ephraem Syrus	ca. 306–373	*Commentarieus in epistolis Pauli nunc primum ex Armenio in Latinum sermonem a partibus Mekhitaristis translati* (Venice, n.p., 1893).
Luke	Aquinas, T.	1260s	*Commentary on the Epistle to the Hebrews*, trans. by C. Baer (South Bend: St. Augustine's Press, 2006).
Apollos	Luther, M.	1522	*Lectures on Genesis Chapters 45-50, LW*, vol. 8.178; *Word and Sacrament, LW*, vol. 35.394.
Silas	Boehme, C. F.	1825	*Epistle to the Hebrews* (Leipzig: Barth, 1825).
Peter	Welch, A.	1898	*The Authorship of the Epistle to the Hebrews* (Edinburgh: Oliphant, Anderson and Ferrier, 1898).
Philip	Ramsay, W. M.	1899	"The Date and Authorship of the Epistle to the Hebrews," *Exp 9* (1899): 401–22.
Priscilla & Aquila (Priscilla dominant)	Harnack, A. von	1900	"Probabilia über die Adresse und den Verfassere des Hebräerbriefs," *ZNW* 1 (1900): 16–41.
Aristion	Chapman, J.	1905	"Aristion, author of the Epistle to the Hebrews," *RBén* 22 (1905): 50–64.

Suggested Author	Proponent	Date	Source
Stephen	Kirby, V. T.	1923	"The Authorship of the Epistle to the Hebrews," *ExpTim* 35 (1923): 375–77.
Voice of Barnabas (translated by Luke)	Badcock, F. J.	1937	*The Pauline Epistles and the Epistle to the Hebrews in their Historical Setting* (NY, 1937).
Jude	Dubarle, A. M.	1939	"Author and Destination of the Epistle to the Hebrews," *RB* 48 (1939): 506–29.
Epaphras	Anderson, C. P.	1966	"The Epistle to the Hebrews and the Pauline Letter Collection," *HTR* 59 (1966): 429–438; "Hebrews among the Letters of Paul," *SR* 5 (1975–76): 258–66.
Timothy	Legg, J. D.	1968	"Our Brother Timothy, A Suggested Solution to the Problem of the Authorship of the Epistle to the Hebrews," *EvQ* 40 (1968): 220–23.
Mary (Mother of Jesus), assisted by Luke and John	Ford, J. M.	1976	"The Mother of Jesus and the Authorship of the Epistle to the Hebrews" *TBT* 82 (1976): 683–94.

Authorship of Hebrews through the Centuries

CHART 2

The Early Church and Church Fathers (C.E. 150 to 600)			
Proposed Author	**Proponent**	**Date**	**Source**
Barnabas	Tertullian	ca. 150–220	*De pudicitia*, 20:2; *On Purity* in ACW, Vol. 28. pp. 115, 277.
Paul	Pantaenus	ca. 190	Eusebius, *Ecclesiastical History*, 6.14.1-4, cf. 6.13.1-2.
Paul (translated by Luke)	Clement of Alexandria	ca. 155–220	Eusebius, *Ecclesiastical History*, 6.14.1-4, cf. 3.38.2, 6.13.1-2.
Unknown	Origen	ca. 185–254	Eusebius, *Ecclesiastical History* 6.25.11-14, cf. 6.23.1.
Paul	Eusebius	ca. 265–339	Eusebius, *Ecclesiastical History* 3.3.5, cf. 2.17.12.
Paul	Athanasius	ca. 296–373	*Patrologiae cursus completus*, 162 vols. (Paris: Migne): 26.148; "Of the Particular Books and their Number..." §5 ("Letter 39" in NPNF[2] 4.552); cf. *On the Incarnation of the Word* 3.2 (NPNF[2] 4.37), *Defence of the Nicene Definition* 5.18 (NPNF[2] 4.161).
Clement of Rome	Ephraem Syrus	ca. 306–373	*Commentarieus in epistolis Pauli nunc primum ex Armenio in Latinum sermonem a partibus Mekhitaristis translati* (Venice: n.p. 1893).
Paul	Didymus the Blind	ca. 309–398	*Patrologiae cursus completus*, 162 vols. (Paris: Migne): 39.317B, 393C.
Paul	Epiphanius	ca. 315–403	*Irenaeus, Adversus Omnes Haereses* 69.37; Patrologiae cursus completus, 162 vol. (Paris: Migne): 42.260.
Barnabas	Gregory of Elvira	ca. 375	*Tractatus Origenis*, Batiffol-Wilmart, ed. (1900), p. 108.

The Early Church and Church Fathers (C.E. 150 to 600)			
Proposed Author	**Proponent**	**Date**	**Source**
Paul	Cyril of Jerusalem	ca. 310–386	*Patrologiae cursus completus*, 162 vols. (Paris: Migne): 33.500.
Barnabas	Filaster (Philastrius)	d. ca. 397	*De Haeresibus.*
Paul	Chrysostom, J.	ca. 344–407	"Homily 1" in *Homilies on the Epistle to the Hebrews* (NPNF[1] 14.363–65).
Paul (tentative)	Jerome	345–419	*Lives of Illustrious Men* §5 (NPNF[2] 3.363); *Against Jovinianus* 2.3 (NPNF[2] 6.389).
Paul	Theodore of Mopsuestia	ca. 350–428	*Patrologiae cursus completus*, 162 vols. (Paris: Migne): 82.673–78; William H. P. Hatch, "The Position of Hebrews in the Canon of the New Testament" *HTR* 29:2 (April 1936): 133–51.
Paul (tentative)	Augustine	354–430	*City of God* 16.22 (NPNF[1] 2.323); *On Christian Doctrine* 2.8 (NPNF[1] 2.539).
Paul	Cyril of Alexandria	d. 444	*Patrologiae cursus completus*, 162 vols. (Paris: Migne): 75.37, 40; 76.1249, 1296.

Middle Ages (C.E. 600 to 1500)			
Proposed Author	**Proponent**	**Date**	**Source**
Paul	John of Damascus	ca. 675–749	*Patrologiae cursus completus*, 162 vols. (Paris: Migne): 95.929. William H. P. Hatch, "The Position of Hebrews in the Canon of the New Testament" *HTR* 29:2 (April 1936): 133–51.
Luke	Aquinas, T.	1260s	*Commentary on the Epistle to the Hebrews*, trans. by C. Baer (South Bend: St. Augustine's Press).

Middle Ages (C.E. 600 to 1500)			
Proposed Author	**Proponent**	**Date**	**Source**
Paul	Nicolaus of Lyra	1265–1349	Koester, *Hebrews* in AB, 30–31.
Paul	Valla, L.	1407–1457	*Collatio Novi Testamenti* 250; *Adnotationes* 1.887

Humanists and Reformers (C.E. 1500 to 1750)			
Proposed Author	**Proponent**	**Date**	**Source**
Apollos	Luther, M.	1522	*Lectures on Genesis Chapters 45-50, LW,* vol. 8.178; *Word and Sacrament, LW,* vol. 35.394.
Unknown	Tyndale, W.	1525–26	"The Prologe to the Epistle of S. Paul to the Hebrues" in *The New Testament* (1525–26).
Paul	Bullinger, H.	1534	*De testamento seu foedere Dei unico et aeterno* (1534).
Luke (or Clement of Rome)	Calvin, J.	1530s	*Calvin's Commentaries: The Epistle… to the Hebrews and the First and Second Epistles of Peter* (Edinburgh, 1963).
Paul	Guilliaud, C.	1543	*Status Epistolae Pauli ad Hebraeos* (1543).
Barnabas	Caméron, J.	1628	*Praelectioni in selectiora quaedam loca Novi Testamenti* (1628).
Luke (independently)	Grotius, H.	1645	*Christ's Passion: A Tragedie, with Annotations* (London)
Paul	Owen, J.	1668	*Exercitation II: On the penman of the Epistle to Hebrews,* 4 vols. (London, reprinted 1790).

Critical Scholarship (C.E. 1750 to Present)			
Proposed Author	**Proponent**	**Date**	**Source**
Silas	Boehme, C. F.	1825	*Epistle to the Hebrews* (Leipzig: Barth, 1825).
Apollos	Bleek, F.	1828	*Der Brief an die Hebräer* (Berlin: F. Dümmler, 1828)
Paul	Forster, C.	1838	*The Apostolical Authority of the Epistle to the Hebrews* (London: James Duncan, 1838).
Paul	Stuart, M.	1876	*A Commentary on the Epistle to the Hebrews*, 4th ed. rev. R. D. C. Robbins (Andover: Warren F. Draper, 1860).
Barnabas	Keil, C. F.	1885	*Commentary on the Book to the Hebrews* (Leipzig: Dörffling and Franke).
Apollos	Farrar, F. W.	1888	*The Epistle of Paul the Apostle to the Hebrews* (Cambridge: University Press, 1888).
Barnabas	Salmon, G.	1888	*A Historical Introduction to the Study of the Books of the New Testament*, 3rd ed. (London: John Murray, 1888).
Unknown	Westcott, B. F.	1889	*The Epistle to the Hebrews* (London: Macmillan, 1889).
Barnabas	Weiss, B.	1897	*Der Brief an die Hebräer* (Göttingen: Vandenoeck & Ruprecht).
Peter	Welch, A.	1898	*The Authorship of the Epistle to the Hebrews* (Edinburgh: Oliphant, Anderson and Ferrier, 1898).
Philip	Ramsay, W. M.	1899	"The Date and Authorship of the Epistle to the Hebrews," *Exp 9* (1899): 401–22.

Critical Scholarship (C.E. 1750 to Present)			
Proposed Author	**Proponent**	**Date**	**Source**
Priscilla & Aquila (Priscilla dominant)	Harnack, A. von	1900	"Probabilia über die Adresse und den Verfassere des Hebräerbriefs," *ZNW* 1 (1900): 16–41.
Aristion	Chapman, J.	1905	"Aristion, author of the Epistle to the Hebrews," *RBén* 22 (1905): 50–64.
Pseudepigraphic	Wrede, W.	1906	*The Literary Riddle of Hebrews* (Göttingen: Vandenhoeck & Ruprecht, 1906).
Paul	Peake, A. S.	1910	*Hebrews* (Edinburgh: Jack, 1910).
Barnabas	Dibelius, F.	1910	*Der Verfasser des Hebräerbriefes* (Strassburg: Heitz).
Barnabas	Edmundson, G.	1913	*The Church in Rome in the First Century* (London: Longmans, Green, and Co.).
Stephen	Kirby, V. T.	1923	"The Authorship of the Epistle to the Hebrews," *ExpTim* 35 (1923): 375–77.
Inspired by Stephen (written by Paul, edited by Luke)	Brown, J. V.	1923	"The Authorship and Circumstances of 'Hebrews'–Again," *BSac* 80 (1923): 505–38.
Voice of Barnabas (translated by Luke)	Badcock, F. J.	1937	*The Pauline Epistles and the Epistle to the Hebrews in their Historical Setting* (New York: Macmillan, 1937).
Apollos	Lenski, R. C. H.	1938	*The Interpretation of the Epistle to the Hebrews and of the Epistle of James* (Minneapolis: Augsburg Pub. House).
Jude	Dubarle, A. M.	1939	"Author and Destination of the Epistle to the Hebrews," *RB* 48 (1939): 506–29.
Paul	Leonard, W.	1939	*The Authorship of the Epistle to the Hebrews* (London: Oates and Washbourne, 1939).

Critical Scholarship (C.E. 1750 to Present)			
Proposed Author	**Proponent**	**Date**	**Source**
Apollos	Manson, T. W.	1949	"The Problem of the Epistle to the Hebrews," *Bulletin of the John Rylands Library* 32 (September 1949): 16–17.
Apollos	Spicq, C.	1952	*The Epistle to the Hebrews*, vol. 1 (Paris: J. Gabalda).
Epaphras	Anderson, C. P.	1966	"The Epistle to the Hebrews and the Pauline Letter Collection" *HTR* 59:4 (1966): 429–438; "Hebrews among the Letters of Paul" *SR* 5 (1975–76): 258–66.
Timothy	Legg, J. D.	1968	"Our Brother Timothy, A Suggested Solution to the Problem of the Authorship of the Epistle to the Hebrews." *EvQ* 40 (1968): 220–23.
Barnabas	Robinson, J. A. T.	1976	*Redating the New Testament* (Philadelphia: Westminster).
Mary (Mother of Jesus), assisted by Luke and John	Ford, J. M.	1976	"The Mother of Jesus and the Authorship of the Epistle to the Hebrews" *TBT* 82 (1976): 683–94.
Barnabas	Pixner, B.	1992	"The Jerusalem Essenes, Barnabas and the Letter to the Hebrews" in *Qumranica Mogilanensia* (1992).
Priscilla	Hoppin, R.	1997	*Priscilla's Letter: Finding the Author of the Epistle to the Hebrews* (Fort Bragg: Lost Coast Press, 1997).
Paul	Voulgaris, C. SP.	1999	"Hebrews: Paul's Fifth Epistle from Prison," *GOTR* 44 (1999): 199–206.
Paul	Linnemann, E.	2000	"A Call for a Retrial in the Case of the Epistle to the Hebrews," trans. David E. Lanier, *Faith and Mission* 19/2 (2002): 19–59.

Critical Scholarship (C.E. 1750 to Present)			
Proposed Author	**Proponent**	**Date**	**Source**
Paul (translated by Luke)	Black, D. A.	2001	"Who Wrote Hebrews? The Internal and External Evidence Reexamined," *Faith and Mission* 18:2 (2001): 3–26.
Apollos	Guthrie, G. H.	2001	"The Case for Apollos as the Author of Hebrews," *Faith and Mission* 18:2 (2001): 41–56.
Pseudepigraphic	Rothschild, C. K.	2009	*Hebrews as Pseudepigraphon* (Tübingen: Mohr Siebeck)
Luke	Allen, D.	2010	*Lukan Authorship of Hebrews* (Nashville: B & H Academic)

Authorship Ascribed by Commentators

CHART 3

Commentator	Commentary Series and Publication	Author
Allen, David L.	New American Commentary, 2010	Luke
Attridge, Harold W.	Hermeneia, 1989	Anonymous
Bruce, F. F.	NICNT, 1990	Unknown
Cockerill, Gareth L.	NICNT, 2012	Unknown
Ellingworth, Paul	NIGTC, 1993	Apollos
Girdwood, Jim and Peter Verkruyse	The College Press NIV Commentary, 1997	Unknown
Guthrie, Donald	Tyndale New Testament Commentaries, 1983	Anonymous
Guthrie, George, H.	NIV Application Commentary, 1998	Apollos
Hagner, Donald A.	New International Biblical Commentary, 1990 Encountering the Book of Hebrews, 2002	Unknown
Hewitt, Thomas	Tyndale New Testament Commentaries, 1960	Silas
Johnson, Luke Timothy	The New Testament Library, 2006	Apollos
Kistemaker, Simon J.	New Testament Commentary, 1984	Unknown
Koester, Craig R.	Anchor Bible, 2001	Unknown
Lane, William L.	Word Biblical Commentary, 1991	Anonymous
Michaels, J. Ramsey	Cornerstone Biblical Commentary Series, 2009	Deutrero-Pauline
Mitchell, Alan C.	Sacra Pagina, 2007	Anonymous
Moffatt, James	International Critical Commentary, 1948	Unknown
O'Brien, Peter T.	The Pillar New Testament Commentary, 2010	Unknown
Pfitzner, Victor C.	Abington New Testament Commentaries, 1997	Apollos
Stedman, Ray C.	IVP New Testament Commentary Series, 1992	Apollos
Wilson, R. McLachlan	The New Century Bible Commentary, 1987	Unknown

Debated Considerations about Authorship of Barnabas

CHART 4

Evidence	Pros	Cons
Early Testimony	Tertullian (*ca.* 150–220) presented Barnabas as the author of Hebrews, a man of equal stature to Paul, and the Epistle of Barnabas as supporting evidence.*	Subsequent North African fathers did not affirm Tertullian's understanding about Barnabas' authorship of Hebrews.
	Gregory of Elvira (4th century): "The most holy Barnabas says, 'Through him we offer to God the sacrifice of lips that acknowledge his name'" (cf. Heb 13.15, *Tractatus Origenis*, p. 108).	Jerome (ca. 345–419) mentioned Barnabas as one of several possibilities: Barnabas, Luke, or Clement (*Lives of Illustrious Men* §5 (NPNF[2] 3.363).
	Filaster, bishop of Brescia, Italy (4th century), suggested Barnabas as the author of Hebrews.	The dominant traditional view during the early church was Pauline authorship.
	The Western church accepted Barnabas as the author of Hebrews.	The Eastern church rejected Barnabas as the author.
Manuscripts	Codex Claromantus (6th century) lists the Epistle of Barnabas among the canonical books, a book considered to be by the same author as Hebrews.	The Epistle of Barnabas and the Book of Hebrews are not by the same author due to differences in style and tone.
Jewish Identification and Character	Barnabas was a Levite born in Cyprus (Acts 4:36) and had ties with the Jewish cultic system, which the author of Hebrews seems to have had as well.	For a Levite, Barnabas' treatment of Levi and the tithe in Hebrews 7 seems odd. In addition, references to the Jewish cultic system depend on the OT system rather than contemporary practices of the first century.
	Barnabas is described as "a good man, full of the Holy Spirit" (Acts 11:24) and was deemed an apostle (1 Cor. 9:6; Acts 14:14).	If Barnabas was considered an apostle, why would the early church need posit Paul as author in order to gain canonicity?

---

* "There is extant an Epistle of Barnabas addressed to the Hebrews, written by a man of such authority that Paul has ranked him with himself: 'I only and Barnabas, have not we power to forbear working?' And certainly this *Epistle of Barnabas* is more received than that apocryphal Shepherd of the adulterer." (*De pudicitia*, 20:2)

Evidence	Pros	Cons
Jewish Identification and Character	Barnabas encouraged people and was nicknamed "son of encouragement" (cp. Acts 4:36 with Heb 13:22).	There is no legitimate connection between the description of Barnabas' character (Acts 4:36) and the statement in Hebrews concerning the author's encouraging words (13:22).
Ministry with Paul	Barnabas was among those who had "heard the message" from the apostles Peter and John (Acts 4:4, 36-7), part of the Hellenistic faction in Jerusalem, and witnessed signs and wonders of the Holy Spirit (Heb 2:3–4).	Barnabas' connection with the original gospel was probably closer than that implied in Hebrews 2:3; he was, after all, associated with the leaders of the Jerusalem church (Acts 4:4, 36-7).
	Barnabas befriended Paul after his conversion and helped dispel suspicions concerning the genuineness of Paul's confession of faith (Acts 9:26–28).	Barnabas is described as a less eloquent speaker than Paul (Acts 14:12), so how could he have written such an effective rhetorical book?
	The leaders in Jerusalem sent Barnabas to the church in Antioch; Barnabas retrieved Paul from Tarsus, and they ministered together in Antioch (Acts 11:22–26).	
	Barnabas and Paul delivered aid from Antioch to the Jewish Christians in Palestine (Acts 11:27–30).	
	The church in Antioch commissioned Barnabas and Paul for missionary service (Acts 13:1–3).	
Ministry with John Mark	Barnabas and Paul evangelized Derbe/ Lystra where Timothy lived (Acts 16:1) and both knew Timothy (Heb 13:23).	Evidence for Barnabas appears to be inferentially derived from the subject matter of the letter.
	Barnabas, along with John Mark, set out on his own and had a ministry apart from Paul (Acts 15:36–39).	The lack of any other extant writings by Barnabas argues against his having written Hebrews.

Debated Considerations about Authorship of Paul

CHART 5

Evidence	Pros	Cons
Early Testimony	Pantaenus (ca. 190), teacher of Clement of Alexandria, held that the epistle was in some sense Pauline.[*]	Clement of Alexandria (ca. 155–220) argues for joint Pauline and Lukan authorship.
	Eusebius (ca. 265–339) held that Paul wrote Hebrews in Hebrew and Luke translated it into Greek (*Hist. eccl.* 6.14.2-4).	Origen (ca. 185–254) argues Paul played no direct role in writing Hebrews (Eusebius, *Hist. eccl.* 6.25.11-14, cf. 6.23.1).
	The Eastern church accepted Pauline authorship (Athanasius, Cyril of Jerusalem, Cyril of Alexandria).	The Western church rejected Pauline authorship and thereby excluded Hebrews from several Old Latin Versions.
Manuscripts	Chester Beatty Papyrus (p⁴⁶, ca. 200) is a codex of the Pauline corpus that lists Hebrews as a Pauline text.	Marcion's Canon (ca. 140), the *Apostolicon*, contains Paul's letters and a revised Gospel of Luke, but excludes Hebrews.
		Muratorian's Canon (*ca.* 160–180) does not include Hebrews as part of the NT canon.
	The council of Hippo (393) and councils of Carthage (28 August 397; 25 May 419) list fourteen works of Paul (including Hebrews).	
Salutation and Identification	Paul omits his name because he was an apostle to the Gentiles and not Hebrews (Eusebius, *Hist. eccl.* 6.14.4).	Unlike Paul's other writings (Rom 1:1; 1 Cor 1:1; Gal 1:1; etc.), a salutation, his name, and his apostleship are missing in Hebrews.
	Paul refrains from identifying his apostleship because he addresses Jesus as the apostle and does not want to equate himself with Jesus (Heb 3:1).	The reference to indirect reception of the gospel in Hebrews 2:3 counters Paul's claim of direct commission from Jesus (Gal 1:11–16; 1 Cor 15:8; Rom 1:1; cp. Acts 9:1–9).
Vocabulary, Style, and Hermeneutic	Similarities in vocabulary identify Hebrews as a Pauline work (see Forster, Linnemann, Black).	The numerous words unique to Hebrews argue against Pauline authorship (see Chart 91; and Ellingworth, Attridge).

---

[*] Clement of Alexandria recalls of Pantaenus' perspective on Hebrews: "But now as the blessed presbyter (Pantaenus) used to say, 'since the Lord who was the Apostle of the Almighty, was sent to the Hebrews, Paul by reason of his inferiority, as if sent to the Gentiles, did not subscribe himself an apostle of the Hebrews; both out of reverence to the Lord, and because he wrote of his abundance to the Hebrews, as a herald and apostle of the Gentiles." (Eusebius, *Hist. eccl.* 6.14.4)

Evidence	Pros	Cons
Vocabulary, Style, and Hermeneutic	The use of *qal wahomer* ("lesser to greater") is a basic argument evident in Pauline works (Rom 5:12–21) and other Jewish forms of exegesis.	The use of *qal wahomer* ("lesser to greater") is a common element in other NT texts (Matt 7:11, 10:25; Luke 11:13; 12:28; John 7:23, 10:34–36).
	Allusions to Psalms 2 and 110 are known in Pauline works (Rom 8:34; Eph 1:20; 1 Cor 15:25; Phil 2:12).	Quotations and allusions of Pss 2 and 110 are known other in NT works (Mark 1:11, 9:7, 12:36, 14:62; John 1:49; Acts 2:34–35, 13:33).
Theology	The use of a period in Hebrews 1:1–4 (cp. 2:2–4; 3:12–14; 4:12–13; 5:1–3, 7–10) is an organizational style also used in two Pauline works (cp. 1 Cor 13; 2 Cor 11:6).	The use of a period in Hebrews is not unique to Paul (cp. Luke 1:1–4; 1 John 1:1–3); in fact, "Paul … does not generally make the effort required by so careful a style" (BDF §464).
	The preeminence of Jesus in Hebrews 1:2–4, particularly as it pertains to creation, is evident in Paul (Eph 1:21; Phil 2:9–10; Col 1:14–19).	The preeminence of Jesus in Hebrews includes an element absent in Pauline works, the royal priesthood of Jesus (7:1–10:18).
		The focused treatment of the Jewish cultic system to interpret and contrast Jesus' salvific work (Heb 5:1–10; 7:1–10:18) is not characteristic of Paul.
Epilogue	The example of Abraham in Heb 6:13–20 recalls Rom 4:1–25 and Gal 3:16–18.	The reference to Abraham and faith is not unique to Paul (James 2:21, 23).
	The epilogue of Hebrews (13:18-25) offers striking parallels to Pauline texts and is an integral part of the book.	The epilogue of Hebrews (13:18–25) alone is Pauline and was added to Hebrews.
	The reference to Timothy (13:23) is a mark of Pauline authorship (e.g. Rom 16:21, 1 Cor 4:17; Phil 1:1; 1 Thess 3:2).	Timothy would have been close to numerous people due to his work in Philippi (Phil 2:19–24); Thessalonica (1 Thess 3:1–10), Corinth (1 Cor 4:17, 16:10–11), and Asia Minor (Acts 19:22; 1 Tim 1:3).

Debated Considerations about Authorship of Luke

CHART 6

Evidence	Pros	Cons
Early Witness	Clement of Alexandria (ca. 155–220) argues for joint Pauline and Lukan authorship.[1]	Luke is credited with only indirect involvement in that he drew his ideas from Paul and is not the sole author.
	Luke as a possible author of Hebrews was a medieval preference of Thomas Aquinas (1200s).	
Identification	Luke is Jewish (see Allen).	Luke is a Gentile.
	Luke was a companion and co-worker of Paul aware of Jewish manners and customs (Col 4:14; 2 Tim 4:11).	If a Gentile, would Jewish recipients be receptive to Luke's criticism of Jewish temple practices?
Style	The use of citation formulae when introducing OT citations in Hebrews is similar to that of Luke/Acts.	The use of citation formulae for introducing OT citations is common among most NT writers and extrabiblical material found at Qumran.
		Luke does not have a theology of the cross, nor does he evidence a high priestly Christology in Luke/Acts.
	Both the Gospel of Luke 1:1–4 and Heb 1:1–4 begin with a similar stylistic use of a period.	The use of a period is not unique to Luke in the NT (cp. 1 Cor 13; 2 Cor 11:6; 1 John 1:1–3).
	Luke/Acts and Hebrews alone have a classical Greek style—namely, remarkable literary and rhetorical skill—which supports Lukan authorship (cp. Acts 7 with Heb 11).	Although Luke/Acts has a classical Greek style, that does not mean Luke *alone* had the rhetorical literary skills necessary to compose Hebrews.
		The style and contents of *1 Clement* are similar to that of Hebrews and there is a co-worker named Clement (Phil 4:3).

Evidence	Pros	Cons
Vocabulary	For Spicq, no less than 30, for Allen no less than 53, similar words are unique to Luke/Acts and Hebrews.	There are only 12 words unique to Luke/Acts and Hebrews. Distinctive vocabulary is shared with 1 Pet (Heb 13:20 with 1 Pet 2:25; Heb 9:24 with 1 Pet 3:21). Hebrews* vocabulary is distinctive enough that it cannot be identified with any known NT author.
	Luke receives his information from others (Luke 1:1–4) as does the author of Hebrews (2:3).	

* Clement of Alexandria argues, "… as for the Epistle to the Hebrews … it is Paul's, but that it was written for Hebrews in the Hebrew tongue, and that Luke, having carefully translated it, published it for the Greeks; hence, as a result of this translation, the same complexion of style is found in the Epistle and in the Acts. (Eusebius, *Hist. eccl.* 6.14.2).

Debated Considerations about Authorship of Apollos

CHART 7

Evidence	Pros	Cons
Early Witness	Martin Luther was the first to suggest Apollos as the author of Hebrews in a sermon on Hebrews 1:1–4 published in 1522.*	Martin Luther admitted that the author of Hebrews is unknown and "will probably not be known for a while" in *Word and Sacrament, LW* (1546), 35.394.
		None of the church fathers mention Apollos as even a possibility.
Jewish Identification and Character	Apollos was a Jew (Acts 18:24) and the author of Hebrews shows an extensive knowledge of Judaism.	Paul was a Jew (Phil 3:4–6) and had extensive knowledge of Judaism (cp. Romans)—a point that might also be made for Barnabas (Acts 4:36).
	Apollos is described as "mighty" or "well-versed" in the Scriptures (Acts 18:24, 28) and the author of Hebrews was well-versed in the Old Testament.	Paul was well-versed in Scripture and used it extensively in his epistle to the Romans.
	Apollos was "an Alexandrian by birth" (Acts 18:24) where Greek thought flourished, and Hebrews reflects Greek perspectives (Platonic and Philonic).	Barnabas was a Hellenistic Jew— a Levite born in Cyprus (Acts 4:36)—as was Paul, who was a Hellenistic Jew from Tarsus (Acts 21:39, 22:3).
	Apollos instructed and taught others (Acts 18:25), and the author of Hebrews also taught (5:9–6:2, then 7:1, 11; 8:1; etc.)	The Alexandrian influences may best be explained through Old Testament presentations of the Levitical system and typology practiced by first century Jews.
	Apollos was "a learned man"—a great orator (Acts 18:24, 26, 28)—and the author of Hebrews employs bold and well-developed forms of rhetoric.	
Hermeneutic	Apollos used an allegorical type of exegesis also evident in Philo's work.	The author of Hebrews readily used exegetical techniques typically seen in other Second Temple Jewish literature (cp. Heb 1:5–13 with 4Q174).

---

* "The author of the Epistle to the Hebrews—whoever he is, whether Paul or, as I think, Apollos—quotes this passage most learnedly when he says: 'By faith Jacob, when dying, blessed each of the sons of Joseph.'" (Martin Luther, *Lectures on Genesis Chapters 45-50, LW* (1522), vol. 8:178.).

Evidence	Pros	Cons
Early Contacts with Christians	Apollos "heard the message" from Priscilla and Aquila (Acts 18:26), which fits the description of the author in Hebrews 2:3.	Barnabas was among those who had "heard the message" from the apostles Peter and John (Acts 4:4), which may fit the description of the author in Hebrews 2:3.
	Apollos was a member of the Pauline circle, which accounts for Pauline influences.	Barnabas, John Mark, Silas, and Timothy were all members of the Pauline circle.
	Apollos was a follower of John the Baptist (Acts 18:25), and the author of Hebrews had moral and religious rigor—especially concerning repentance—that parallels John's.	There are no extant works of Apollos to support authorship.
Epilogue	The destination was not Rome but Corinth (1 Cor 16:19), and Aquila and Priscilla are the referents in Heb 13:24.	The contrast of the triumphalism of the Corinthian believers versus the discouraged community of Hebrews would appear to argue against Corinth.
	Apollos ministered in Corinth (1 Cor 3:4–5), which explains the similarity between comments about foods in Heb 9:10; 13:9–10 and 1 Cor 8:1–13 (Johnson. pp. 35, 43).	The Eucharistic community of Corinth (1 Cor 11:17–34) does not sound like the non-Eucharistic community of Hebrews, nor does the strong refusal of Apollos (1 Cor 16:12) sound like the author of Hebrews 13:19.
	Apollos was closely associated with Timothy (1 Cor 16:10–12) as was the author of Hebrews in 13:23.	Barnabas and Paul evangelized Derbe/Lystra where Timothy lived (Acts 16:1) and both knew Timothy (Heb 13:23).

Debated Considerations about the Destination of Hebrews

CHART 8

Options	Rome and Italy	Jerusalem and Judea
Location	City of Rome: East Bank of the Tiber River, Central Italy	City of Jerusalem: Mountains of Judah, Central Palestine
Founding	City of Rome: 753 B.C.E. (by Romulus)	City of Jerusalem: 3300 B.C.E. (by Semites: perhaps Jebusites)
First Century Ethnicity	Latins, Etruscans, Greeks, Hellenistic Jews, and others	Canaanites, Hebrew Jews, Hellenistic Jews, Greeks, Romans, and others.
Sources	Founding: *T. Levi* 1.4.1–1.9.1; cp. Strabo 5.3.2 Early Jewish Presence: 1 Macc 14:24; 15:15–24; Cicero, *Flacc.* 66–69; Josephus, *Ant.* 14.69–79 Jews from Rome: Acts 2:5, 10 Jewish Christians: Acts 2:10, 41; 18:1–2; Rom 2:17–18; 16:3	Founding: Perhaps Gen 10:14; cp. Strabo 16.2.34–37 Early Jewish Presence: Josh 18 :11–28; 2 Sam 5:6–10; cp. Josephus, *Ant.* 5.80-87; 7.61–68 Jews Return from Babylon: Ezra 1:1–11; 1 Esd 2:1–15; Acts 2:5, 9 Jewish Christians: Acts 2:5, 9, 41

Options	Antioch of Syria	Colossae	City of Cyrene
Location	Orontes River in Syria	Lycus River in Phrygia	North Africa
Founding	300 B.C.E. (by Seleucus I)	Prior to 480 B.C.E. (by Phrygians)	630 B.C.E. (by Greeks)
First Century Ethnicity	Native Syrians, Greeks, Cretans, Cypriots, Romans, Hellenistic Jews	Phrygians, Greeks, Romans, Hellenistic Jews, and others	Greeks, Libyans, Romans, Hellenistic Jews, and others

Options	Antioch of Syria	Colossae	City of Cyrene
Sources	Founding: Strabo 16.2.6–7 Early Jewish Presence: Josephus, *Ag. Ap.* 2.39; *Ant.* 12.17, 23–27, 119, 121–34; *J.W. 7.*43; 2 Macc 4:33–38 Jews from Syria Antioch: Josephus, *Ant.* 13.137; 1 Macc 11:44–47 Jewish Christians: Acts 11:19–30; 13:1–3; 14:24–28; 15:30–35; 18:22	Founding: Herodotus 7.30; Strabo 12.8.12, 16 Early Jewish Presence: Jews from Colossae: Cicero, *Flacc.* 68 Jewish Christians: Col 2:16–26; 4:12–13; Phlm 1:23–24; (Perhaps 2 Tim 4:10)	Founding: Herodotus 4.156–161; Strabo 8.3.20; 17.3.21 Early Jewish Presence: Isa 49:12; Josephus, *Ant.* 14.114–18 Jews from Cyrene: 2 Macc 2:19–32; Mark 15:21 (Matt 27:32); Acts 2:5, 10; 6:9 Jewish Christians: Acts 2:10, 41; 11:20; 13:1

Destination Ascribed by Commentators

CHART 9

Commentator	Commentary Series and Publication	Destination
Allen, David L.	New American Commentary, 2010	Antioch of Syria
Attridge, Harold W.	Hermeneia, 1989	Rome
Bruce, F. F.	NICNT, 1990	Unknown
Cockerill, Gareth L.	NICNT, 2012	Rome
Ellingworth, Paul	NIGTC, 1993	Rome
Girdwood, Jim and Peter Verkruyse	The College Press NIV Commentary, 1997	Rome
Guthrie, Donald	Tyndale New Testament Commentaries, 1983	Rome
Guthrie, George, H.	NIV Application Commentary, 1998	Rome
Hagner, Donald A.	New International Biblical Commentary, 1990 Encountering the Book of Hebrews, 2002	Rome Rome
Hewitt, Thomas	Tyndale New Testament Commentaries, 1960	Rome
Johnson, Luke Timothy	The New Testament Library, 2006	Unknown
Kistemaker, Simon J.	New Testament Commentary, 1984	Rome
Koester, Craig R.	Anchor Bible, 2001	Rome
Lane, William L.	Word Biblical Commentary, 1991	Rome
Michaels, J. Ramsey	Cornerstone Biblical Commentary Series, 2009	Rome
Mitchell, Alan C.	Sacra Pagina, 2007	Rome
Moffatt, James	International Critical Commentary, 1948	Unknown
O'Brien, Peter T.	The Pillar New Testament Commentary, 2010	Rome
Pfitzner, Victor C.	Abington New Testament Commentaries, 1997	Rome
Stedman, Ray C.	IVP New Testament Commentary Series, 1992	Colossae
Wilson, R. McLachlan	The New Century Bible Commentary, 1987	Rome

Debated Considerations About the Recipients of Hebrews

CHART 10

Jewish Christian Audience		
Evidence	**Pros**	**Cons** ("Pros" for Gentile recipients)
External Evidence	The traditional title "To the Hebrews" occurs in very early manuscripts (p[46]).	The heading "To the Hebrews" does not demand that the readers were Hebrews.
	Pantaenus attributes the work to be written to Jews (Eusebius, *Hist. eccl.* 6.14.4).	The idea that Hebrews is written to Jewish Christians is assumed on the basis of church tradition.
	Tertullian ascribes the work to be written to Jews (*On Morals* 20).	The use of the Septuagint, "the codex of their religion," suggests a Gentile Christian audience (Moffatt, xvi).
Internal Evidence	The direct address of "brothers and sisters" (ἀδελφοὶ in 2:11, 17; 3:1, 12; 10:19; 13:22), and the referencing of the readers as "holy" (2:11; 10:14, 29), "sanctified" (10:10), and sharers in God's holiness (12:10, 28) support a converted audience.	The description of a repentance from dead works suggests a conversion from paganism and supports a Gentile audience (6:1).
	The recipients are converted Jews who the author fears will fall away from the living God as did their ancestors (2:1–4; 3:12–14; 5:11–6:8; 10:26–31; 12:25–29).	Concern about "falling away from God" points to Hellenistic syncretism and supports a Gentile audience (13:12).
	The author compares and contrasts the Jewish wilderness generation with the early church (3:7–4:11), the Levitical priesthood with the Melchizedekan priesthood of Jesus (4:14–5:10), and the old with the new covenant (9:1–20), suggesting a converted Jewish audience.	The mention of an "enlightenment" suggests a conversion from paganism and supports a Gentile Christian audience (6:4; 10:32).
	The expectation of the audience to recognize Jewish traditions like angelic mediation of the Mosaic law (2:2–3), regulations about food (9:10; 13:9–10), and Jewish exegesis (1:5–13; 5:5–6) supports a Jewish audience.	The exhortation to avoid "strange teachings" points to Hellenistic syncretism and supports a Gentile Christian audience (13:9).

Recipients Ascribed by Commentators		
CHART 11		
Commentator	**Commentary Series and Publication**	**Recipients**
Allen, David L.	New American Commentary, 2010	Jewish Christians
Attridge, Harold W.	Hermeneia, 1989	Unknown
Bruce, F. F.	NICNT, 1990	Jewish Christians
Cockerill, Gareth L.	NICNT, 2012	Jewish Christians
Ellingworth, Paul	NIGTC, 1993	Jewish Christians
Girdwood, Jim and Peter Verkruyse	The College Press NIV Commentary, 1997	Jewish Christians
Guthrie, Donald	Tyndale New Testament Commentaries, 1983	Jewish Christians
Guthrie, George, H.	NIV Application Commentary, 1998	Jewish Christians
Hagner, Donald A.	New International Biblical Commentary, 1990 Encountering the Book of Hebrews, 2002	Jewish Christians Jewish Christians
Hewitt, Thomas	Tyndale New Testament Commentaries, 1960	Jewish Christians
Johnson, Luke Timothy	The New Testament Library, 2006	Jewish Christians
Kistemaker, Simon J.	New Testament Commentary, 1984	Jewish Christians
Koester, Craig R.	Anchor Bible, 2001	Jewish\Gentile Christians
Lane, William L.	Word Biblical Commentary, 1991	Jewish Christians
Michaels, J. Ramsey	Cornerstone Biblical Commentary Series, 2009	Jewish Christians
Mitchell, Alan C.	Sacra Pagina, 2007	Jewish Christians
Moffatt, James	International Critical Commentary, 1948	Gentile Christians
O'Brien, Peter T.	The Pillar New Testament Commentary, 2010	Jewish Christians
Pfitzner, Victor C.	Abington New Testament Commentaries, 1997	Jewish Christians
Stedman, Ray C.	IVP New Testament Commentary Series, 1992	Jewish Christians
Wilson, R. McLachlan	The New Century Bible Commentary, 1987	Jewish\Gentile Christians ?

Evidence of Recipients' Regeneration in Hebrews

CHART 12

Terminology	Past	Present
Brothers (and sisters) (ἀδελφοί)		Holy brothers and sisters, partners of the heavenly calling, consider … (3:1) Take care brothers and sisters not to turn away from God … (3:12) Brothers and sisters have confidence to enter the sanctuary … and we have a great High Priest over God's house (10:19, 21; cp. 3:1–6) Brothers and sisters heed this word of exhortation (13:22)
Confession (ὁμολογία)		Consider Jesus, the apostle and high priest of our confession (3:1) Let us hold fast to our confession (4:14) Let us hold fast to the confession of our hope without wavering (10:23)
Confidence (παρρησία)		Hold onto your confidence (3:6) Approach God in prayer with confidence (4:16) We have confidence to enter the heavenly sanctuary (10:19) Do not throw away your confidence (10:35)
Partners (μέτοχοι)	We have become partners with Christ (3:14)	Holy brothers and sisters, partners of the heavenly calling, consider … (3:1)
Perfect (τελειόω)	Those sanctified (see 10:10 below) have been perfected (10:14)	Let us move on to perfection (6:1)
Salvation (σωτηρία)	*Our* great salvation was confirmed to us (2:3)	We are confident of better things that accompany *your* salvation (6:9, cp. 7:25)
Sanctified (ἁγιάζω)	By God's will, we have been sanctified (10:10)	

Debated Considerations About the Dating of Hebrews

CHART 13

Agreed Upon Considerations — No Debate among Commentators		
Evidence	**Date**	**Explanation**
Jesus' earthly ministry has ended (Hebrews 2:17; 5:7–10; 13:20–21).	29–33	Emphasis throughout Hebrews is upon Jesus' ruling presence in heaven (1:3, 13; 2:28; 4:14; 8:1–6; 10:12).
Clement of Rome is the first to quote Hebrews (1:3, 4, 5, 7, 13; 2:18; 3:1, 2, 5; 6:18; 11:5, 7, 17, 31, 37; 12:2, 6, 9)	95–96	Eighteen quotes from Hebrews appear in *1 Clement*: *1 Clement* 9.3-4; 10.1-7; 12.1; 17.1, 5; 19.2; 27.2; 43.1; 56.3-4; 64.1
Broadest Parameters for Dating Hebrews: 29 to 96		

Neutral Considerations for Determining Date		
Evidence	**Date**	**Explanation**
Second Generation: The author speaks of certain people having heard the gospel from Jesus (Hebrews 2:3). Does "us" in v. 3 indicate that the author is part of an older (first) generation?	30–70 90s	The two options are inconclusive: • For some, the author receives the gospel from Jesus, and he is a first generation believer ("us"). • For others, the author is *silent* about his being part of the first generation but views himself ("us") as part of the second generation of saints.
Timothy: Hebrews is written during Timothy's lifetime (Hebrews 13:23). How might the reference to Timothy affect the dating of Hebrews?	50–52 64–68 90s?	Timothy first appears during Paul's second missionary journey (Acts 16:1). If 2 Timothy is Pauline, Timothy is still alive at the time of Paul's death (4:9). Timothy's death an unknown factor.
Neutral considerations appear to narrow the dating of Hebrews: 50s to 90s		

Debated Considerations for Dating		
Evidence	**Date**	**The Debates**
Persecution: Hebrews identifies that the readers are experiencing • periods of trials (2:18; 4:15), • periods of opposition (12:3–4), • periods of persecution (10:32–34; 13:3). Determining what the persecution is becomes a determinative factor for dating the book as pre-70.	49 64–68 66–70 81–96	Three options support a **pre-70** dating for Hebrews: • Claudius' persecution of the Jews (Acts 18:2; Seutonius, *Life of Claudius* 25.4), • Nero's persecution of Christians (Tertullian *Ad. Nat.* 1.7.8/9; *Apol.* 5.3/4; Eusebius, *Hist. eccl.* 4.26.9), • Jewish Wars (if to Jerusalem Jews) (Josephus, *Ant.* 20.179-184; *J.W.* 1.10; 2.272–76; Tacitus, *Ann.* 15.44). One option supports a **post-70** dating for Hebrews: • Domitian's persecution of Christians (Pliny, *Ep.* 10.96.1; Eusebius, *Hist. eccl.* 3.18.4).
Temple: Hebrews is silent about the destruction of Jerusalem's temple in 70 C.E. • The sacrificial system appears to be in operation (8:4; 9:6–9; 10:1–4; 13:11). • The present tense describes the appointment of high priest, Levites' priestly office, and service (5:1–4; 7:5; 8:3–4; 10:11; 13:11). • The law and the cultic system is presented as coming to an end (7:12; 8:7, 13; 9:10–11; 10:18) Answering the issue about the temple seems to be *most* determinative for a post-70 date.	70 130 90–96	Two arguments for a pre-70 date: • Hebrews' author shows no awareness of the temple's destruction. • In the *Epistle of Barnabas*, while discussing temple practices, the author notes clearly the temple's destruction (16:4). Two arguments for a **post-70** date: • Though both *Ant.* and *Ag. Ap.* published 93 C.E. or later, Josephus still speaks of temple practices in the present tense (*Ant.* 3.224–257; *Ag. Ap.* 2.77). • The author of Hebrews does not discuss the temple, he appeals to the tabernacle (8:5; 9:1–9).
You now, make the call! When was Hebrews written?		

Dating Ascribed by Commentators

CHART 14

Commentator	Commentary Series and Publication	Dating
Allen, David L.	New American Commentary, 2010	Before 70
Attridge, Harold W.	Hermeneia, 1989	60 to 90
Bruce, F. F.	NICNT, 1990	shortly before 70
Cockerill, Gareth L.	NICNT, 2012	64
Ellingworth, Paul	NIGTC, 1993	64 to 70
Girdwood, Jim and Peter Verkruyse	The College Press NIV Commentary, 1997	64–68
Guthrie, Donald	Tyndale New Testament Commentaries, 1983	during the 60s
Guthrie, George, H.	NIV Application Commentary, 1998	mid 60s
Hagner, Donald A.	New International Biblical Commentary, 1990 Encountering the Book of Hebrews, 2002	during the 60s
Hewitt, Thomas	Tyndale New Testament Commentaries, 1960	around 65
Johnson, Luke Timothy	The New Testament Library, 2006	between 45 and 70
Kistemaker, Simon J.	New Testament Commentary, 1984	early 80s
Koester, Craig R.	Anchor Bible, 2001	between 60 to 90
Lane, William L.	Word Biblical Commentary, 1991	64 to June 68
Michaels, J. Ramsey	Cornerstone Biblical Commentary Series, 2009	Shortly before/after 70
Mitchell, Alan C.	Sacra Pagina, 2007	early 70s
Moffatt, James	International Critical Commentary, 1948	81–96
O'Brien, Peter T.	The Pillar New Testament Commentary, 2010	before 70
Pfitzner, Victor C.	Abington New Testament Commentaries, 1997	before 64
Stedman, Ray C.	IVP New Testament Commentary Series, 1992	67–68
Wilson, R. McLachlan	The New Century Bible Commentary, 1987	80–90

Dating Ascribed by Authors of New Testament Studies

CHART 15

	Brown	Carson	Fiensy	Gromacki
Matthew	80–90	70	50–55	50–70
Mark	between 68 & 73	between 50–60	66–67	45–68
Luke	85	mid to late 60s	before 62	before 60
John	80–110	80–85	90	85–95
Acts	85	mid 60s	62–64	before 64
Romans	Winter 57–58	57	56	55–56
1 Corinthians	late 56–early 57	55	54	Winter 55
2 Corinthians	Autumn 57	56	55	55
Galatians	54–55	48	48	48–49
Ephesians	90s	early 60s	61–62	59–61
Philippians	56	mid 50s to 60s	61–62	60–61
Colossians	80s	early 60s	61–62	59–61
I Thessalonians	50 or 51	50	50–52	51
2 Thessalonians	late 1st century	50–early 51	50–52	51
1 Timothy	end 1st century	early 60s	62–65	62
2 Timothy	end 1st century	mid 60s	65	64–67
Titus	end 1st century	mid 60s	62–65	62
Philemon	56	mid 60s	61–62	60
Hebrews	60s; prob 80s	before 70	around 64	before 70
James	80s or 90s	mid 40s	late 50s	45–50
1 Peter	70–90	after 63	65	63–65
2 Peter	130	before 65	64–65	64–67
1 John	100	early 90s	100	between 85–95
2 John	100	early 90s	100	between 85–95
3 John	100	early 90s	100	between 85–95
Jude	90–100	mid–late 60s	75	66–80
Revelation	92–96	68–69	95	95

	Guthrie, D.	**Kümmel**	**Robinson**	**Zahn**
Matthew	prior to 63	80–100	62	61–63
Mark	65–70	70	62	64–70
Luke	63–64	70–90	62	75
John	80–95	90s	65	80–90
Acts	62–64	80–90	65	75
Romans	57–59	55–56	early 57	March 58
1 Corinthians	57	54–55	Spring 55	April 57
2 Corinthians	57	55–56	early 56	November 57
Galatians	49–50	53–55	late 56	April/May 53
Ephesians	50–51	80–100	Summer 58	62
Philippians	50–51	56/58 or 58/60	Spring 58	Spring 63
Colossians	50–51	56/58 or 58/60	Summer 58	Winter 62–63
I Thessalonians	49	50–52	early 50	June 53
2 Thessalonians	49	50–52	early 50 or 51	Aug/Sept 53
1 Timothy	64–67	turn 2nd century	Autumn 55	64–65
2 Timothy	64–67	turn 2nd century	Autumn 58	Summer 66
Titus	64–67	turn 2nd century	late Spring 57	64–65
Philemon	50–51	56/58 or 58/60	Summer 58	Spring 63
Hebrews	64–70	80–90	67	before 90
James	40–50	end 1st century	early 48	44–51
1 Peter	58–68	end 1st century	Spring 65	64
2 Peter	60–68	150	61–62	75?
1 John	90–100	90–110	60–65	80
2 John	90–100	90–110	60–65	after 80
3 John	90–100	90–110	60–65	after 80
Jude	65–80	turn 2nd century	61–62	75
Revelation	90–95	90–95	68–70	95

Debated Considertions about Hebrews as a Sermonic Letter

CHART 16

Sermonic Letter		
Evidence	**Pros**	**Cons**
External Evidence	Manuscripts (cf. Chart 26) place Hebrews with other New Testament letters.	Manuscripts typically place Hebrews with Pauline letters as well, but such a placement does not necessitate the work to be a letter any more than it deems Hebrews to be authored by Paul.
	Hebrews follows the pattern of the sermon in Acts 13:16–41, which like Hebrews is described to be a "word of exhortation" (cp. Hebrews 13:22).	Hebrews develops an argument along the lines of classic rhetoric with a prologue (1:1–4), a thematic statement (1:5–4:16), a statement of the plausibility of the case (5–6), demonstration of the proof for the case (7:1–10:18), and a peroration (10:19–13:25) (Aristotle, *Rhetoric* 1.3.1–9 ; 3.13-19).
Internal Evidence	There are indications that Hebrews is a friendship letter: the author has a good opinion of the readers (6:9), he recalls their generosity to other believers (6:10), he knows of their persecutions (10:32; 12:4), they have a mutual friend (13:23), and he longs to visit them (13:19, 23).	The absence of an epistolary salutation and thanksgiving argues against Hebrews being a letter.
	The oscillating presentation of material in Hebrews of a formal introduction (3:1–6; 8:1–6; 12:1–3), scriptural citations (3:7–11; 8:7–13; 12:4–6), exposition (3:12–4:13; 9:1–10:18; 12:7–11), and application (4:14–16; 10:19–25; 12:12–16) is evidence of an ancient Jewish homily or sermon.	Hebrews follows the pattern of rhetoric, perhaps deliberative rhetoric urging readers to follow a course of action (4:11; 6:18; 10:35–36; 12:1–2) or epideictic that reinforces the values of the readers (3:6; 4:14; 10:23), as an art of persuasion.
	The distinctive use of the first person (we, us, and our) is a customary feature for both personal letters and oral discourse.	The presence of the author's declaration of peace (13:20–21), news of Timothy (13:23), exchange of greetings (13:24), and final prayer (13:25) are evidence of a postscript that argues more for Hebrews being a letter than a homily.

Hebrews: A "Mixed" Christian Letter of Exhortation

CHART 17

Paraenetic Features: exhorts readers to a certain positive behavior	Admonishing Features: warns or dissuades readers from adverse behavior	Encouraging Features: reminds readers of past or ongoing behavior	Consoling Features: consoles the readers over troubles that befell them
We must pay closer attention to what we have heard (2:1)	The position of the Son in relation to the angels (1:5–2:18)		For surely his concern is not for angels, but for Abraham's descendants (2:16)
Consider Jesus, the apostle and high priest of our confession (3:1)	Exposition of Psalm 95 and warning against an evil, unbelieving heart (3:7–19, especially 12).		For since he himself suffered when he was tempted, he is able to help those who are tempted (2:18)
Exhort one another every day, that none of you become hardened (3:13)			
Let us fear, lest any of you appear to have come short of reaching God's rest (4:1)	Admonition by reminder of the rebellious Israelites that failed to enter the promised land (4:2–13).		
Let us make every effort to enter that rest (4:11)			
Let us confidently approach the throne of grace (4:16)			
Let us advance beyond the elementary teachings about Christ and move on to maturity (6:1)	Admonition against immaturity and being slow to obey and mature (5:11–6:3)		
But we want each of you to demonstrate the same diligence (6:11)	Warning against falling away by apostasy (6:4–8)		

Paraenetic Features: exhorts readers to a certain positive behavior	Admonishing Features: warns or dissuades readers from adverse behavior	Encouraging Features: reminds readers of past or ongoing behavior	Consoling Features: consoles the readers over troubles that befell them
Hold fast to the hope set before us (6:18)			
Let us draw near with a sincere heart (10:22)			
Let us consider how to stir up one another toward love and good deeds (10:23–24)	Admonition against abandoning community assemblies and willfully sinning (10: 25–31)		
Remember the former days (10:32)	Warning against loss of their eternal reward (10: 35–38)	Encouragement that readers exhibit continued faith and preservation of life (10:39)	Consolation by reminder of past suffering endured and the readers' positive example (10:32–34)
Let us lay aside every weight and the sin that easily entangles (12:1)			
Let us run with patient endurance the race that is set before us (12:1)			
Consider closely him who endured such hostility against himself from sinners (12:3)			
Strengthen your weakened hands and your weak knees and make straight paths for your feet (12:12–13)			
Pursue peace with everyone, and holiness (12:14)			

Paraenetic Features: exhorts readers to a certain positive behavior	Admonishing Features: warns or dissuades readers from adverse behavior	Encouraging Features: reminds readers of past or ongoing behavior	Consoling Features: consoles the readers over troubles that befell them
See to it that no one comes short of the grace of God (12:15)			
Let us give thanks, since we are receiving an unshakeable kingdom (12:28)			
Let us render worship that is pleasing to God (12:28)			

Genre Ascribed by Commentators

CHART 18

Commentator	Commentary Series and Publication	Genre
Allen, David L.	New American Commentary, 2010	Sermonic Letter
Attridge, Harold W.	Hermeneia, 1989	Synagogue Sermon
Bruce, F. F.	NICNT, 1990	Midrash in Rhetorical Prose
Cockerill, Gareth L.	NICNT, 2012	Sermonic Letter
Ellingworth, Paul	NIGTC, 1993	Sermonic Letter
Girdwood, Jim and Peter Verkruyse	The College Press NIV Commentary, 1997	Sermonic Letter
Guthrie, Donald	Tyndale New Testament Commentaries, 1983	Letter
Guthrie, George, H.	NIV Application Commentary, 1998	Sermon
Hagner, Donald A.	New International Biblical Commentary, 1990 Encountering the Book of Hebrews, 2002	Sermonic Letter Sermonic Letter
Hewitt, Thomas	Tyndale New Testament Commentaries, 1960	Epistle
Johnson, Luke Timothy	The New Testament Library, 2006	Rhetorical Sermon
Kistemaker, Simon J.	New Testament Commentary, 1984	Epistle
Koester, Craig R.	Anchor Bible, 2001	Rhetorical Sermon
Lane, William L.	Word Biblical Commentary, 1991	Synagogue Homily
Michaels, J. Ramsey	Cornerstone Biblical Commentary Series, 2009	
Mitchell, Alan C.	Sacra Pagina, 2007	Christian Church Homily
Moffatt, James	International Critical Commentary, 1948	Letter
O'Brien, Peter T.	The Pillar New Testament Commentary, 2010	Sermonic Letter
Pfitzner, Victor C.	Abington New Testament Commentaries, 1997	Sermonic Letter
Stedman, Ray C.	IVP New Testament Commentary Series, 1992	Letter
Wilson, R. McLachlan	The New Century Bible Commentary, 1987	Sermonic Letter

Debated Considerations About the Structure of Hebrews

CHART 19

Structural Options	Pros	Cons
Thematic arrangements…	… tend to be more descriptive and explain the content of Hebrews (or more "content-oriented").	… do little to reveal the author's flow of thought (i.e., "better than," "greater than," and "superior than" descriptions do not always fit nor do they reflect the entirety of the book).
	… tend to divide Hebrews into blocks based upon major themes.	… tend to ignore repetition of themes evidenced in Hebrews.
	… tend to be built on the expositional sections of Hebrews.	… miss the significant literary shifts from exposition to exhortation evident throughout Hebrews.
Rhetorical arrangements…	… draw attention to the literary devices in Hebrews (repetition, inclusio, parallelism, hook words, etc.) that highlight the flow of thought from one section to another.	… are not easily categorized according to any one form of ancient Greek rhetorical speech (deliberative or epideictic).
	… are sensitive to the oral features in Hebrews (repetition of sounds and words).	… suggest the author's manner of argumentation follows the rhetorical and exegetical skills of a Jewish author.
	… are consistent with the strongly pastoral character of Hebrews in that it helps readers identify with Jesus.	… that designate units of thought as exordium, narration, and argumentation, are less helpful to the modern interpreter.

Structural Options	Pros	Cons
Chiastic literary arrangements…	… emphasize literary features of Hebrews (i.e., inclusio, chiasmus) that reveal a concentric composition.	… over dramatize the balance of literary features to form a concentric center for Hebrews.
	… identify aspects of style, genre shifts, repetition, and vocabulary.	… ignore the linear manner in which author of Hebrews moves from the beginning to the end of his letter.
	… are more concerned with the interpretation of the text and less concerned with Greek rhetorical developments.	… miss some of the intertwining and the repetition of themes prominent throughout Hebrews.
Text-linguistic literary arrangements …	… incorporate the best features of rhetorical and chiastic arrangements.	… are not based upon a systemic-functional linguistics developed for Hellenistic Greek that examines the function and use of language.
	… emphasize the literary parts (exposition and exhortation) and how they contribute to the literary whole.	… lack scholarly agreement on the major and minor divisions in Hebrews.
	… draw attention to the literary and thematic relationship between paragraphs.	

Structure Ascribed by Commentators

CHART 20

Commentator	Commentary Series and Publication	Structure
Allen, David L.	New American Commentary, 2010	Chiastic Arrangement
Attridge, Harold W.	Hermeneia, 1989	Epideictic Rhetorical Arrangement
Bruce, F. F.	NICNT, 1990	Thematic Arrangement
Cockerill, Gareth K.	NICNT, 2012	Chiastic Arrangement
Ellingworth, Paul	NIGTC, 1993	Chiastic Arrangement
Girdwood, Jim and Peter Verkruyse	The College Press NIV Commentary, 1997	Chiastic Arrangement
Guthrie, Donald	Tyndale New Testament Commentaries, 1983	Thematic Arrangement
Guthrie, George, H.	NIV Application Commentary, 1998	Text-Linguistic Arrangement
Hagner, Donald A.	New International Biblical Commentary, 1990	Text-Linguistic Arrangement
Hewitt, Thomas	Tyndale New Testament Commentaries, 1960	Thematic Arrangement
Johnson, Luke Timothy	The New Testament Library, 2006	Deliberative Rhetorical Arrangement
Kistemaker, Simon J.	New Testament Commentary, 1984	Thematic Arrangement
Koester, Craig R.	Anchor Bible, 2001	Epideictic / Deliberative Rhetorical Arrangement
Lane, William L.	Word Biblical Commentary, 1991	Text-Linguistic Arrangement
Mitchell, Alan C.	Sacra Pagina, 2007	Chiastic Arrangement
Moffatt, James	International Critical Commentary, 1948	Rhetorical Arrangement
O'Brien, Peter T.	The Pillar New Testament Commentary, 2010	Text-Linguistic Arrangement
Pfitzner, Victor C.	Abington New Testament Commentaries, 1997	Chiastic Arrangement
Stedman, Ray C.	IVP New Testament Commentary Series, 1992	Thematic Arrangement
Wilson, R. McLachlan	The New Century Bible Commentary, 1987	Thematic Arrangement (?)

Thematic Arrangements of Hebrews

CHART 21

Thematic Structural Scheme of Philip E. Hughes

    I.   Christ superior to the prophets (1:1–3)

   II.   Christ superior to the angels (1:4–2:18)

  III.   Christ superior to Moses (3:1–4:13)

  IV.   Christ superior to Aaron (4:14–10:18)

   V.   Christ superior as the new and living way (10:19–12:29)

  VI.   Concluding exhortations, requests, and greetings (13:1–25)

Thematic Structural Scheme of F. F. Bruce (NICNT)

    I.   The Finality of Christianity (1:1–2:18)

   II.   The True Home of the People of God (3:1–4:13)

  III.   The High Priesthood of Christ (4:14–6:20)

  IV.   The Order of Melchizedek (7:1–28)

   V.   Covenant, Sanctuary, and Sacrifice (8:1–10:18)

  VI.   Call to Worship, Faith, and Perseverance (10:19–12:29)

 VII.   Concluding Exhortations and Prayer (13:1–21)

VIII.   Postscript (13:22–25)

Thematic Structural Scheme of Donald Guthrie (Tyndale)

    I.   The Superiority of the Christian Faith (1:1–10:18)

       A.   God's revelation through the Son (1:1–4)

       B.   The superiority of the Son to the angels (1:5–2:18)

       C.   The superiority of Jesus to Moses (3:1–19)

       D.   The superiority of Jesus to Joshua (4:1–13)

       E.   A superior high priest (4:14–9:14)

       F.   The mediator (9:15–10:18)

   II.   Exhortations (10:19–13:25)

       A.   The believer's present position (10:19–39)

       B.   Faith (11:1–40)

       C.   Discipline and its benefits (12:1–29)

       D.   Concluding advice (13:1–25)

Rhetorical Arrangements of Hebrews

CHART 22

Rhetorical Analysis of Harold W. Attridge

Exordium (1:1–4)

I. Christ exalted and humiliated, a suitable High Priest (1:5–2:18)

    A. Christ exalted above the angels (1:5–14)

    B. Paraenetic interlude: Hold fast (2:1–4)

    C. Christ the Savior, a faithful and merciful High Priest (2:5–18)

II. Christ faithful and merciful (3:1–5:10)

    A. A homily on faith (3:1–4:13)

    B. Christ the merciful High Priest (4:14–5:10)

III. The difficult discourse (5:11–10:25)

    A. Paraenetic prelude (5:11–6:20)

    B. Christ and Melchizedek (7:1–28)

    C. An exegetical homily on Christ's sacrificial act (8:1–10:18)

    D. Paraenetic application: Have faith, hope, and charity (10:19–25)

IV. Exhortation to faithful endurance (10:26–12:13)

    A. Paraenetic prelude (10:26–31)

    B. An encomium on faith (11:1–40)

    C. A homily on faithful endurance (12:1–13)

V. Concluding exhortations (12:14–13:21)

    A. Paraenetic prelude: A final warning against failure (12:14–17)

    B. The serious, but encouraging situation (12:18–29)

    C. The life of the covenant (13:1–21)

Concluding benediction and greetings (13:20–25)

Rhetorical Analysis of Craig Koester

I. Exordium (1:1–2:4)

II. Proposition (2:5–9)

III. Arguments (2:10–12:27)

    A. First Series (2:10–6:20)

        1. Argument: Jesus received glory through faithful suffering—a way that others are called to follow (2:10–5:10)

        2. Transitional Digression: Warning and Encouragement (5:11–6:20).

    B. Second Series (7:1–10:39)

        1. Argument: Jesus' suffering is the sacrifice that enables others to approach God (7:1–10:25).

        2. Transitional Digression: Warning and Encouragement (10:26–39).

    C. Third Series (11:1–12:27)

        1. Argument: God's people persevere through suffering to glory by faith (11:1–12:24).

        2. Transitional Digression: Warning and Encouragement (12:25–27).

IV. Peroration (12:28–13:21)

V. Epistolary Postscript (13:22–25)

Chiastic Arrangements of Hebrews

CHART 23

Chiastic Structural Scheme of Albert Vanhoye

1:1–4 Exordium

A¹   1:5–2:18 A name different from the name of angels

   B¹ 3:1–4:14   Jesus is faithful

     B² 4:15–5:10   Jesus is a compassionate high priest

       C¹ 5:11–6:20 First exhortation

         C² 7:1–28 Jesus is a high priest in the order of Melchizedek

         C³ 8:1–9:28 Jesus comes to fulfillment

         C⁴ 10:1–18 Jesus is the cause of an eternal salvation

       C⁵ 10:19–39 Second exhortation

   B³ 11:1–40 The faith of men and women of old

   B⁴ 12:1–13 The endurance required

A²   12:14–13:19 The peaceful fruit of justice

13:20–25 Peroration

Chiastic Structural Scheme of Gareth L. Cockerill

A   1:1–2:4 Sinai Picture

   B 2:5–4:13 Pilgrimage Picture

     C 4:14–10:31 High Priest Picture

   B 10:32–12:13 Pilgrimage Picture

A   12:14–29 Sinai Picture

13:1–25 Final Application and Farewell

Chiastic Structural Scheme of Victor C. Pfitzner

A   1:1–2:18 God's Final Revelation in the Son

   B 3:1–4:13 The Son, as Faithful High Priest, Calls to Faith

     C 4:14–7:28   The Son as Merciful High Priest

     C 8:1–10:31   The Perfect Sacrifice of the Heavenly High Priest

   B 10:32–12:17   A Call to Persevering Faith

A   12:18–13:25   The Call to Heavenly Worship

Chiastic Structural Scheme of Albert Vanhoye

1:1–4 Exordium

A¹   1:5–2:18 A name different from the name of angels

   B¹ 3:1–4:14   Jesus is faithful

      B² 4:15–5:10   Jesus is a compassionate high priest

         C¹ 5:11–6:20 First exhortation

            C² 7:1–28 Jesus is a high priest in the order of Melchizedek

            C³ 8:1–9:28 Jesus comes to fulfillment

            C⁴ 10:1–18 Jesus is the cause of an eternal salvation

         C⁵ 10:19–39 Second exhortation

      B³ 11:1–40 The faith of men and women of old

   B⁴ 12:1–13 The endurance required

A²   12:14–13:19 The peaceful fruit of justice

13:20–25 Peroration

Text-Linguistic Structure of Hebrews

CHART 24 (GEORGE GUTHRIE)

1:1-4	Introduction: *God Has Spoken to Us in a Son*

	exposition	*exhortation*
1:5-14	I. The Position of the Son in Relation to the Angels	
2:1-4	A. The Son Superior to the Angels	**WARNING:** *Do not Reject the Word Spoken Through God's Son*
2:5-9	ab. The Superior Son for a Time Became Positionally Lower than the Angels	
2:10-18	B. The Son Lower than the Angels (i.e., among men) to Suffer for the sons	
3:1-6		*Jesus, the Supreme Example of a Faithful Son*
3:7-19		*The Negative Example of Those Who Fell through Faithfulessness*
4:1-2		*[Intermediary Transition]*
4:3-11		*The Promise of Rest for Those Who are Faithful*
4:12-13		**WARNING:** *Consider the Power of God's Word*
	II. The Position of the Son, Our High Priest, in Relation to the Earthly Sacrificial System	
4:14-16	Opening: Since We Have a High Priest… [Overlap]	Closing: Hold Fast and Draw Near
	A. The Appointment to the Son As a Superior High Priest	
5:1-10	1. Introduction: The Son taken from Among Men and Appointed According the Order of Melchizedek	
5:11-6:3		*The Present Problem with the Hearers*
6:4-8		**WARNING:** *The Danger of Falling Away from the Christian Faith*
6:9-12		*Mitigation: The Author's Confidence in & Desire for the Hearers*
6:13-20	God's Promise Our Basis of Hope	
7:1-10	2. The Superiority of Melchizedek	
7:11-28	3. The Superiority of Our Eternal, Melchizedekan High Priest	
8:1-2	ab. We Have Such a High Priest Who is a Minister in Heaven	
	B. The Superior Offering of the Appointed High Priest	
8:3-6	1. Introduction: The More Excellent Ministry of the Heavenly High Priest	
8:7-13	2. The Superiority of the New Covenant	
9:1-10:18	3. The Superiority of the New Covenant Offering	
10:19-25	Closing: Since We Have a Great Priest Who takes Us into Heaven [Overlap]	Closing: Hold Fast and Draw Near
10:26-31		**WARNING:** *The Danger of Rejecting God's Truth and God's Son.*
10:32-39		*The Positive Example of the Hearers' Past and an Admonition to Endure to Receive the Promise*
11:1-40		*The Positive Example of the Old Testament Faithful*
12:1-2		*Reject Sin and Fix Your Eyes on Jesus, Supreme Example of Endurance*
12:3-17		*Endure Discipline as Sons*
12:18-24		*The Blessings of the New Covenant*
12:25-29		**WARNING:** *Do not Reject God's Word!*
13:1-19		*Practical Exhortations*
13:20-21		Benediction
13:22-25		Conclusion

Canonical Overview of the New Testament

CHART 25

Legend:
- X = Citation or allusion
- O = Named as authentic
- ? = Named as disputed

BOOK	Pseudo-Barnabas (ca. 70–130)	Clement of Rome (ca. 95–97)	Ignatius (ca. 110)	Polycarp (ca. 110–50)	Hermas (ca. 115–40)	Didache (ca. 115–40)	Papias (ca. 130–40)	Irenaeus (ca. 130–202)	Diognetus (ca. 150)	Justin Martyr (ca. 150–55)	Clement of Alexandria (ca. 150–55)	Tertullian (ca. 150–215)	Origen (ca. 185–254)	Cyril of Jerusalem (ca. 185–254)	Eusebius (ca. 315–86)	Jerome (ca. 340–420)	Augustine (ca. 400)	Marcion (ca. 140)	Muratorian (ca. 170)	Barococcio (ca. 206)	Apostolic (ca. 300)	Cheltenham (ca. 360)	Athanasius (367)	Tatian Diatessaron (ca. 170)	Old Latin (ca. 150–170)	Old Syriac (ca. 200)	Nicea (ca. 325–40)	Hippo (393)	Carthage (397)	Carthage (419)
Matthew	X	X	X	X	X	X		O		X	X	X	X	X	O	O	O		O	O	O	O	O	O	O	O	O	O	O	O
Mark	X	X	X					O		X	X	X	X	X	O	O	O		O	O	O	O	O	O	O	O	O	O	O	O
Luke	X	X	X			X		O		X	X	X	X	X	O	O	O	O	O	O	O	O	O	O	O	O	O	O	O	O
John		X	X	X			X	O		X	X	X	X	X	O	O	O		O	O	O	O	O	O	O	O	O	O	O	O
Acts	X	X			X			O		X	X	X	X	X	O	O	O		O	O	O	O	O	O	O	O	O	O	O	O
Romans	X	X	X	X		X		O		X	O	X	X	X	O	O	O	O	O	O	O	O	O	O	O	O	O	O	O	O
1 Corinthians	O	X	X	X		X		O		X	O	X	X	X	O	O	O	O	O	O	O	O	O	O	O	O	O	O	O	O
2 Corinthians		X	X					O		X		X	X	X	O	O	O	O	O	O	O	O	O	O	O	O	O	O	O	O
Galatians		X	X	X				O		X		X	X	X	O	O	O	O	O	O	O	O	O	O	O	O	O	O	O	O
Ephesians	X	X	X	X				O		X	O	X	X	X	O	O	O	O	O	O	O	O	O	O	O	O	O	O	O	O
Philippians		X	X	X				O			O	X	X	X	O	O	O	O	O	O	O	O	O	O	O	O	O	O	O	O
Colossians		X	X					O				X	X	X	O	O	O	O	O	O	O	O	O	O	O	O	O	O	O	O
1 Thessalonians		X	X	X				O		X	X	X	X	X	O	O	O	O	O	O	O	O	O	O	O	O	O	O	O	O
2 Thessalonians		X	X					O		X	X	X	X	X	O	O	O	O	O	O	O	O	O	O	O	O	O	O	O	O
1 Timothy	X			X				X		X	X	X	X	X	O	O	O		O	O	O	O	O	O	O	O	O	O	O	O
2 Timothy	X			X				X		X		X	X	X	O	O	O		O	O	O	O	O	O	O	O	O	O	O	O
Titus	X	X		X				X		O		X	X	X	O	O	O		O	O	O	O	O	O	O	O	O	O	O	O
Philemon												X			O	O	O			O	O	O	O	O	O	O	O	O	O	O
Hebrews	X	X			X					O	O	X	O	O	O	O	O			O	O	O	O	?	O	O	O	O	O	O
James	X				X								?	O	?	O	O			O	O	?	O	?	?	O	?	O	O	O
1 Peter	X			X				O			O	X	O	O	O	O	O			O	O	O	O	O	O	O	O	O	O	O
2 Peter	X	X									X	?	?	?	?	O	O			O	?	?	O	?	?	O	?	O	O	O
1 John				X				O			O	X	O	O	O	O	O			O	O	O	O	O	O	O	O	O	O	O
2 John				X							X	?	?	?	O	O	O			O	?	?	O	?	?	O	?	O	O	O
3 John												?	?	?	O	O	O			O		?	O		?	O		O	O	O
Jude		X		X				X			O	X	?	?	O	O	O		O	O	O	?	O		?	O	?	O	O	O
Revelation					X	X		O	X	X	X	O	O		O	O			O	O	O		O	O	O		O	O	O	O

Taken with adaptation from William E. Nix and Norman L. Geisler, *Introduction to the Bible* (Chicago: Moody, 1968). Used by permission.

Canonical Placement of Hebrews in the New Testament

CHART 26

Canonical Placement*	Manuscript Evidence	Date of Manuscript	Family Text-type
After Romans	P[46]	200 C.E.	Alexandrian
	103	11th century	Byzantine†
	455	13th/14th century	Byzantine (?)
	1961	14th century	Byzantine (?)
	1964	15th century	Byzantine
	1977	14th century	Byzantine (?)
	1994	16th century	Byzantine (?)
	2104	12th century	Byzantine (?)
	2576	1287	Byzantine (?)
	2685	15th century	Byzantine (?)
After 2 Corinthians	1930	16th century	Byzantine
	1978	15th century	Byzantine
	1992	1232	Byzantine
	2000	14th century	Byzantine (?)
	2248	14th century	Byzantine (?)
	Coptic Version (Southern Dialect: Sahidic)	3rd to 4th centuries	Alexandrian

* Canonical Placement of Hebrews = Metzger's listing in *A Textual Commentary of the Greek New Testament* (p. 591).

† Entries marked "Byzantine (?)" are printed editions of the Greek New Testament that have not been checked (see UBS 4th edition, NA27). Yet, they were labeled "Byzantine (?)" because other printed editions (103 1964 1930 1978 1992 2690) were labeled clearly as Byzantine by Aland in *The Text of the New Testament* (pp. 129–40).

Canonical Placement*	Manuscript Evidence	Date of Manuscript	Family Text-type
After Galatians	B (03)	4th century	Alexandrian
After Ephesians	606	11th century	Byzantine (?)
After Philippians	2690	16th century	Byzantine
	2739	14th century	Byzantine (?)
After 2 Thessalonians	א (01)	4th century	Alexandrian
	A (02)	5th century	Alexandrian
	B (03)[3]	4th century	Alexandrian
	C (04)	5th century	Alexandrian
	H (015)	6th century	Independent
	P (025)	9th century	Independent
	0150	9th century	Independent
	0151	9th century	Byzantine
	33	9th century	Alexandrian
	81	1044	Alexandrian
	1739	10th century	Alexandrian
	1877	14th century	Independent
	1881	14th century	Alexandrian
	1962	11th/12th century	Alexandrian
	2127	12th century	Alexandrian
After Titus	1311	1090	Byzantine (?)
	2183	1042	Byzantine

---

*   For an explanation concerning the appearance of Hebrews "After Galatians" and then later "After 2 Thessalonians" see Bruce Metzger, *A Textual Commentary on the Greek New Testament* (2nd edition), 591 n. 2.

Canonical Placement	Manuscript Evidence	Date of Manuscript	Family Text-type
	D (06)	6th century	Western (?)*
	L (019)	8th century	Byzantine
	044	9th/10th century	Alexandrian
	048	5th century	Alexandrian
	056	10th century	Byzantine
	075	10th century	Independent
	0142	10th century	Byzantine
	104	1087	Independent (?)†
	326	12th century	Independent (?)
	330	12th century	Independent
After Philemon (Today's Ordering)	451	11th century	Independent
	614	13th century	Western (?)
	629	14th century	Western (?)
	630	14th century	Independent
	1984	14th century	Independent (?)
	1985	1561	Independent (?)
	2492	13th century	Independent
	2495	14th/15th century	Independent
	it^d	5th century	Western
	Coptic Version (Northern Dialect: Bohairic)	4th to 5th centuries	Alexandrian

---

*   "Western (?)" = manuscripts labeled by Aland as Independent, though their description by Aland in *The Text of the New Testament* (p. 133) shows a Western influence.

†   Independent (?) = Greek minuscules that exhibit a significant degree of independence from the so-called Byzantine family (see UBS 4th edition, xix-xx). Yet, they were labeled Independent (?) because other minuscules (405 1984 1985 2492 2495) were labeled clearly as Independent by Aland in *The Text of the New Testament* (pp. 129–37).

Citations of Hebrews by Early Church Leaders

CHART 27

Figure/Text	Date	Hebrews	Writings
Clement of Rome	ca. 95–97	1:3–4, 5, 7, 13; 2:18; 3:1	*Letter to the Corinthians (1 Clement) 36.1-5*
Ignatius of Antioch	ca. 110	4:14–5:10	*Letter to the Philadelphians 9.1*
Polycarp	ca. 110–150	6:20; 7:3	*Letter to the Philippians 12.2*
The Didache	ca. 120–150	13:7	*Didache 4:1*
Papias of Hierapolis	ca.130–140	No citation	
Irenaeus	ca. 130–202	1:3	*Against Heresies 2.30.9*
Epistle to Diognetus	ca. 150	No citation	
Justin Martyr	ca. 148–155	3:1	*First Apology 12*
Clement of Alexandria	ca. 150–215	2:14–16 2:11; 8:10–12 10:32–39; 11:1–4, 36–40; 12:1–2	*The Instructor 3.3* *Exhortation to the Heathen §11* *Miscellanies 2.2, 4; 4.16*
Tertullian	ca. 150–220	6:1, 4–6	*Modesty 20.3*
Origen	ca. 185–254	2:9	*Commentaries on Romans 3.8*
Cyril of Jerusalem	ca. 315–386	3:13; 10:22; 12:16; 13:4	*Catechetical Lectures 23.15; 3.4; 4.24–25*
Eusebius*	ca. 325–340	5:6; 10:34; 12:6	*Ecclesiastical History 1.3.17; 6.41.6; 10.4.33*
Jerome*	ca. 340–420	2:1; 6:4, 9; 7:3 7:6; 11:17–19, 32 12:6	*Against Jovinianus 1.3, 5, 23, 28; 2.3* *Letter to Julian (Letter 118) 5* *Against the Pelagians 1.28*
Hilary of Poitiers	ca. 315–368	7:27 1:4; 3:1	*Homilies on the Psalms: Ps 53, §13* *On the Trinity: 4.11*
Basil "The Great"	ca. 330–379	11:6 11:14	*Letter to Amphilochius, Bishop of Iconium 234.2* *On the Spirit 27.66*

Figure/Text	Date	Hebrews	Writings
Didymus the Blind	ca. 313–398	11:3	*The Trinity* 3.2.8
Gregory of Nazianzen	ca. 330–389	2:14; 5:12–14; 7:23; 8:8–13	*In Defense of his Flight to Pontus* 23, 24, 45, 62
		7:3; 13:8	*On the Theophany* 2, 12
		4:15	*Second Oration on Easter* 13
Gregory of Nyssa	ca. 335–394	11:1, 3	*Dialogue on the Soul and Resurrection* (NPNF2, pp. 450, 457)
		1:6–12, 14; 2:14; 6:20; 7:21	*Against Eunomius* 6.2; 11.3; 12.1
Ambrose of Milan	ca. 339–397	10:10–12; 4:12	*On the Christian Faith* 4.6.70, 74
		11:33, 34, 37	*Letter LXIII (to the Church at Vercellæ)* 67
John Chrysostom	ca. 344–407	11:6	*The Incomprehensible Nature of God* 5.40
		1:1–2, 3, 6–8; 2:5–7, 16–17; 3:7–11, etc.	*Homilies on the Epistle to the Hebrews* (34 homilies on various verses)
		1:3; 4:12, 13; 13:4	*Letters to the Fallen Theodore* 1.12; 2.2,3
Augustine*	ca. 400	11:1; 1:13	*Enchiridion* 8; 58
		9:15; 11:7, 11–12; 12:14; 13:2	*City of God* 17.6; 18.38; 15.6; 16.29
		13:4	*On the Good of Marriage* 8
Cyril of Alexandria	ca. 423–431	2:11–12	*Dialogues on the Holy Trinity* 6
		1:3	*Memorials on the True Faith* 2.3
		2:14; 3:1	*The Twelve Anathemas* (end of letter 17, the third to Nestorius) 5, 10
Fulgence of Ruspe	ca. 467–527	12:2	*Letter to Count Reginus* 18.9
Gregory I ("The Great")	ca. 590–604	9:4; 12:5–6, 9–10	*Book of Pastoral Rule* 2.6; 3.12
John of Damascus	ca. 645–749	2:17; 13:4	*Exposition of the Orthodox Faith* 4.13, 24

* See the "Chart Comments" for the items marked with an * (asterisk).

Inclusion of Hebrews in Early Church Canons

CHART 28

Barococcio's Canon (*circa* 206)	Apostolic Canon (*circa* 300)	Athanasius's Canon (*circa* 367)
Matthew	Matthew	Matthew
Mark	Mark	Mark
Luke	Luke	Luke
John	John	John
Acts	Acts	Acts
Romans	Romans	Romans
1 Corinthians	1 Corinthians	1 Corinthians
2 Corinthians	2 Corinthians	2 Corinthians
Galatians	Galatians	Galatians
Ephesians	Ephesians	Ephesians
Philippians	Philippians	Philippians
Colossians	Colossians	Colossians
1 Thessalonians	1 Thessalonians	1 Thessalonians
2 Thessalonians	2 Thessalonians	2 Thessalonians
1 Timothy	1 Timothy	1 Timothy
2 Timothy	2 Timothy	2 Timothy
Titus	Titus	Titus
Philemon	Philemon	Philemon
Hebrews	Hebrews	Hebrews
James	James	James
1 Peter	1 Peter	1 Peter
2 Peter	2 Peter	2 Peter
1 John	1 John	1 John
2 John	2 John	2 John
3 John	3 John	3 John
Jude	Jude	Jude
		Revelation

Omission of Hebrews from Early Church Canons

CHART 29

Marcion's Canon (*circa* 140)	Muratorian's Canon (*circa* 160–180)	Cheltenham's Canon (*circa* 360)
	Matthew	Matthew
	Mark	Mark
Luke	Luke	Luke
	John	John
	Acts	Acts
Romans	Romans	Romans
1 Corinthians	1 Corinthians	1 Corinthians
2 Corinthians	2 Corinthians	2 Corinthians
Galatians	Galatians	Galatians
Ephesians	Ephesians	Ephesians
Philippians	Philippians	Philippians
Colossians	Colossians	Colossians
1 Thessalonians	1 Thessalonians	1 Thessalonians
2 Thessalonians	2 Thessalonians	2 Thessalonians
	1 Timothy	1 Timothy
	2 Timothy	2 Timothy
	Titus	Titus
Philemon	Philemon	Philemon
		1 Peter
		2 Peter (?)
	1 John	1 John
	2 John	2 John (?)
		3 John (?)
	Jude	
	Revelation	Revelation
	(*Apocalypse of Peter*)	
	(*Wisdom of Solomon*)	

Part Two

OLD TESTAMENT AND SECOND TEMPLE INFLUENCES IN HEBREWS

Old Testament Quotations in Hebrews

CHART 30

Quotation	Hebrews	Quotation	Hebrews
Psalm 2:7	1:5	Psalm 110:4	7:17, 21
2 Samuel 7:14	1:5		
Deuteronomy 32:43 (LXX)	1:6	Exodus 25:40	8:5
Psalm 104:4	1:7	Jeremiah 31:31–34	8:8–12
Psalm 45:6–7	1:8-9		
Psalm 102:25–27	1:10–12	Exodus 24:8	9:20
Psalm 110:1	1:13		
		Psalm 40:6–8	10:5–7
Psalm 8:4–6	2:6–8	Jeremiah 31:33–34	10:16–17
Psalm 22:22	2:12	Deuteronomy 32:35	10:30
Isaiah 8:17–18	2:13	Deuteronomy 32:36	10:30
		Psalm 135:14	10:30
Psalm 95:7–11	3:7–11	Habakkuk 2:3–4	10:37–38
Psalm 95:7–8	3:15		
		Genesis 21:12	11:18
Psalm 95:11	4:3, 5		
Genesis 2:2	4:4	Proverbs 3:11–12	12:5–6
Psalm 95:7–8	4:7	Exodus 19:12–13	12:20
		Deuteronomy 9:19	12:21
Psalm 2:7	5:5	Haggai 2:6	12:26
Psalm 110:4	5:6	Deuteronomy 4:24	12:29
Genesis 22:17	6:14	Deuteronomy 31:6	13:5
		Psalm 118:6 (LXX)	13:6

Direct Quotes Categorized by Old Testament Divisions

CHART 31

Pentateuch

OT Book	English Bible	Hebrew Bible	Septuagint	Hebrews
Deuteronomy	32:43	32:43	32:43	1:6
Genesis	2:2	2:2	2:2	4:4
Genesis	22:17	22:17	22:17	6:14
Exodus	25:40	25:40	25:40	8:5
Exodus	24:8	24:8	24:8	9:20
Deuteronomy	32:35	32:35	32:35	10:30
Deuteronomy	32:36	32:36	32:36	10:30
Genesis	21:12	21:12	21:12	11:18
Exodus	19:12–13	19:12–13	19:12–13	12:20
Deuteronomy	4:24	4:24	4:24	12:29
Deuteronomy	31:6	31:6	31:6	13:5

Historical and Prophetic Books

OT Book	English Bible	Hebrew Bible	Septuagint	Hebrews
2 Samuel	7:14	7:14	7:14	1:5
Isaiah	8:17–18	8:17–18	8:17–18	2:13
Jeremiah	31:31–34	31:31–34	38:31–34	8:8–12
Jeremiah	31:33–34	31:33–34	38:33–34	10:16–17
Habakkuk	2:3–4	2:3–4	2:3–4	10:37–38

Poetic Books				
OT Book	**English Bible**	**Hebrew Bible**	**Septuagint**	**Hebrews**
Psalm	2:7	2:7	2:7	1:5
Psalm	104:4	104:4	103:4	1:7
Psalm	45:6–7	45:7–8	44:7–8	1:8
Psalm	102:24–26	102:25–27	101:25–27	1:10–12
Psalm	110:1	110:1	109:1	1:13
Psalm	8:4–6	8:5–7	8:5–7	2:6–8
Psalm	22:22	22:23	21:23	2:12
Psalm	95:7–11	95:7–11	94:7–11	3:7–11
Psalm	95:7–8	95:7–8	94:7–8	3:15
Psalm	95:11	95:11	94:11	4:3, 5
Psalm	95:7–8	95:7–8	94:7–8	4:7
Psalm	2:7	2:7	2:7	5:5
Psalm	110:4	110:4	109:4	5:6
Psalm	110:4	110:4	109:4	7:17, 21
Psalm	40:6–8	40:7–9	39:7–9	10:5–7
Psalm	135:14	135:14	134:14	10:30
Proverbs	3:11–12	3:11–12	3:11–12	12:5–6
Psalm	118:6	118:6	117:6	13:6

Old Testament Allusions in Hebrews

CHART 32

Allusion	Hebrews	Allusion	Hebrews
Psalm 2:8	1:3	Psalm 110:1	8:1
Psalm 110:1	1:3	Exodus 25:40	8:5
		Isaiah 53:12	9:28
Numbers 12:7	3:5		
Numbers 14:13, 19, 22	3:16	Psalm 110:1	10:12
Numbers 14:26–35	3:17	Psalm 110:1	10:13
Numbers 14:34–35	3:18	Exodus 24:3–8	10:22
		Ezekiel 36:25–26	
Psalm 110:4	5:10	Isaiah 26:11	10:27
		Deuteronomy 17:6	10:28
Numbers 14:35, 39–45	6:4	Isaiah 26:20	10:37
Deuteronomy 11:11; 28:12	6:7		
Genesis 3:17–18	6:8	Genesis 22:17	11:12
Deuteronomy 29:23, 27	6:8	Genesis 47:31 (cp. LXX)	11:21
Psalm 110:4	6:20		
		Psalm 110:1	12:2
Genesis 14:17–20	7:1–2	Isaiah 35:3	12:12
Genesis 14:20	7:4	Deuteronomy 29:18	12:15

Allusions Categorized by Old Testament Divisions

CHART 33

Pentateuch				
OT Book	English Bible	Hebrew Bible	Septuagint	Hebrews
Genesis	3:17–18	3:17–18	3:17–18	6:8
Genesis	14:17–20	14:17–20	14:17–20	7:1–2
Genesis	14:20	14:20	14:20	7:4
Genesis	22:17	22:17	22:17	11:12

Pentateuch				
OT Book	**English Bible**	**Hebrew Bible**	**Septuagint**	**Hebrews**
Genesis	47:31	47:31	47:31	11:21
Exodus	25:40	25:40	25:40	8:5
Numbers	12:7	12:7	12:7	3:5
Numbers	14:13, 19, 22	14:13, 19, 22	14:13, 19, 22	3:16
Numbers	14:26–35	14:26–35	14:26–35	3:17
Numbers	14:34–35	14:34–35	14:34–35	3:18
Deuteronomy	11:11	11:11	11:11	6:7
Deuteronomy	17:6	17:6	17:6	10:28
Deuteronomy	28:12	28:12	28:12	6:7

Pentateuch				
OT Book	**English Bible**	**Hebrew Bible**	**Septuagint**	**Hebrews**
Deuteronomy	29:18	29:18	29:18	12:15
Deuteronomy	29:23, 27	29:23, 27	29:23, 27	6:8

Prophetic Books				
OT Book	**English Bible**	**Hebrew Bible**	**Septuagint**	**Hebrews**
Ezekiel	36:25–26	36:25–26	36:25–26	10:22
Isaiah	53:12	53:12	53:12	9:28
Isaiah	26:11	26:11	26:11	10:27
Isaiah	26:20	26:20	26:20	10:37
Isaiah	35:3	35:3	35:3	12:12

Poetic Books				
OT Book	**English Bible**	**Hebrew Bible**	**Septuagint**	**Hebrews**
Psalm	2:8	2:8	2:8	1:3
Psalm	110:1	110:1	109:1	1:3
Psalm	110:1	110:1	109:1	8:1

Poetic Books				
OT Book	**English Bible**	**Hebrew Bible**	**Septuagint**	**Hebrews**
Psalm	110:1	110:1	109:1	10:12
Psalm	110:1	110:1	109:1	10:13
Psalm	110:1	110:1	109:1	12:2
Psalm	110:4	110:4	109:4	5:10
Psalm	110:4	110:4	109:4	6:20

Old Testament People Named in Hebrews

CHART 34

People in the Pentateuch Mentioned			
Person	**OT Reference**	**OT Event**	**Hebrews**
Cain	Gen 4:3–7	Cain offered an unacceptable sacrifice to God.	11:4
Abel	Gen 4:2–5	Abel offered an acceptable sacrifice to God.	11:4
Abel	Gen 4:8–11	Cain killed Abel whose blood cried out from the ground.	12:24
Enoch	Gen 5:22–24	Enoch was a righteous person who did not experience physical death.	11:5
Noah	Gen 6:9–22	Noah built an ark and saved his family.	11:7
Abraham	Gen 22:16–17	Abraham obeyed; God promised to multiply his offspring.	6:13–15
Abraham	Gen 14:20b–24	Abraham paid a tithe to Melchizedek.	7:1–2
Abraham	Gen 12:1–8; 23:4	Abraham left Sumer for a new land.	11:8
Abraham	Gen 22:1–12	Abraham offered Isaac as a sacrifice.	11:17
Sarah	Gen 17:15–21; 18:9–15	Sarah, via an angel, is promised she will conceive a son.	11:11
Melchizedek	Gen 14:18–20a	Melchizedek brought bread and wine to Abraham, and blessed him.	7:1
Melchizedek	Gen 14:20b	Melchizedek accepted a tithe from Abraham.	7:2a
Isaac	Gen 27:27–29, 39–40	Isaac blessed Esau and Jacob.	11:20
Jacob	Gen 48:14–20	Jacob blessed the sons of Joseph.	11:21

People in the Pentateuch Mentioned			
Person	**OT Reference**	**OT Event**	**Hebrews**
Levi	Lev 27:30–34; Num 18:21, 26	The descendants of Levi were to receive Israel's tithe offered to the Lord.	7:9
Judah	Gen 49:10	From the line of Judah came kings and not priests.	7:14
Joseph	Gen 50:24–25	Joseph gave instructions about his burial in the land.	11:22
Moses	Num 12:7	Moses was the Lord's servant.	3:2, 3, 5
Moses	Num 14:2–4	The people rebelled against Moses at Kadesh.	3:16
Moses	Num 18:21, 26	Moses never spoke of Judah and the priesthood.	7:14
Moses	Exod 25:40	Moses was to pattern the earthly tabernacle after the one he saw on the mountain.	8:5
Moses	Exod 24:3, 6–8	Moses, having received the Lord's commands, offered a sacrifice.	9:19
Moses' Parents	Exod 2:1–2	After Moses was born, his parents hid him for three months.	11:23
Moses	Exod 2:11–15	Moses identified himself with the Jewish people, killed an Egyptian, fled from Pharaoh.	11:24–26
Moses	Exod 12:21–28	Moses kept (inaugurated) the Passover in Egypt.	11:28
Moses	Exod 14:5–31	Moses led the exodus community across the Red Sea.	11:29
Moses	Exod 19:16–25	Moses approached the Lord on the sacred Mt. Sinai.	12:21

People in the Historical Books Mentioned			
Person	**OT Reference**	**OT Event**	**Hebrews**
Joshua	Josh 22:4	Joshua told the eastern tribes (Reubenites, Gadites, and half-tribe of Manasseh) to return home because "God has given rest … as he promised."	4:8
Rahab	Josh 2:1–24; 6:17, 23–25	Rahab hid two Israelite spies and escaped the destruction of Jericho .	11:31
Gideon	Judg 6:11–12; 7:1–25	An angel of the Lord appeared to Gideon and addressed him as a mighty warrior. Gideon defeated the Midianites.	11:32
Barak	Judg 4:6–24	Barak defeated Sisera, army commander of King Jabin of Canaan, at Mount Tabor.	11:32
Samson	Judg 13:24–16:31	Samson wreaked havoc with the Philistines and died destroying a Dagon temple.	11:32
Jephthah	Judg 11:1–29; 12:1–7	Jephthah defended the Gadites against the Ammonites and later the Ephraimites.	11:32
Samuel	1 Sam 7:3–16	Samuel subdued the Philistines at Mizpah and served as a judge in Israel.	11:32
David	Ps 95:7b-8	A psalm of worship attributed to David.	4:7
David	1 Sam 16–17	David served Saul, defeated Goliath and numerous enemies of Israel, and ruled as king over the nation of Israel.	11:32

The Tabernacle in Exodus

CHART 35

The Outer Court Yard	The Gate of the Court Yard	The Sanctuary	The Sanctuary's Screen	The Sanctuary's Veil	Priestly Garments
27:9–19;	27:16;	26:1–37;	26:36–37;	26:31–35;	28:1–43;
38:9–17;	38:18–20;	36:14–34;	36:8–13;	36:35–38;	39:1–41;
40:8–9, 33	40:8	40:18–19	40:28	40:3b, 21	40:13–15

Brazen Altar for Sacrifices	Laver	Golden Lampstand	Table of Showbread	Altar of Incense	Ark
27:1–8;	30:18–21;	25:31–40;	25:23–30;	30:1–10;	25:10–22;
38:1–7;	38:8;	37:17–24;	37:10–16;	37:25–29;	37:1–9;
40:6, 10, 29	40:7, 11, 30–32	40:4b, 24–25	40:4a, 22–23	40:5, 26–27	40:3a, 20–21

The Tabernacle's Sanctuary in the Old Testament

CHART 36

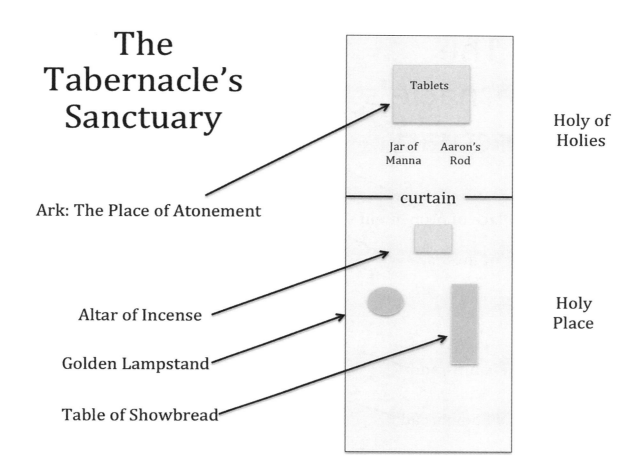

The Tabernacle's Sanctuary

Ark: The Place of Atonement

Altar of Incense

Golden Lampstand

Table of Showbread

Tablets

Jar of Manna   Aaron's Rod

Holy of Holies

curtain

Holy Place

Scripture	Holy Place	Golden Lampstand	Table of Showbread	Altar of Incense	Inner Curtain	Holy of Holies	Ark
Exodus	26:33–34	25:31–40; 37:17–24; 40:4b, 24–25	25:23–30; 37:10–16; 40:4a, 22–23	30:1–10; 37:25–29; 40:5, 26–27	26:31–35	26:33–34	25:10–22; 37:1–9; 40:3a, 20–21
Leviticus		24:1–4	24:5–9	16:13	16:12, 15	16:12	16:13–19
Numbers		4:9–10	4:7–8	4:11–14			4:5–6

The Tabernacle's Sanctuary in Hebrews

CHART 37

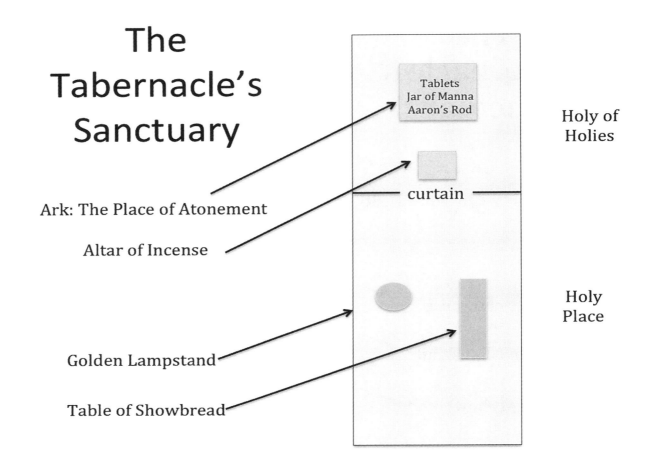

The
Tabernacle's
Sanctuary

Tablets
Jar of Manna
Aaron's Rod

Holy of
Holies

curtain

Ark: The Place of Atonement

Altar of Incense

Holy
Place

Golden Lampstand

Table of Showbread

Sources	Holy Place	Golden Lampstand	Table of Showbread	Inner Curtain	Holy of Holies	Altar of Incense	Ark
Hebrews	9:2, 6	9:2	9:2	10:20	9:3, 7	9:4	9:4, 5

The Old Testament Tabernacle's Sanctuary
Compared with Hebrews
CHART 38

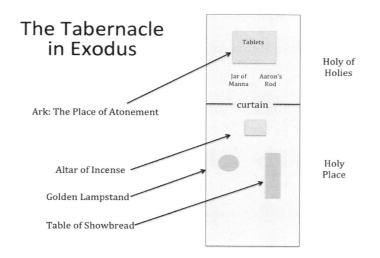

The Tabernacle in Exodus

Ark: The Place of Atonement

Altar of Incense

Golden Lampstand

Table of Showbread

Tablets

Jar of Manna   Aaron's Rod

curtain

Holy of Holies

Holy Place

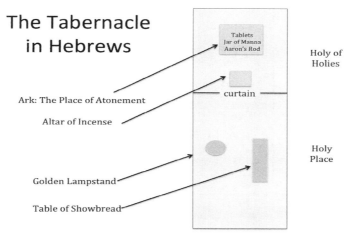

The Tabernacle in Hebrews

Ark: The Place of Atonement

Altar of Incense

Golden Lampstand

Table of Showbread

Tablets
Jar of Manna
Aaron's Rod

curtain

Holy of Holies

Holy Place

Sources	Holy Place	Golden Lampstand	Table of Showbread	Inner Curtain	Holy of Holies	Altar of Incense	Ark
Hebrews	9:2, 6	9:2	9:2	10:20	9:3, 7	9:4	9:4, 5

	Holy Place	Golden Lampstand	Table of Showbread	Inner Curtain	Holy of Holies	Altar of Incense	Ark
Exodus	26:33–34	25:31–40; 37:17–24; 40:4b, 24–25	25:23–30; 37:10–16; 40:4a, 22–23	26:31–35	26:33–34	30:1–10; 37:25–29; 40:5, 26–27	25:10–22; 37:1–9; 40:3a, 20–21
Josephus, *Antiquities*	3.122, 124–133	3.144–146	3.139–143	3.126	3.122, 124–126	3.147–150	3.134–138

Old Testament Feasts and Celebrations in Hebrews

CHART 39

Feast	When	OT Texts	Description	Reference in Hebrews
Sabbath (and Jubilee)	Every 7th day of the week	Exod 23:10–12; Lev 23:3	Patterned after God's 6 days of creation, all work stops on the 7th day of the week.	4:3–4
Passover	March/April	Exod 12:1–14; Lev 23:5; Num 28:16	People celebrate the nation's escape from Egypt under the leadership of Moses.	11:28
Feast of Unleavened Bread	The week following Passover	Exod 23:15–20; Lev 23:6–8; Num 28:17	For 7 days, people eat bread without leaven as a reminder of women who had no time to let bread rise when they left Egypt.	Not Cited
First fruits	April	Exod 23:16a; Lev 23:9–14; Num 28:26	Once the harvest season begins, people are to bring the first fruits of harvest to the priest.	Not Cited
Feast of Weeks (Pentecost)	June Fifty days after Passover.	Exod 23:16b; Lev 23:15–21	At the end of the grain harvest, people bring their offerings to God as a reminder that God provides.	Not Cited
Feast of Trumpets	Sept/Oct 1st day of the month	Lev 23:23–25; Num 29:1–2	On the first day of the month, a blast of trumpets sounded to mark the start of the New Year festival.	Not Cited
Day of Atonement	Sept/Oct 10th day of the month	Lev 16:1–34; Num 29:7–11	The entire nation fasts, confesses their sins, and asks God's forgiveness.	9:7, 25
Feast of Tabernacles (Shelters)	Sept/Oct 15th day of the month	Lev 23:34–43; Num 29:12–40	For 7 days, after arriving in Jerusalem, people build shelters of branches as a reminder of desert living during the Exodus.	Not Cited

The Day of Atonement in Leviticus and Hebrews

CHART 40

Questions	Leviticus 16	Reference in Hebrews
Who officiates?	As the levitical high priest, he alone enters a tabernacle made with human hands (16:2–3, 17; cp. Exod 25–26).	As regal high priest, Jesus alone enters the heavenly tabernacle (9:12, 25–28; 10:1–3, 10:14).
What is needed?	1. A young bull is needed for a sin offering (16:3, 6, 11, 14, 18–19) 2. Two male goats are needed (16:5, 7–10): one as a sin offering (16:3, 15, 18–19), one as a scapegoat (16:5, 8, 10, 20–22).	1. One person is needed: Jesus (9:11–14). 2. Compare the concept of human atonement in Rom 9:3.
What happens to the animals?	1. The bull is sacrificed as a sin offering and its blood is sprinkled on the atonement plate (16:6, 11, 14). 2. The sin offering goat is sacrificed and its blood is sprinkled on the atonement plate (16:15). 3. The scapegoat is sent into the wilderness (16:10, 21–22).	Jesus' death on the cross serves as atonement in the heavenly holy of holies (9:11–12; 10:4–10). Some may argue that Jesus dies and offers his own blood in the heavenly sanctuary.
Who benefits?	1. The blood of the sacrificed bull benefits the high priest and his household (16:6, 11–14). 2. The blood of the sacrificed goat benefits the people (16:15). 3. The blood of the sacrificed bull and goat benefits the tabernacle (16:18–19) 4. The scapegoat benefits the community (16:21–22).	1. The blood of Jesus benefits all who are called (9:15). 2. The blood of Jesus benefits all who eagerly await him (9:28). 3. Compare: The sufferings of Jesus benefits all who obey him (5:9).
How often is this to occur?	1. On the Day of Atonement, the high priest enters the holy of holies three times on behalf of himself, the people, and then the tabernacle (16:11, 15, 18–19, 33). 2. The Day of Atonement and its expectations were repetitious and needed to be practiced annually (16:29, 34).	1. Jesus enters the heavenly holy of holies _once_ for all people (9:28). 2. Jesus enters the heavenly holy of holies _once_ for all, never to be repeated (9:11–12, 25–28; 10:1–3, 10–14).

Overview of Jewish High Priesthood (539 B.C.E. –70 C.E.)

CHART 41

High Priests	Dates	Primary Sources	Historical Issues
Joshua to Jaddua	539–332 B.C.E. (Temple rebuilt, 515)	Nehemiah; Haggai; Zechariah; Josephus *Antiquities*; *Elephantine Papyri*	Persian control of Judah (539–332 B.C.E.)
Onias I to Alcimus	309–159 B.C.E.	Josephus *Antiquities*; 1, 2, 3 Maccabees	Grecian control of Judah (332–159 B.C.E.)
Jonathan to Antigonus	159–37 B.C.E.	Josephus; 1 Maccabees; 4QPesher Nahum	Hasmonean control of Judea (152–37 B.C.E.)
Ananel to Phannias	37 B.C.E.-70 C.E. (Temple destroyed, 70 C.E.)	Josephus *Antiquities* and *Jewish War*	Herodian control of Judea (37 B.C.E. – 70 C.E.)

High Priests of the Persian Period (539–332 B.C.E.)

CHART 42

High Priest	Dates (B.C.E.)	Primary Sources	Historical Issues
Joshua	Time of Cyrus (539–530) and during the reign of Darius (520)	Hag 1:1, 12, 14; 2:2, 4; Zech 3:1, 3, 6, 8, 9; 6:11; Neh 12:22	First high priest of the Second Temple period
Joiakim		Neh 12:10, 12, 26; Josephus, *Ant.* 11.121–58	
Eliashib	445–433	Neh 3:1, 20–21; 12:10, 22; 13:28; Josephus, *Ant.* 11.158–83	Contributes to the construction of Jerusalem's walls by building the Sheep gate
Joiada	433	Neh 12:10-11, 22; 13:28; Josephus, *Ant.* 11.297	
Johanan	410	Neh 12:22, 23; Josephus, *Ant.* 11.297–301; *Elephantine Papyri, AP 30 = TAD A4.7*	Jews of Elephantine write to Johanan for support to rebuild their temple. (Porten, *The Elephantine Papyri in English*, 148–51)
Jaddua	332	Neh 12:11, 22; Josephus, *Ant.* 11.302–47	Meets Alexander the Great (Josephus, *Ant.* 11.304–32)

High Priests of Early Hellenistic Period (332–159 B.C.E.)

CHART 43

High Priest	Dates (B.C.E.)	Primary Sources	Historical Issues
Onias I	Contemporary of the Spartan Monarch Areus I (309–265)	Josephus, *Ant.* 11.347; 12.226–27	Spartan monarch writes to Onias to generate relations (cp. 1 Macc 12:20–23)
Simon I (Surnamed the Just)		Josephus, *Ant.* 12.43	
Eleazar	Contemporary of Ptolemy II Philadelphus (283–246)	Josephus, *Ant.* 12.44-45; *Letter of Aristeas* 41–46	Ptolemy II requests Eleazar for a Greek translation of the Jewish books about their laws (see *Letter of Aristeas*)
Manassah		Josephus, *Ant.* 12.157	
Onias II	Contemporary of Ptolemy III Euergetes (246–221)	Josephus, *Ant.* 12.154–224	Onias II loses the right to collect taxes in Judah to Joseph, son of Tobias.
Simon II	Contemporary of Ptolemy IV Philopator (221–204)	3 Macc 2:1–3; Josephus, *Ant.* 12.224–29.	Ptolemy IV's victory over Antiochus III at Raphia; Antiochus III's victory over Ptolemy V at Panion (198/200 B.C.E.)
Onias III	? – September 175 (died 3 years later)	2 Macc 3:1–4:6 Death: 2 Macc 4:30–38; Dan 9:26	Is forced out of the high priestly position by his brother, Jason; Antiochus IV appoints Jason as high priest
Jason	175–172	2 Macc 4:7–23 (cp. 1 Macc 1:11–15); Josephus, *Ant.* 12.240–41.	Jason's appointment is based upon promises to convert Jerusalem to Hellenism; but eventually forced out of the high priestly position; Antiochus IV appoints Menelaus as high priest
Menelaus	172–162	2 Macc 4:24–5:10; 11:27–33; 13:3–8; Josephus, *Ant.* 12.383–85	Jason revolts against Menelaus; Antiochus IV reappoints Menelaus as high priest; Maccabean Revolt
Interlude: Onias IV	164 – ?	Josephus, *J. W.* 1.31–33; 7.420–36	Flees Judah to Egypt; founded a temple in Heliopolis; assumes for himself the title high priest
Alcimus	162–160 or 159	1 Macc 7:12–16, 21–25; 9:54–57; 2 Macc 14:1–4; Josephus, *Ant.* 12.385; 12.413	Replaces Menelaus as high priest; was at odds with Judas Maccabeus; dies of a heart attack

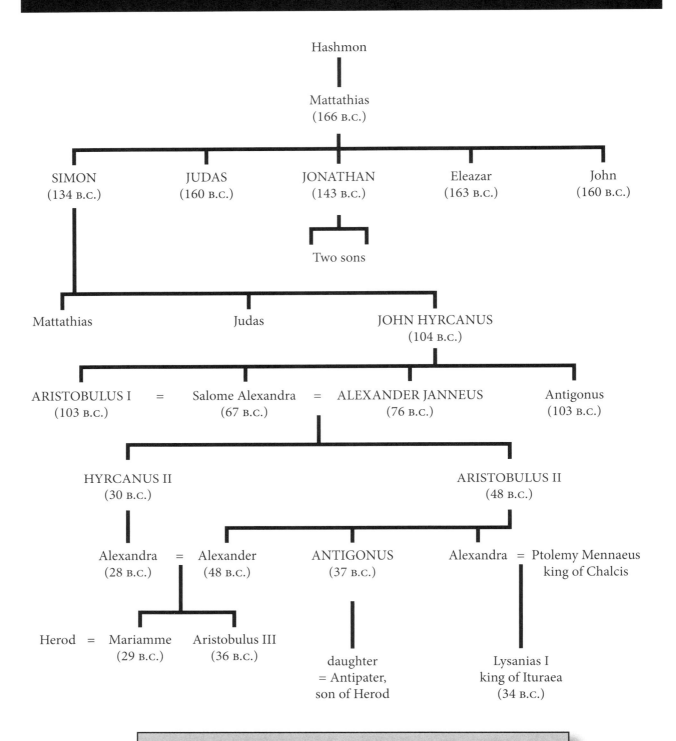

Hasmonean Family Tree

CHART 44

Hashmon

Mattathias
(166 B.C.)

SIMON
(134 B.C.)

JUDAS
(160 B.C.)

JONATHAN
(143 B.C.)

Eleazar
(163 B.C.)

John
(160 B.C.)

Two sons

Mattathias

Judas

JOHN HYRCANUS
(104 B.C.)

ARISTOBULUS I
(103 B.C.)

=

Salome Alexandra
(67 B.C.)

=

ALEXANDER JANNEUS
(76 B.C.)

Antigonus
(103 B.C.)

HYRCANUS II
(30 B.C.)

ARISTOBULUS II
(48 B.C.)

Alexandra
(28 B.C.)

=

Alexander
(48 B.C.)

ANTIGONUS
(37 B.C.)

Alexandra

=

Ptolemy Mennaeus
king of Chalcis

Herod

=

Mariamme
(29 B.C.)

Aristobulus III
(36 B.C.)

daughter
= Antipater,
son of Herod

Lysanias I
king of Ituraea
(34 B.C.)

Names in capitals denote those Hasmoneans who were rulers.
The dates following (unless otherwise indicated) are the dates of death.
The symbol "=" denotes "marriage to."

High Priests of the Early Hasmonean Period
(152–37 B.C.E.)

CHART 45

High Priest	Dates (B.C.E.)	Primary Sources	Historical Issues
Jonathan	152–142	1 Macc 9:23–10:66	Appointed high priest by Alexander Balas/Epiphanes.
Simon	142–134	1 Macc 10:67–14:49	Acquires independence from King Demetrius; recognized as high priest, leader, governor, ethnarch, protector of the Jewish people; and has national recognition.
John Hyrcanus	134–104	1 Macc 16:11–22; Josephus, *Ant.* 13.230–58	Assumes the high priesthood after the murder of Simon, expands the Hasmonean kingdom, and favors the Sadducees.
Aristobulus I	104–103	Josephus, *Ant.* 13.301–19; *J. W.* 1.70–84	the high priesthood after the death of John Hyrcanus, declares himself king and priest, expands the Hasmonean kingdom, and favors the Sadducees.
Alexander Jannaeus	103–76	Josephus, *Ant.* 13.320–405; *J. W.* 1.85–106; 4QpNah 3–4 I, 1–9	Assumes the royal priesthood from his brother, expands the Hasmonean kingdom, and favors the Sadducees.
Hyrcanus II	76–67, 63–40	Josephus, *Ant.* 13.408; 14.46–57; *J. W.* 1.109–137, 141-43, 153	Appointed high priest by Alexandra and eventually the royal crown; thwarted by his brother; reappointed as high priest by Pompey.
Aristobulus II	67–63	Josephus, *Ant.* 14.46–67; *J. W.* 1.142–152	Usurped the royal priesthood from Hyrcanus II; defeated by Pompey in 63; carried off to Rome and eventually murdered.
Antigonus	40–37	Josephus, *Ant.* 14.140–491; *J. W.* 1.195–357	Usurped the royal priesthood from Hyrcanus II, was defeated by Herod the Great; carried off to prison and died.

Herodian Family Tree

CHART 46

Names in capitals denote those Hasmoneans who were rulers.
The dates following (unless otherwise indicated) are the dates of death.
The symbol "=" denotes "marriage to."

THE HERODS OF JUDEA

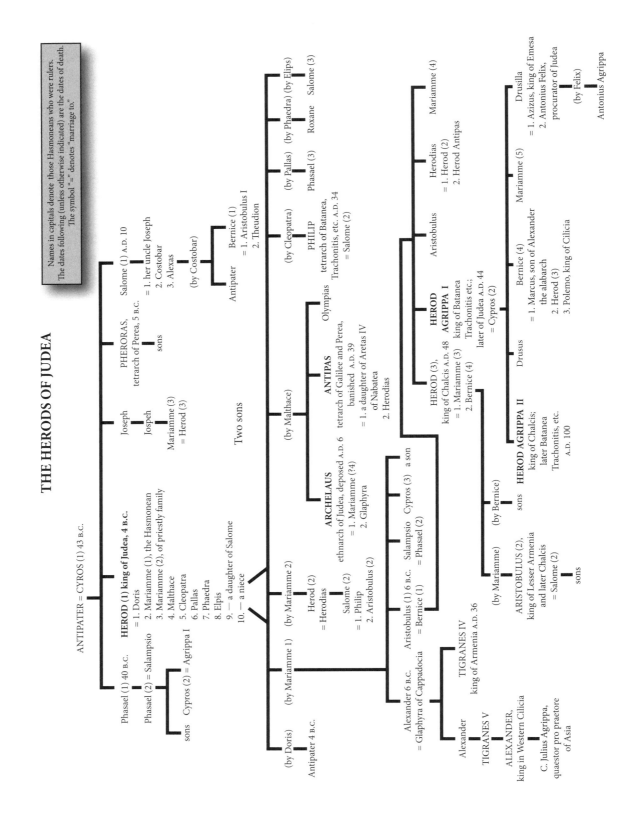

High Priests of the Herodian Period (37 B.C.E. - 70 C.E.)

CHART 47

High Priest	Dates	Primary Sources	Historical Issues
Ananel	37–35 B.C.E.	Josephus, *Ant.* 15.22, 39–40	First high priest appointed by Herod the Great.
Aristobulus III	35 B.C.E.	Josephus, *Ant.* 15.31–36, 40–53	Second high priest appointed by Herod the Great, who drowned "accidentally."
Ananel (reappointed)	35–30? B.C.E.	Josephus, *Ant.* 15.56	High priest reappointed by Herod, after Herod's brother-in-law, Aristobulus III, died.
Jesus son of Phiabi	30?–between 24–22 B.C.E.	Josephus, *Ant.* 15.322	Third high priest appointed by Herod the Great.
Simon son of Boethus	24–22 to 5 B.C.E.	Josephus, *Ant.* 15.319–22	Fourth high priest appointed by Herod the Great, whose daughter, Mariamme II, Herod married, and under whom Herod began rebuilding the temple.
Matthias son of Theophilus	5–4 B.C.E.	Josephus, *Ant.* 17.149–67	Fifth high priest appointed by Herod the Great.
Joazar son of Boethus	4 B.C.E.(?)–6 C.E.	Josephus, *Ant.* 17.164, 339	Sixth and last high priest appointed by Herod the Great.
Eleazar son of Boethus	4 B.C.E.	Josephus, *Ant.* 17.339	First high priest appointed by Archelaus.
Jesus son of Seë	4 B.C.E. – ?	Josephus, *Ant.* 17.341	Second high priest appointed by Archelaus.
Joazar son of Boethus (reappointed)	6 C.E.	Josephus, *Ant.* 18.2–3, 26	High priest reappointed by Quirinius, legate of Syria.
Ananus son of Seth/Sethi	6–15 C.E.	Josephus, *Ant.* 18.26, 34	First high priest appointed by Quirinius, legate of Syria.

High Priest	Dates	Primary Sources	Historical Issues
Ishmael son of Phiabi	15–16? C.E.	Josephus, *Ant.* 18.34	First high priest appointed by Gratus, a prefect of Rome who governed Judea, Samaria, and Idumea.
Eleazar son of Ananus	16–17? C.E.	Josephus, *Ant.* 18.34	Second high priest appointed by Gratus, a prefect of Rome.
Simon son of Camith	17–18 C.E.	Josephus, *Ant.* 18.34; *t. Yoma* 3:20; *m. Yoma* 7:4	Third high priest appointed by Gratus, a prefect of Rome.
Joseph Caiaphas	18–36/37 C.E.	Josephus, *Ant.* 18.35, 55–64; Matt 26:3, 51–57; Mark 14:47, 53; Luke 3:2; 22:50, 54; John 11:45–53; 18:10–14; Acts 4:5-21	Fourth high priest appointed by Gratus, a prefect of Rome, who questioned Jesus and was instrumental in Jesus' subsequent crucifixion.
Jonathan son of Ananus	36/37 C.E.	Josephus, *Ant.* 18.95; 20.162–64	First high priest appointed by Vitellius, a prefect of Rome.
Theophilus son of Ananus	37–41 C.E.	Josephus, *Ant.* 18.123	Second high priest appointed by Vitellius, a prefect of Rome, but removed from office by Agrippa I.
Simon Cantheras son of Boethus	41–42 C.E.	Josephus, *Ant.* 19.297	First high priest appointed by Herod Agrippa I, grandson of Herod the Great.
Matthias son of Ananus	42–43? C.E.	Josephus, *Ant.* 19.312–16; Acts 12:1-2	Second high priest appointed by Herod Agrippa I; was in office when Agrippa had James, the son of Zebedee murdered.
Elionaeus son of Cantheras	43?–45 C.E.	Josephus, *Ant.* 19.342	Third high priest appointed by Herod Agrippa I.
Joseph son of Camei	45–48 C.E.	Josephus, *Ant.* 20.15–16	Fourth high priest appointed by Herod Agrippa I.
Ananias son of Nedebaeus	48–59 C.E.	Josephus, *Ant.* 20.102–03	High priest appointed by Herod of Chalcis.
Ishmael son of Phiabi	59–61 C.E.	Josephus, *Ant.* 20.179–81	First high priest appointed by Agrippa II.

High Priest	Dates	Primary Sources	Historical Issues
Joseph son of Simon	61–62 C.E.	Josephus, *Ant.* 20.195–96	Second high priest appointed by Agrippa II.
Ananus son of Ananus	62 C.E.	Josephus, *Ant.* 20.197–203	Third high priest appointed by Agrippa II and who took part in the Jewish war 66–68 C.E.
Jesus son of Damnaeus	62–63? C.E.	Josephus, *Ant.* 20.203	Fourth high priest appointed by Agrippa II.
Jesus son of Gamaliel	63–64 C.E.	Josephus, *J. W.* 4.160, 238–69, 314–25 (cp. *Ant.* 20.213)	High priest appointed by Agrippa II, and the year Herod's temple was completed.
Matthias son of Theophilus	64–66? C.E.	Josephus, *Ant.* 20.223	High priesthood given to Matthias by Agrippa II, under whom Jewish war against Rome began.
Phannias son of Samuel	68? C.E.	Josephus, *Ant.* 20.227; *t. Yoma* 1:6–7	High priest when Jerusalem was captured and destroyed and served as Jerusalem's last high priest.

Anointed Figures in the Old Testament

and Second Temple Literature

CHART 48

Figures Anointed	Old Testament "Anointed Ones"	Second Temple "Anointed Ones"
Prophet	Elisha (1 Kgs 19:15–16)	CD II, 12 CD V, 21–VI, 1 (=4Q267 II, 5–6 = 6Q15 III, 4) 1QM XI, 7–8 4Q270 2 II, 13–14 4Q377 1 II, 4–5 (of Moses) 4Q521 2 II, 1 (cf. 12–13) 4Q521 VIII, 9 (messianic prophets)
High Priest	Aaron (Exod 40:13; cp. Lev 7:36) Subsequent Priests (Exod 40:14–15; Lev 16:32)	CD XII, 23–XIII, 1; XIX, 10–11; XX, 1 CD XIV, 19 (= 4Q266 10 I, 12) 1QS IX, 11 4Q375 I, 9 4Q376 1 I, 1
King	Saul (1 Sam 10:1; 15:1) David (1 Sam 16:12–13; cp. Sir 46:13) Solomon (1 Kgs 1:45; cp. 1 Chr 29:22) Subsequent kings called "the Lord's anointed" (2 Sam 22:51; Pss 2:2; 18:50; cp. Lam 4:20)	CD XII, 23–XIII, 1; XIX, 10–11; XX, 1 CD XIV, 19 (= 4Q266 10 I, 12) 1QS IX, 11 1Q28a II, 11–12, 14–15, 20–21 4Q252 V, 3–4 4Q458 2 II, 6 4Q521 2 II, 1, 7, 12–13 *Pss. Sol.* 17:32; 18 (title); 18:5, 7 *4 Ezra* 7:26–36 ("messiah" = king) *1 En.* 46:3–4; 48:2; 62:5, 7, 8, 14; 63:11; 69:27, 29; 70:1; 71:17 ("son of man" = king)
Heavenly or Apocalyptic Figure	Daniel	11Q13 II, 18 (11QMelch) 4Q171 IV, 25 (4QpPs[a]) (king = holy spirit) *1 Enoch* 48:10; 52:4 *2 Baruch* 29:3; 30:1; 39:7; 40:1; 70:9; 72:2 *4 Ezra* 7:28–29; 11:37–12:34 *3 Enoch* 45:5; 48A:10

Portraits of Messiah in Second Temple Literature

CHART 49

Humanity (Lineage)	Hasmonean Period			Herodian Period				
	Early 150–125 B.C.E.	Mid 125–75 B.C.E.	Late 75–50 B.C.E.	Pre 50–30 B.C.E.	Early 30–1 B.C.E.	Mid 1–30 C.E.	Late 30–68 C.E.	Post 68–135 C.E.
Davidic Scion	*Jubilees, T. Jud.*	1Q28 1Q28a 4Q266=CD	4Q161 *Pss. Sol.*	1QM 4Q246 4Q376	4Q174 4Q252 4Q285		4Q369	*4 Ezra 2 Baruch*
Human	*Jubilees, T. Jud.*	1Q28 1Q28a 1Q28b 4Q266=CD 4Q521	4Q161 4Q382 (UK) 4Q458 *Pss. Sol.*	1QM 4Q246 4Q376	4Q174 4Q252 4Q285		4Q369 4Q423 (UK)	*4 Ezra 2 Baruch*
Offspring			*Pss. Sol.*		4Q174 4Q252		4Q369	

Authority (Leadership)	Hasmonean Period			Herodian Period				
	Early 150–125 B.C.E.	Mid 125–75 B.C.E.	Late 75–50 B.C.E.	Pre 50–30 B.C.E.	Early 30–1 B.C.E.	Mid 1–30 C.E.	Late 30–68 C.E.	Post 68–135 C.E.
Military Leader	*Jubilees, T. Jud.*	1Q28a 1Q28b 4Q266=CD	4Q161 4Q382 4Q458 *Pss. Sol.*	1QM 4Q246 4Q376	4Q174 4Q285			*4 Ezra 2 Baruch*
Political Leader	*Jubilees, T. Jud.*	4Q266=CD 4Q521	4Q161 4Q382 (UK) *Pss. Sol.*	4Q246	4Q174		4Q369 4Q423	*4 Ezra 2 Baruch*
Righteous Leader/Judge	*Jubilees, T. Jud.*	1Q28 1Q28b 4Q266=CD	4Q161 4Q458 *Pss. Sol.*		4Q252 4Q285 *1 Enoch*		4Q369 4Q423	*4 Ezra 2 Baruch*

Relationship with God (Chosen)	Hasmonean Period			Herodian Period				
	Early 150–125 B.C.E.	Mid 125–75 B.C.E.	Late 75–50 B.C.E.	Pre 50–30 B.C.E.	Early 30–1 B.C.E.	Mid 1–30 C.E.	Late 30–68 C.E.	Post 68–135 C.E.
Empowered by God's Spirit	*T. Jud.*	1Q28b	4Q161		4Q174			
Unique Relationship with God		1Q28a	*Pss. Sol.*	4Q246	4Q174		4Q369	
Interpreter of the Law	*Jubilees, T. Jud.*	4Q266=CD			4Q252			*4 Ezra 2 Baruch*

Second Temple Messianic Titles Paralleled in Hebrews

CHART 50

Title	Second Temple Literature	Hebrews
Son	1Q28a II, 11–15 ("father" within Ps 2:7); 4Q174 1 I, 10–11/III, 10–11 4Q369 1 II, 6–12 *Psalms of Solomon* 17:21–25 (Son of David) 4 Ezra 7:26–36	1:2, 5 (within Ps 2:7), 8; 3:6; 5:5 (within Ps 2:7), 8; 7:28
Son of God	4Q246 2:1–9	4:14; 6:6; 7:3; 10:29
Son of Man	*1 Enoch* 46:3–4; 48:2; 62:5, 7, 8, 14; 63:11; 69:27, 29; 70:1; 71:17	2:6 (within Ps 8:4–6)
Christ or Messiah	CD XII, 23–XIII, 1; XIX, 10–11; XX, 1 CD XIV, 19 (= 4Q266 10 I, 12) 1QS IX, 11 1Q28a II, 11–12, 14–15, 20–21 4Q252 V, 3–4 4Q458 2 II, 6 4Q521 2 II, 1, (cf. 12–13) *Psalms of Solomon* 17:32; 18 (title); 18:5, 7 4 Ezra 7:26–36 *1 Enoch* 48:10; 52:4	3:6, 14; 5:5; 6:1; 9:11, 14, 24, 28; 10:10; 11:26; 13:8, 21
Heir (In Second Temple literature, prince = heir)	CD VII, 19b–20 (4Q266 3 III, 21) 1Q28b V, 20–28 1QM V, 1 1QM III, 15 (= 4Q496 X, 3–4) 4Q161 2–6 II, 15 4Q285 6–4 I, 2, 6; 5 I, 4 4Q376 1 III, 1, 3 4Q423 5 I, 2	1:2
Melchizedekan Figure	11Q13 (11QMelch) II, 13, 24–25 (possible allusion to Ps 110)	5:6; 7:17 (within Ps 110:4)
High Priest	CD XII, 23–XIII, 1; XIX, 10–11; XX, 1 CD XIV, 19 (= 4Q266 10 I, 12) 1QS IX, 11 4Q375 I, 9 4Q376 1 I, 1	2:17; 3:1; 4:14, 15; 5:10; 6:20; 7:26; 8:1; 9:11; 10:21

Melchizedek Cited in Hebrews & Other Jewish Literature

CHART 51

Literature	Past, Present, and Future Presentations of Melchizedek	Reference
Old Testament	**Past**: Melchizedek king of Salem brought bread and wine to Abraham. He was the priest of the Most High God.	Genesis 14:18
	Past: Abram gave Melchizedek a tenth of everything.	Genesis 14:20
	Present: "You (David's heir) are a priest forever after the order of Melchizedek."	Psalm 110:4
Dead Sea Scrolls	**Future**: It will be "decreed for 'the year of Melchizedek's favor' (Isa 61:2, modified), [and] by his might he w[i]ll judge God's holy ones and so establish a righteous ki[n]gdom" (Wise, p. 456).	11Q13 II, 9
	Future: "Melchizedek will thoroughly prosecute the veng[ea]nce required by Go[d's] statu[te]s. [Also, he will deliver all the captives from the power of B]elial (the devil), and from the power of [all the spirits predestined to him] (Wise, p. 456).	11Q13 II, 13 (cp II, 25)
Hebrews	**Present**: God designated Jesus (David's heir) as a regal priest according to the order of Melchizedek.	5:6, 10; 6:20; 7:17
	Past: Melchizedek was a king of Salem, priest of the Most High God, who met Abram as he was returning from the slaughter of the kings and who blessed him.	7:1
	Past: Abram paid tithes to Melchizedek.	7:2, 4, 6, 9–10
Josephus	**Past**: Melchizedek means the righteous king; and he was without dispute … thus, he was made the priest of God.	*Antiquities* 1.180
	Past: Melchizedek supplied Abram's army in a hospitable manner … when Abram gave him the tenth part of his prey, he accepted of the gift.	*Antiquities* 1.181
Philo	**Past**: God made Melchizedek, the king of peace (i.e., the city of Salem) … and he was worthy of his priesthood. For he is called a just king … because he is the interpreter of law.	*Allegorical Interpretation* 3.79
	Past: Melchizedek defined the Most High, from his conceiving of God not in a low and groveling spirit, but one of exceeding greatness and sublimity …	*Allegorical Interpretation* 3.82
	Past: Melchizedek received a self-instructed and self-taught priesthood.	Philo, *Congr.* 99

Comparison of Mechizedek in Genesis 14, Psalm 110, 11Q13, and Hebrews 1–7

CHART 52

Genesis 14	Psalm 110	11Q13	Hebrews 1–7
Return of captives and property (14:16)	N/A	Return of captives and property in the year of Jubilee (Lines 2–6)	N/A
Captives freed by Abram (14:16)	N/A	Captives freed (Line 6). Melchizedek will free the people from the hand of Belial (Line 25)	Jesus frees captives from the devil (2:14–15)
Melchizedek was the regal priest of Salem (Jerusalem) (14:18)	The Davidic regal priest ruled in Jerusalem (110:2; cf. 2 Sam 5:1–7)	Melchizedek will reign over Zion (Jerusalem) (Lines 16, 23)	Melchizedek was the regal priest of Salem (Jerusalem) (7:1–2)
Melchizedek, the regal priest, functioned under the authority of God Most High (YHWH) (14:18)	YHWH tells the Davidic regal priest to sit at his right hand, under his authority (110:1)	Melchizedek, the regal priest, will function under the authority of YHWH (Lines 13–14)	Melchizedek, the regal priest, functioned under the authority of God Most High (YHWH) (7:1) Jesus sat down at God's right hand, the place of authority (1:3, 13; cf. Eph 1:20)
N/A	YHWH is at the Davidic regal priest's right hand (110:5)	N/A	N/A
Abram returned from defeating enemies in battle (14:14–17)	The Davidic regal-priest is in the midst of his enemies who will be defeated (110:1–2, 5–6)	Melchizedek will defeat God's enemies (Lines 13–14, 25)	Abraham slaughtered his enemies (7:1)
N/A	YHWH tells the Davidic regal priest to rule in the midst of his enemies (110:2)	N/A	N/A

Genesis 14	Psalm 110	11Q13	Hebrews 1–7
N/A	YHWH will make the Davidic regal priest's enemies a footstool, [promise of peace in the future] (110:1)	Melchizedek delivers God's people from the power of Belial and reigns over Zion (lines 23-25)	Melchizedek's name means king of peace (7:2) YHWH will make Jesus' enemies a footstool, [guarantee of future peace] (1:13; cf. 2:8)
N/A	YHWH stretches forth the king's scepter from Zion (110:2)	N/A	The son (Jesus) is God and the scepter of his kingdom is righteousness (1:8)
N/A	The Davidic regal priest's people will volunteer for military service (110:3)	Melchizedek, the regal priest, will lead the army of God's holy ones (Line 9) (Martínez, p. 1207)	N/A
Melchizedek brought out bread and wine (14:17)	N/A	N/A	N/A
God blessed Abram (12:1–3) Melchizedek, the regal priest, blessed Abram (14:19)	N/A	N/A	God blessed Abraham (6:13–14) Melchizedek, the regal priest, blessed Abraham (7:1, 6–7)
N/A	Holy garments are mentioned, possibly alluding to priesthood (110:3)	N/A	N/A
Melchizedek was a regal priest of God Most High (YHWH) (14:18)	The Davidic regal priest functioned as a priest of YHWH (110:4)	Use of the Day of Atonement implies the idea of a high priest of YHWH (Line 7)	Melchizedek was a regal priest of God Most High (YHWH) (7:1)
N/A	The regal priesthood after the order of Melchizedek will last forever (110:4)	N/A	The regal priesthood after the order of Melchizedek will last forever (5:6; 6:20; 7:3, 17, 21)
N/A	YHWH swore an oath concerning the enduring nature of the Davidic regal priesthood after the order of Melchizedek (110:4)	N/A	YHWH swore an oath concerning Jesus' eternal priesthood after the order of Melchizedek (7:17, 20–21)

Genesis 14	Psalm 110	11Q13	Hebrews 1–7
God Most High is the creator of heaven and earth (14:19)	N/A	N/A	God is referred to as resting from his work on the seventh day (4:4; cf. Gen 2:2)
God Most High (YHWH) defeated Abram's enemies (14:20)	YHWH will defeat (shatter) the Davidic regal priest's enemies (110:1, 5–6)	Melchizedek will defeat God's enemies (Lines 13–14, 25)	Jesus defeated the devil (2:14–15)
N/A	YHWH will execute judgment on the nations (110:6)	Melchizedek will administer justice (Lines 9, 13) YHWH will judge the nations (Lines 11, 23)	God acts as a judge (4:12; cf 10:26–27; 12:23; 13:4
N/A	YHWH will lift up the head of the Davidic regal priest [figurative] (110:7)	N/A	N/A
Abram gave Melchizedek a tithe (14:20)	N/A	N/A	Abraham gave Melchizedek a tithe which showed his superiority over Abraham (7:2, 4, 6–7)
Melchizedek was the first regal priest mentioned in Scripture (14:18)	The Davidic regal priest functioned after the order of Melchizedek (110:4)	N/A	Jesus functioned as a Davidic regal priest after the order of Melchizedek (5:6, 10; 6:20; 7:17, 24)
Melchizedek's regal priesthood occurred within a limited historical time frame	The Davidic regal priest was promised an enduring priesthood (110:4)	N/A	Jesus functions as an eternal regal priest (5:6; 7:17, 21)
Focuses on a present historical reality	Focuses on a future reality	Focuses on a future reality	Focuses on a present and future reality
N/A	N/A	Captives and teachers have been hidden and kept secret (Lines 4–5) (Martínez, p. 1207)	N/A

Genesis 14	Psalm 110	11Q13	Hebrews 1–7
N/A	N/A	Captives and teachers are the inheritance of Melchizedek (Line 5) (Martínez, p. 1207)	N/A
N/A	N/A	Focus on the Day of Atonement (Line 7)	Jesus is the high priest who went behind the veil—a likely reference to the Day of Atonement (6:19–20)
N/A	N/A	Atonement is made for the sons of light and the "lot of Melchizedek" (Line 8)	No mention of atonement, however, people being able to draw near to God through Jesus implies atonement (7:25)
Chedorlaomer and the kings with him took people captive, including Lot, Abram's nephew (14:5 -12)	N/A	Belial leads people away from God (Line 12)	N/A
Abram's rescue of the captives implies salvation from an enemy (14:14–16)	N/A	Melchizedek reigns and delivers God's people from the power of Belial (lines 23-25)	Jesus offers salvation (2:10; 5:9; 6:9 7:25)
N/A	N/A	N/A	Jesus is the Son of God and regal high priest (3:1; 4:14)
N/A	N/A	N/A	Melchizedek's name means king of righteousness. He is the king of peace (7:2)
N/A	N/A	N/A	Melchizedek had no father or mother (7:3)
N/A	N/A	N/A	Melchizedek had no genealogy (7:3)
N/A	N/A	N/A	Melchizedek had no birth or death (7:3)

Comparisons of Old Testament Regal Priests with Jesus in Hebrews

CHART 53

Regal Priest	Comparisons	References in OT and Hebrews
His Person	Unlike OT Davidic regal priests, mere men who were to be *like* God in how they ruled, and who died and were succeeded by another Davidic heir…	2 Sam 6:12–15; 24:17–25; 1 Kgs 1:47–48; 2:10–12; 8:27–30; 11:43; etc.; Pss 45:2–7; 72:1–2, 4, 12–14; cf. Jer 22:2–5
	in Hebrews, Jesus is a divine regal priest who rules and intercedes on behalf of his people in perfect righteousness.	Hebrews 1:1–14; 4:15; 7:25
His Ministry	Unlike OT Davidic regal priests whose function was primarily ruling over the nation with *limited* priestly roles like temple upkeep and making intercession …	David: 2 Sam 6:13–18; 24:10–25; 1 Chr 21:23–26, 22:7–19) Solomon: 1 Kgs 2:27, 35; 3:4–15; 8:12–14, 54–55, 62–64; 2 Chr 1:6; 5:1–6; 6:12–7:1, 5–8 Uzziah: 2 Chr 26:18
	in Hebrews, Jesus as regal priest has expanded priestly functions that include a one-time atoning sacrifice, entrance into and cleansing of the inner heavenly sanctuary, and making intercession.	One-time sacrifice: 1:3; 9:12, 14, 24–28 Intercession: 2:18; 4:15; 7:25; 9:24
His Location	Unlike the symbolic picture of Yahweh, the "Divine King" of Israel enthroned in heaven giving the Davidic regal priest, the "earthly king" of Israel, a special place of honor and authority to rule at his right hand …	Compare Pss 2:1–4; 80:1–15; 89:5–18 with Pss 80:17; 89:20–24; 110:1.
	in Hebrews Jesus as regal priest quite literally resides and reigns in heaven with God.	Hebrews 1:2–3, 13; 4:14; 7:25; 9:24; 10:12–13
His Dominion	Unlike OT Davidic regal priests whose political dominion was over the limited and earthly territory of Israel …	2 Sam 7:8–14; 1 Kgs 9:4–5; 1 Chr 28:5–7; 2 Chr 13:5
	in Hebrews Jesus' dominion as regal priest includes all of heaven and earth (in part now—in full later).	Hebrews 2:8; 3:1–6; 10:21
His Duration	Unlike OT Davidic regal priests whose ruling duration was always spoken of in figurative language but expected to endure through marriage and subsequent heirs …	Ps 45:17; cf. 2 Sam 7:11b–12, 14a, 16; 1 Chr 17:11–14
	in Hebrews Jesus has no heirs and his duration is literally an eternal one.	Hebrews 7:24; 13:8

Position and Character of Jesus as Regal Priest in Hebrews

CHART 54

Position & Character	Description	Hebrews
Position: Jesus is …	seated at the right hand of the throne of God.	1:3 (cp. 8:1); 1:13 (via Ps 110:1)
	a regal priest after the order of Melchizedek.	5:6, 10; 6:20; 7:17 (via Ps 110:4)
	an appointed regal priest by God.	5:5–6 (via Pss 2:7, 110:4) (cp. 5:1, 4)
	a regal priest exalted above the heavens.	7:26 (cp. 4:14)
	a minister in the heavenly sanctuary.	8:2
	a regal priest of the good things that have come.	9:11
Character: Jesus is …	a merciful and faithful regal priest.	2:17
	able to help believers who are tempted.	2:18
	able to sympathize with the weaknesses of believers.	4:15
	tempted just like everyday believers, yet without sin.	4:15
	a forerunner of all people who believe (via his regal priesthood).	6:20
	holy, blameless, unstained, separated from sinners.	7:26
	made perfect forever.	7:28
	securing an eternal redemption for believers.	9:12

The Role of Divine Beings in Jewish Theology

CHART 55

Categories	Old Testament	Extrabiblical Material
Terms used for divine beings	The term אֱלֹהִים (*Elohim*) can be translated "God" or "gods." In Ps 82:1, 6; 97:9; 138:1 it is translated "gods" and is indicative of angels. אֵל (*El*, "God") and אֵלִים (*Elim*, "gods") are also closely identified with angels. See "sons of God" below.	LXX = "gods": θεούς (Pss 81:1; 96:9); θεοί (Ps 81:6)
	"sons of God": (בְּנֵי אֵלִים or בְּנֵי־הָאֱלֹהִים), Gen 6:2, 4; Ps 29:1; 89:7; Job 1:6 The sons of God appear to have been interpreted as angels; however, in other OT contexts "sons of God" refers to Israel.	LXX = The "sons of God" (οἱ υἱοὶ τοῦ θεοῦ) are fallen angels in Gen 6:2, 4, but holy angels in Pss 28.1; 88.7 (υἱοὶ θεοῦ/υἱοῖς θεοῦ). *1 Enoch* has a theology of fallen angels and presents an account of the "sons of God" who had sexual relations with women (6:1–7:1; cf. *Jub.* 5:1–2; Sir 16:7; Josephus, *Ant.* 1.72–73) Some *pesharim* employ similar terms to describe fallen angels: "sons of Belial" (the devil) (בני בליעל), e.g., 4Q174 1 I, 7–9. But in 11QMelch II, 14, the "sons of God" (בני אל) help Melchizedek defeat Belial.
	"holy ones" (קְדֹשִׁים) The "holy ones," often refer to the angelic assembly (Zech 14:5).	LXX = The "holy ones" (ἁγίων) are an angelic assembly in Ps 88:6, 8. In 1QapGen II, 1; VI, 20, fallen "holy ones" (קדוש) (Martínez, pp. 29, 33) conceive children with women. But in 11Q17 II, 4, "eternal holy ones" (Martínez, p. 1213) are to praise God. In 1QM I, 13–16 "holy ones" fight with God and holy humans ("sons of light") to defeat Belial (Martínez, p. 115).
	"angels" (מַלְאָכִים) Often used for messengers of God (Gen 19:1). Appear with God in theophanies (Gen 28:12) and encamp around the faithful (Ps 34:8).	LXX: "angels" (ἀγγέλων) in Ps 137:1 vs. "gods" (*elohim*) of MT in Ps 138:1. Angels can also appear in human form (ἄγγελοι; Gen 19:1). 4Q180 1 I, 78: fallen "angels" (מלאך) (Martínez, p. 371).

Categories	Old Testament	Extrabiblical Material
Terms used for divine beings	"spirits" (רוּחוֹת) The term "spirits" occurs once, possibly in reference to angels. In Ps 104:4 "he (God) makes (עֹשֶׂה) his messengers/angels (מַלְאָכָיו) spirits/winds" (רוּחוֹת). In his divine activity, the superiority of the spirit of God (רוּחַ אֱלֹהִים) is distinct from the activity of these angelic spirits (Gen 1:2; cp. Judg 16:34; 2 Chr 24:20).	The LXX may also correlate "spirits" with angels in Ps 103:4 (MT Ps 104:4), using the same terminology in Greek: τοὺς ἀγγέλους αὐτοῦ πνεύματα. Angels as "spirits" underscore that they are supernatural beings. 11Q17 (*Songs of the Sabbath Sacrifice*) is replete with holy angelic spirits. 1QM XIII, 2 and 4 refer to spirits loyal to Belial and 1QHᵃ IV, 23 refers to "[fiendish] spirits" (Martínez, p. 149).
	"hosts" (צבא) This term is often used for the angels under God and frequently has a military connotation (1 Kgs 22:19; cp. 2 Chr 18:18; Isa 13:4).	The LXX translates 1 Kgs 22:19 "army" or "host" (στρατιὰ); 2 Chr 18:18 "power" or "host" (δύναμις); Isa 13:4 "Lord Sabaoth (σαβαωθ)" = Lord of hosts. The term צבא is used for God's angelic army in the *War Scroll* (1 QM XII, 1, 8, 9).
	"watcher, watchers" (עִירִין ;עִיר) The term "watchers" occurs three times in the book of Daniel (4:10, 14, 20 [Eng. 4:13, 17, 23]).	LXX = ιρ The Theodotian recension of the book of Daniel employs this term, transliterated from עִיר (watcher, Dan [TH] 4:17). See also *1 En.* 1:5; 10:9; 12:2, 4; 20:1.
	The OT does not appear to develop the concept of "spirit" for "angel." (רוּחוֹת in Ps 104:4 can also be translated "winds.")	A striking feature of angelology in the Dead Sea Scrolls concerns the development of the term "spirit" for "angel" (11Q17; 1QHᵃ IV, 23; 1QM XIII, 2, 4).
Named angels	"Gabriel" (גַּבְרִיאֵל), an archangel, occurs only twice in the OT (Dan 8:16; 9:21).	Gabriel, mentioned in *1 En. 10:9 and 20:7,* is among seven archangels listed in *1 En.* 20: Suru'el, Michael, Raphael, Raguel, Remiel and Saraqa'el).
	"Michael," an archangel, governs Israel (Dan 10:13, 21; cf. 12:1).	Michael is often mentioned in the DSS. His name, along with Gabriel, Sariel and Raphael, are to be written on battle shields (1QM IX, 15–16). These archangels also appear in *1 Enoch* (9:1; 10:11; 20:1-7; 24:6).

Categories	Old Testament	Extrabiblical Material
Named angels	"Satan" (שָׂטָן) appears with the other angels that present themselves before God (Job 1:6, 7, 9; 2:1–7; cp. Zech 3:1–2).	In *2 Enoch*, a group of 200 angels, referred to as the Grigori, rejected the Lord. They are led by a prince named Satanail (*2 Enoch* 18:1, 3).
	"Angel of the Lord," (מלאך יהוה) is equated with Yahweh in some contexts (e.g., Gen 16:7, 9, 10, 11; cf. 22:11, 15), yet appears distinctive in others (Zech 12:8).	Second Temple literature predominantly distinguishes Yahweh above the angels, including the Cherubim (11Q17 VII, 10–11).
Activities of divine beings	In the OT, angels are limited to the four angels mentioned above (cp. Melchizedek, Chart 51).	Angels unique to early Jewish apocalyptic literature: Belial and his angels are the enemies of God's people, (1QM I, 10–11, 13–16). Semyaz (or Semyaza) conspires against God and leads some 200 angels to enter into a shocking sexual union with humans (*1 Enoch* 7:1–2). Azaz'el also leads angels in evil deeds (8:1–2). Lists of numerous angels are found in in *1 Enoch* 6:7–8; 8:1–4; 20:1–7; 54:6.
	Angels are part of the "divine council" (1 Kgs 22:19–23; cf. Job 1:6–12; 2:1–6).	Among the angelic participants in his court Yahweh has no rival (*1 Enoch* 14:22).
	Angels serve as mediators of the divine message (Job 33:23).	*Holy ones* and *sons of heaven* are common terms for angels in the DSS and are often in parallel with *spirits of knowledge* (1QHᵃ XI, 22–23) and announce God's message.
	Isaiah envisions seraphim surrounding God as he is seated on a high and exalted throne (Isa 6:1–6)	A divine messenger, seraphim, holy creatures, and other heavenly beings are in God's heavenly throne room (*3 En.* 1:6–8, 12; cf. 28:7; 36:2, etc).

Categories	Old Testament	Extrabiblical Material
Angelic Activities in relationship to God	Cherubim surround God as he is seated on a high and exalted throne (Isa 6; cf. Ezek 1; 10:1–22; Dan 7:9–10).	Cherubim are winged angels (4Q405 20 II, 4, 8). Later Judaism depicts them as a separate class of angels (*1 En.* 61:10; cf.; *2 En.* 21.1; *Sib. Or.* 3.1).
		Examples of some angelic activities unique to early Jewish apocalyptic literature appear in *Songs of the Sabbath Sacrifice* (4Q400–407; cf. 11Q17)
Angelic Activities in relationship to People	Genesis 18 does not seem to identify Abraham's three visitors as angelic beings.	The Ages of Creation (4Q180 2–4 II, 3–4) identify the three men who visit Abraham as angels.
	Angels are a benefit to people (Pss 103:20; 78:25; cf. 2 Sam 14:17, 20; 19:27; Zech 14:5; Job 25:3)	Angels are perceived at Qumran to have a dualistic division like that of humanity: the Sons of Light and the Sons of Darkness (1QS III, 13–IV, 26).
	Angels execute divine judgment or justice (Num 22:23; Josh 5:13; 2 Sam 24:16; 1 Chr 21:16; Ezek 9:2; Zech 1:8–11; 12:5). Often they are portrayed as being armed with weapons (Josh 5:13; cf. Num 22:23; 1 Chr 21:16, 30).	Angels are perceived at Qumran to execute judgment alongside human beings (*War Scroll* 1QM I, 13–16).
	Angels provide divine deliverance (Gen 48:16; cf. Exod 23:20–23; Judg 2:1). It is the angel of the Lord who went out and put to death 185,000 of Sennacherib's army (Isa 37:14–21; 33–37; cp. 2 Kgs 19:32–34).	Josephus portrays the Sennacherib event as God delivering a sickness upon the army (Josephus, *Ant.* 10.20–22).
	The OT appears to be silent about communion between human beings and angelic beings.	The members at Qumran commune with angelic beings during the eschatological battle against that of Belial and his angels (1QM I, 10–11).

Part Three

THEOLOGY IN HEBREWS

Portraits of God in Hebrews

CHART 56

Characteristic	Depiction	Reference in Hebrews
God is living	God is the living God.	3:12; 9:14; 10:31; 12:22; cf. 4:12
God is Creator	God is creator through the regal priest, Jesus.	1:2; 2:10; 11:3, 10
	God provides the universe with a ruler.	1:1–14; 3:4, 6; 5:5–6, 10
	God maintains the earth as does the Son.	6:7; 1:3
	God is creator of the unseen world in which all believers will find their resting place.	4:4, 9, 10; 11:10
	God controls the end of history via his granting Jesus the rights of ownership over all creation.	1:2
God is relational	God speaks through OT prophets.	1:1
	God speaks through Jesus.	1:2
	God's grace is available to all people through the death of Jesus.	2:9
	God warns his people through his Spirit.	3:7 (cf. 12:25)
	God calls people to service.	5:4
	God calls Jesus to service.	5:5
	God makes promises to people.	6:13–18
	God confirms his message via miraculous signs.	2:4
	God is trustworthy and will keep his promises.	10:23
	God speaks with his children.	12:5
	God disciplines his children.	12:7
	God is approachable through Jesus	7:19, 25; 11:6 (cp. 4:16; 10:22)
God is judge	God is the judge of all things, which is predominantly a future event.	4:12; 10:31; 12:23; 13:4
	God's judgment is to be feared.	4:1; 10:27, 31; 12:21

Portraits of Jesus in Hebrews

CHART 57

Characteristic	Depiction	Reference in Hebrews
Jesus is a human	Jesus was (and still lives as) a human being.	5:7; 12:14 (cf. 1:6)
	Jesus was tempted.	2:18; 4:15
	Jesus suffered and died.	2:9, 14
	Jesus feared death.	5:7
	Jesus learned obedience through what he suffered.	5:8
Jesus' character as royal priest	Jesus is a merciful and faithful regal priest.	2:17
	Jesus is able to help believers who are tempted.	2:18
	Jesus is able to sympathize with human weaknesses.	4:15
	Jesus was tempted just like people, yet did not sin.	4:15
	Jesus is a forerunner of all who believe in him.	6:20
	Jesus is holy, blameless, unstained, separated from sinners.	7:26
Jesus' position as exalted royal priest	Jesus is appointed (Davidic) heir seated at the right hand of God enthroned in heaven.	1:2 with 1:13
	Jesus made purification for sins and sat at the right hand of God enthroned in heaven.	1:3 (cp. 8:1)
	Jesus is a regal priest after the order of Melchizedek.	5:6, 10; 6:20; 7:17
	Jesus is a regal priest appointed by God.	5:1–5 (cp. 5:1, 4)
	Jesus is a regal priest exalted above the heavens.	7:26 (cp. 4:14)
	Jesus is a regal priest made perfect forever.	7:28
	Jesus ministers in the heavenly sanctuary.	8:2
	Jesus is a regal priest of the good things that have come.	9:11
	Jesus is securing an eternal redemption for believers.	9:12

Characteristic	Depiction	Reference in Hebrews
Jesus is God (Divine Wisdom)	Jesus is creator of all things.	1:2, 10
	Jesus is the radiance and image of God.	1:3a
	Jesus sustains creation.	1:3b
	Jesus is worshiped.	1:6
	Jesus is called both Lord and God.	1:8, 9, 10

Portraits of God Shared with Jesus in Hebrews

CHART 58

Characteristic	God in the OT and Book of Hebrews	Applied to Jesus by Author of Hebrews
Creator	Gen 1:1; 14:19, 22 (see Heb 4:3; cp. 3:4; 11:3) Ps 104:1-5 Ps 102:25	1:2; 2:10 1:7 (Ps 104:4 applied to Jesus) 1:10 (Ps 102:25 applied to Jesus)
Sustains creation by his word	Ps 104:7–30 (cp. Deut 11:11–12 with Heb 6:7)	1:3b
God's glory	Exod 40:34–35 (cp. 1 Kgs 8:10–11; 2 Chr 7:1–2; Ezek 10:1–19)	1:3a "radiance of God's glory"
Called God	Ps 45:6–7	1:8–9 (Ps 45:6-7 applied to Jesus)
Eternal	Ps 102:12, 26, 27	1:11–12 (Ps 102:26 applied to Jesus; cp. Heb 13:8) 7:24
Eternal king	Jer 10:10	1:8 with 1:5 and 1:13 (eternal divine Davidic king)
Creator king	Isa 43:15	1:5–13 (Jesus as divine Creator Davidic king)
Rules justly	Pss 7:11; 11:7 (Heb 10:23)	1:8–9 (Ps 45:6-7 applied to Jesus)
Rules over all	Heb 12:23	1:2, 2:8a (cp. 3:6)
Family-oriented	Prov 3:11–12 (Heb 12:3–8)	2:11–13 via the psalmist (22:22) and the prophet Isaiah (8:18)
Worshiped	Ps 97:7	1:6

Portraits of God's Spirit in Hebrews Compared with the Dead Sea Scrolls

CHART 59

God's Involvement	Dead Sea Scroll Citation	Dead Sea Scroll Translation	Reference in Hebrews
God speaks through his Spirit	lQS VIII, 16	and by what the prophets have revealed by His holy spirit. No man belonging to the Covenant of the …	Hebrews 3:7–11 10:15–17
	4Q266 2 II, 12	with their descendants. He taught them through those anointed by the holy spirit, the seers of truth.	
	4 Q258 VI, 8	from age to age, and as the prophets have revealed by His holy spirit. And no man from men of the covenant Community who removes from any commandment …	
	1 Q34bis 3 II, 7	Your holy spirit, by the works of Your hands and the writing of Your right hand, in order to declare to them the foundations of glory, and the eternal works	
God guides or encourages through his Spirit	1 QHa IV, 26*	I give thanks to You, O Lord, for] You have spread Your holy spirit over Your servant [...] his heart …	Hebrews 3:7–11 9:8
	1 QHa VIII, 15†	… encouraging myself by Your holy spirit, clinging to the truth of Your covenant, serving You in truth and a perfect heart, and loving Your holy name.	
	1 QHᵃ XVII, 32	With a sure truth You have supported me, and by Your holy spirit You have delighted me; even until this day	
God indwells or anoints through his Spirit	CD-A II, 12	… the surface of the earth with their descendants. He taught them through those anointed by the holy spirit, the seers of …	Hebrews 1:1 2:4
	4Q504 1-2 V, 15	Indeed, You have poured out Your holy spirit upon us,	
	4Q‡	[...] against the anointed of [His] hol[y] spirit [....]	
	4Q266 2 II, 12	with [their] descendants. He taught them through those anointed by the holy spirit, the seers of truth.	

---

* 1QHa 4:38 (Accordance only).

† 1QHa 8:25 (Accordance only)

‡ 4Q287 10:13 (Accordance only).

God's Involvement	Dead Sea Scroll Citation	Dead Sea Scroll Translation	Reference in Hebrews
God empowers through his Spirit	4Q444 I, 1	And I am among those who fear God, who opens his mouth aided by His veritable knowledge, and [...] empowered by His holy spirit. [...]	Hebrews 2:4
God illuminates through his Spirit	CD-A II, 12	the surface of the earth with their descendants. He taught them through those anointed by the holy spirit, the seers of truth.	Hebrews 9:8 10:15–17
	1QHᵃ*	that by Your favor for m[an ...] Your holy spirit, and thus ...	
	1QHᵃ XX, 11-12†	You bring me to Your understanding. As which You gave me, and I have listened faithfully to Your wondrous counsel by Your holy spirit.	
	4Q427 2-3 II, 13	by Your holy spirit. (1QHᵃ XX, 12) You have opened within me knowledge in the mystery of Your insight, and a spring of Your strength and your ... (1QHᵃ XX, 13)	
	4Q266 2 II, 12	with their descendants. He taught them through those anointed by the holy spirit, the seers of truth.	
God saves or sanctifies through his Spirit	1QHᵃ VIII, 20‡	Your mercy with Your servant forever, to cleanse me by Your holy spirit, and to bring me near by Your grace according to Your great mercy [...] in [...]	Hebrews 9:14
	1QHᵃ XXIII *bottom*, 13§	[...] Your holy spirit You have spread out, atoning for guilt	
	4Q⁵	... and so be joined to His truth by His holy spirit purified from all	

---

*   1QHa 6:24 (Accordance only)

†   1QHa 20:15 (Accordance only)

‡   1QHa 8:30 (Accordance only)

§   1QHa 23:33 (Accordance only)

⁵   4Q 255 2:1 (Accordance only)

Overview of Jesus and Wisdom Parallels

CHART 60

Characteristic	Old Testament	Wisdom of Solomon	New Testament	Hebrews
Creator	Prov 8:27–30	9:2, 9	Col 1:16 1 Cor 8:6	1:2b
Radiance of God's glory		7:15–26	John 14:9 (cf. 2 Cor 4:6)	1:3a
Image of God		7:26	Col 1:15 2 Cor 4:4	1:3b
Sustainer of creation		7:27; 8:1	Col 1:17	1:3c
Enthroned with God		9:4, 10	Eph 1:20	1:3d

Jesus as Wisdom Paralleled with the Old Testament

CHART 61

Compared with Old Testament Parallel	
Hebrews	**Proverbs 8:27–30**
The Son is Creator (1:2b) "through whom also he made the world" (δἰ οὗ καὶ ἐποίησεν τοὺς αἰῶνας)	**Wisdom is Creator** "When he established the heavens, I [Wisdom] was there; when he [God] marked out the horizon over the face of the deep, when he established the clouds above, when the fountains of the deep grew strong, when he gave the sea his decree that the waters should not pass over his command, when he marked out the foundations of the earth, then I was beside him as a master craftsman, and I was his delight day by day, rejoicing before him at all times." (NET)

Jesus as Wisdom Paralleled with Wisdom of Solomon

CHART 62

Characteristic	Hebrews	Wisdom of Solomon
Creator	(1:2b) "through whom also he made the world" (δι᾽ οὗ καὶ ἐποίησεν τοὺς αἰῶνας)	(9:2, 9) "… by your wisdom [you] created (κατασκευάσας) humankind" (cp. Prov 8:27–28) "With you is Wisdom, she who knows your works and was present when you made (ἐποίεις) the world"
Radiance of God's glory	(1:3a) "who is the radiance of his glory" (ὃς ὢν ἀπαύγασμα τῆς δόξης)	(7:15–26) "For she [Wisdom] is … an emanation (ἀπόρροια) of the glory (δόξης) of the Almighty" (25a) "She [Wisdom] is a reflection (ἀπαύγασμα) of eternal light" (26a)
Image of God	(1:3b) "the exact imprint of God's very being" (καὶ χαρακτὴρ τῆς ὑποστάσεως αὐτοῦ)	(7:26b) "She [Wisdom] is … an image (εἰκών) of his goodness"
Sustains creation	(1:3c) "and who sustains all things by his powerful word" (φέρων τε τὰ πάντα τῷ ῥήματι τῆς δυνάμεως αὐτοῦ)	(7:27; 8:1) "while remaining in herself, she [Wisdom] renews (καινίζει) all things" "She [Wisdom] orders (διοικεῖ) all things well"
Sits alongside God	(1:3d) "He sat (ἐκάθισεν) down at the right hand of the Majesty on high" (cp. 1:13) (ἐκάθισεν ἐν δεξιᾷ τῆς μεγαλωσύνης ἐν ὑψηλοῖς)	(9:4, 10) "give me the wisdom sitting (πάρεδρον) by your throne" "Send her [Wisdom] forth from the holy heavens, and from the throne of your glory send her"

Jesus as Wisdom Paralleled with the New Testament

CHART 63

Characteristic	Hebrews	New Testament Parallels
Creator	(1:2b) "through whom also he made the world" (δἰ οὗ καὶ ἐποίησεν τοὺς αἰῶνας)	(Col 1:16) "by Him all things were created (ἐκτίσθη)" (1 Cor 8:6; cp. John 1:1–3) "through whom are all things and through whom we live"
Radiance of God's glory	(1:3a) "who is the radiance of his glory" (ὅς ὢν ἀπαύγασμα τῆς δόξης)	(John 14:9; cp. 2 Cor 4:6) "The person who has seen me has seen the Father"
Image of God	(1:3b) "the exact imprint of God's very being" (καὶ χαρακτὴρ τῆς ὑποστάσεως αὐτοῦ)	(Col 1:15) "who is the image (εἰκὼν) of the invisible God" (2 Cor 4:4) "who is the image (εἰκὼν) of God"
Sustains creation	(1:3c) "and who sustains all things by his powerful word" (φέρων τε τὰ πάντα τῷ ῥήματι τῆς δυνάμεως αὐτοῦ)	(Col 1:17) "all things hold together (συνέστηκεν) in him"
Sits alongside God	(1:3d) "He sat (ἐκάθισεν) down at the right hand of the Majesty on high" (cp. 1:13) (ἐκάθισεν ἐν δεξιᾷ τῆς μεγαλωσύνης ἐν ὑψηλοῖς)	(Eph 1:20) "he [God] raised him [Jesus] from the dead and seated (καθίσας) him at his right hand in the heavenly realm"

Jesus as Wisdom Paralleled in the Septuagint and the New Testament

CHART 64

Characteristic	Wisdom of Solomon	Hebrews	NT Parallels
Creator	(9:2, 9) "… by your wisdom [you] created (κατασκευάσας) humankind" (cf. Prov 8:27–28) "With you is Wisdom, she who knows your works and was present when you made (ἐποίεις) the world"	(1:2b) "through whom also he made (ἐποίησεν) the world"	(Col 1:16) "by Him all things were created (ἐκτίσθη)" (1 Cor 8:6) "through whom are all things and through whom we live"
Radiance of God's glory	(7:25a; 7:26a) "For she [Wisdom] is … an emanation (ἀπόρροια) of the glory (δόξης) of the Almighty" "She [Wisdom] is a reflection (ἀπαύγασμα) of eternal light"	(1:3a) "who is the radiance (ἀπαύγασμα) of his glory (δόξης)"	(John 14:9; cf. 2 Cor 4:6) "The person who has seen me has seen the Father"
Image of God	(7:26b) "She [Wisdom] is … an image (εἰκὼν) of his goodness"	(1:3b) "the exact imprint (χαρακτήρ) of God's very being"	(Col 1:15) "He is the image (εἰκών) of the invisible God" (2 Cor 4:4) "who is the image (εἰκών) of God"
Renews all things	(7:27; 8:1) "while remaining in herself, she [Wisdom] renews (καινίζει) all things" "She [Wisdom] orders (διοικεῖ) all things well"	(1:3c) "and who sustains (φέρων) all things by his powerful word"	(Col 1:17) "all things hold together (συνέστηκεν) in him"
Sits alongside God	(9:4, 10) "give me the wisdom sitting (πάρεδρον) by your throne" "Send her [Wisdom] forth from the holy heavens, and from the throne of your glory send her"	(1:3d) "He sat (ἐκάθισεν) down at the right hand of the Majesty on high" (cp. 8:1; 10:12)	(Eph 1:20) "he [God] raised him [Jesus] from the dead and seated (καθίσας) him at his right hand in the heavenly realm"

Titles Ascribed to Jesus in Hebrews

CHART 65

Messianic & Regal Priest Titles

Son (υἱός)	1:2, 5 (within Ps 2:7), 8; 3:6; 5:5 (within Ps 2:7), 8; 7:28
Son of God (υἱός τοῦ θεοῦ)	4:14; 6:6; 7:3; 10:29
Son of Man (υἱός ἀνθρώπον)	2:6 (within Ps 8:4–6)
Christ (Χριστός)	3:6, 14; 5:5; 6:1; 9:11, 14, 24, 28; 10:10; 11:26; 13:8, 21
*Heir (κληρονόμος)	1:2
*Melchizedekan priest (ἱερεύς)	5:6; 7:17 (within Ps 110:4)
*Great priest (ἱερέυς μέγασ)	10:21
*High priest (ἀρχιερεύς)	2:17; 3:1; 4:14, 15; 5:10; 6:20; 7:27; 8:1; 9:11

Non-Regal Titles

*Apostle (ἀπόστολος)	3:1
*Forerunner (πρόδρομος)	6:20
*Minister (λειτουργός)	8:2
Pioneer (ἀρχηγός)	2:10; 12:2
Perfecter (τελειωτής)	12:2
Mediator (μεσίτης)	9:15; 12:24
Great Shepherd (μέγασ ποιμήν)	13:20

Divine Titles

God (θεός)	1:8 (within Ps 45:6–7)
Lord (κύριος)	1:10 (within Ps 102:25–27); 7:14; 13:20

References marked with an * indicate that these titles for Jesus occur only in Hebrews.

Titles Ascribed to Jesus in Hebrews and Shared in the New Testament

CHART 66

Title	Hebrews	Gospels & Acts	Pauline	General Epistles
Son	1:2 1:5a (Ps 2:7) 1:5b (2 Sam 7:14) 1:8 3:6 5:5 (Ps 2:7) 5:8 7:28	Matt **2**:15; **3**:17 (Ps 2:7); **11**:27; **17**:5 (Ps 2:7); **24**:36; **28**:19 Mark 1:11 (Ps 2:7); **9**:7 (Ps 2:7); 13:32 Luke 3:22 (Ps 2:7); **9**:35; 10:22 John 3:16, 17, 35, 36; 5:19, 20, 21, 22, 23, 26; 6:40; 8:36; 14:13; 17:1 Acts 13:33 (Ps 2:7)	Rom **1**:3, 9; **5**:10; **8**:3, 29, 32 1 Cor **1**:9; **15**:28 Gal **1**:16; **4**:4, 6 Col **1**:13 1 Thess **1**:10	2 Pet **1**:17 (Ps 2:7) 1 John **1**:7; **2**:22, 23, 24; **3**:23; **4**:9, 10, 14; **5**:9, 11, 12, 20 2 John 3, 9 Rev **21**:7
Son of God	4:14 6:6 7:3 10:29	Matt 4:3, 6; 8:29; 14:33; 16:16; 26:63; 27:40, 43, 54 Mark 1:1, 3:11; 5:7; 15:39 Luke 1:35; 4:3, 9, 41; 8:28; 22:70 John 1:34, 49; 3:18; 5:25; 10:36; 11:4, 27; 19:7; 20:31 Acts 9:20	Rom **1**:4 2 Cor **1**:19 Gal **2**:20 Eph **4**:13	1 John **3**:8; **4**:15; 5:5, 10, 12, 13, 20 Rev **2**:18
Son of Man	2:6 (Ps 8:4–6)	Matt **8**:20; **9**:6; **10**:23; **11**:19; **12**:8, 32, 40; **13**:37, 41; **16**:13, 27, 28; **17**:9, 12, 22; **18**:11; **19**:28; **20**:18, 28; **24**:27, 30, 37, 39, 44; **25**:31; **26**:2, 24, 45, 64 Mark 2:10, 28; **8**:31, 38; **9**:9, 12, 31; **10**:33, 45; **13**:26; **14**:21, 41, 62 Luke **5**:24; **6**:5, 22; 7:34; **9**:22, 26, 44, 56, 58; **11**:30; **12**:8, 10, 40; **17**:22, 24, 26, 30; **18**:8, 31; **19**:10; **21**:27, 36; **22**:22, 48, 69; **24**:7 John **1**:51; **3**:13, 14; **5**:27; **6**:27, 53, 62; **8**:28; **9**:35; **12**:23, 34; **13**:31 Acts 7:56		Rev **1**:13; **14**:14 (?)

Title	Hebrews	Gospels & Acts	Pauline	General Epistles
Christ	3:6 3:14 5:5 6:1 9:11 9:14 9:24 9:28 10:10 11:26 13:8 13:21	Matt **1**:1, 16, 17, 18; **11**:2; **16**:16, 20; **22**:42; **23**:10; **26**:63; **27**:17, 22 Mark **1**:1; **8**:29; **9**:41; **14**:61; **15**:32 Luke **2**:11, 26; **4**:41; **9**:20; **22**:67; **23**:2, 35, 39; **24**:26, 46 John **1**:17, 41; **4**:29; **7**:26, 41; **9**:22; **10**:24; **11**:27; **17**:3; **20**:31 Acts **2**:36, 38; **3**:6, 20; **4**:10; **5**:42; **8**:5, 12, 37; **9**:22, 34; **10**:36, 48; **11**:17; **15**:26; **16**:18; **17**:3; **18**:5, 28; **20**:21; **24**:24; **28**:31	Rom **1**:1, 4, 6, 7, 8; **2**:16; **3**:22, 24; **5**:1, 6, 8, 11, 15, 17, 21; **6**:3, 4, 8, 9, 11, 23; **7**:4, 25; **8**:1, 2, 9, 10, 11, 17, 34, 35, 39; **9**:1, 3, 5; **10**:4, 6, 7, 17; **12**:5; **13**:14; **14**:9, 15, 18; **15**:3, 5, 6, 7, 8, 16, 17, 18, 19, 20, 29, 30; **16**:3, 5, 10, 16, 18, 25, 27 1 Cor **1**:1, 2, 3, 4, 6, 7, 8, 9, 10, 12, 13, 17, 23, 24, 30; **2**:2, 16; **3**:1, 11, 23; **4**:1, 10, 15, 17; **5**:7; **6**:11, 15; **7**:22; **8**:6, 11, 12; **9**:12, 21; **10**:4, 16; **11**:1, 3; **12**:12, 27; **15**:3, 12, 13, 14, 15, 16, 17, 18, 19, 20, 22, 23, 31, 57; **16**:24 2 Cor **1**:1, 2, 3, 5, 19, 21; **2**:10, 12, 14, 15, 17; **3**:3, 4, 14; **4**:4, 5, 6; **5**:10, 14, 16, 17, 18, 19, 20; **6**:15; **8**:9, 23; **9**:13; **10**:1, 5, 7, 14; **11**:2, 3, 10, 13, 23; **12**:2, 9, 10, 19; **13**:3, 5, 14 Gal **1**:1, 3, 6, 7, 10, 12, 22; **2**:4, 16, 17, 20, 21; **3**:1, 13, 14, 16, 22, 24, 26, 27, 28, 29; **4**:14, 19; **5**:1, 2, 4, 6, 24; **6**:2, 12, 14, 18 Eph **1**:1, 2, 3, 5, 10, 12, 17, 20; **2**:5, 6, 7, 10, 12, 13, 20; **3**:1, 4, 6, 8, 11, 17, 19, 21; **4**:7, 12, 13, 15, 20, 32; **5**:2, 5, 14, 20, 21, 23, 24, 25, 29, 32; **6**:5, 6, 23, 24 Phil **1**:1, 2, 6, 8, 10, 11, 13, 15, 17, 18, 19, 20, 21, 23, 26, 27, 29; **2**:1, 5, 11, 16, 21, 30; **3**:3, 7, 8, 9, 12, 14, 18, 20; **4**:7, 19, 21, 23 Col **1**:1, 2, 3, 4, 7, 24, 27, 28; **2**:2, 5, 6, 8, 11, 17, 20; **3**:1, 3, 4, 11, 15, 16, 24; **4**:3, 12 1 Thess **1**:1, 3; **2**:6, 14; **3**:2; **4**:16; **5**:9, 18, 23, 28 2 Thess **1**:1, 2, 12; **2**:1, 14, 16; **3**:5, 6, 12, 18 1 Tim **1**:1, 2, 12, 14, 15, 16; **2**:5; **3**:13; **4**:6; **5**:11, 21; **6**:3, 13, 14 2 Tim **1**:1, 2, 9, 10, 13; **2**:1, 3, 8, 10; **3**:12, 15; **4**:1 Titus **1**:1, 4; **2**:13; **3**:6 Phlm 1, 3, 6, 8, 9, 20, 23, 25	Jas **1**:1; **2**:1 1 Pet **1**:1, 2, 3, 7, 11, 13, 19; **2**:5, 21; **3**:15, 16, 18, 21; **4**:1, 11, 13, 14; **5**:1, 10, 14 2 Pet **1**:1, 8, 11, 14, 16; **2**:20; **3**:18 1 John **1**:3; **2**:1, 22; **3**:23; **4**:2; **5**:1, 6, 20 2 John 3, 7, 9 Jude 1, 4, 17, 21, 25 Rev **1**:1, 2, 5; **12**:10; **20**:4, 6

Title	Hebrews	Gospels & Acts	Pauline	General Epistles
Mediator	8:6 9:15 12:24		1 Tim **2**:5	
Great Shepherd	13:20	John **10**:11,14; cp. 10:16		1 Pet **2**:25; 5:4
Pioneer	2:10; 12:2	Acts **3**:15; **5**:31		
God	1:8 (Ps 45:6–7)	John **20**:28	Rom **9**:5 Phil **2**:6 Titus **2**:13	1 John 5:20
Lord	7:14 13:20	Matt **7**:21, 22; **8**:2, 6, 8, 21, 25; **9**:28; **12**:8; **14**:28, 30; **15**:22, 25, 27; **16**:22; **17**:4, 15; **18**:21; **20**:30, 31, 33; **21**:3; **24**:42; **26**:22 Mark **2**:28; **7**:28; **11**:3; **16**:19, 20 Luke **2**:11; **5**:8, 12; **6**:5, 46; **7**:6, 13, 19; **9**:54, 59, 61; **10**:1, 2, 17, 39, 40, 41; **11**:1, 39; **12**:41, 42; **13**:15, 23; **17**:5, 6, 37; **18**:6, 41; **19**:8, 31, 34; **22**:33, 38, 49, 61; **24**:3, 34 John **4**:1, 11, 15, 19, 49; **5**:7; **6**:23, 34, 68; **8**:11; **9**:36, 38; **11**:2, 3, 12, 21, 27, 32, 34, 39; **13**:6, 9, 13, 14, 25, 36, 37; **14**:5, 8, 22; **15**:15; **20**:2, 13, 18, 20, 25, 28; **21**:7, 12, 15, 16, 17, 20, 21 Acts **1**:6, 21, 24; **2**:36; **4**:33; **5**:14; **7**:59; **8**:16; **9**:1, 5, 10, 11, 13, 15, 17, 27, 28, 35, 42; **10**:36; **11**:16, 17, 20, 21, 23, 24; **13**:12, 44, 48, 49; **14**:3, 23; **15**:11, 26, 35, 36; **16**:15, 31, 32; **18**:8, 9, 25; **19**:5, 10, 13, 17, 20; **20**:19, 21, 24, 35; **21**:13; **22**:8, 10, 19; **26**:15; **28**:31	Rom **1**:4, 7; **4**:8, 24; **5**:1, 11, 21; **6**:23; **7**:25; **8**:39; **10**:9, 12, 13; **12**:11; **13**:14; **14**:4, 6, 8, 9, 11, 14; **15**:6, 30; **16**:2, 8, 11, 12, 13, 18, 20, 22, 24 1 Cor **1**:2, 3, 7, 8, 9, 10; **2**:8; **4**:17; **5**:4, 5; **6**:11, 14, 17; **8**:6; **9**:1, 2, 5, 14; **10**:21; **11**:11, 20, 23, 26, 27; **12**:3, 5; **15**:31, 57, 58; **16**:7, 10, 19, 22, 23 2 Cor **1**:2, 3, 14; **4**:5, 14; **5**:6, 8; **8**:5, 9; **11**:31; **12**:1, 8; **13**:14 Gal **1**:3, 19; **6**:14, 18 Eph **1**:2, 3, 15, 17; **3**:11; **5**:20; **6**:23, 24 Phil **1**:2; **2**:11, 19; **3**:8, 20; **4**:23 Col **1**:3; **2**:6; **3**:17, 24 1 Thess **1**:1, 3, 6; **2**:15, 19; **3**:11, 13; **4**:1, 2, 15, 16, 17; **5**:2, 9, 23, 28 2 Thess **1**:1, 2, 7, 8, 12; **2**:1, 8, 13, 14, 16; **3**:6, 12, 18 1 Tim **1**:2, 12; **6**:3, 14, 15 2 Tim **1**:2, 8 Phlm 3, 5, 25	Jas **1**:1; **2**:1; 5:8 1 Pet **1**:3; **3**:15 2 Pet **1**:2, 8, 11, 14, 16; **2**:20; 3:18 Jude 4, 17, 25 Rev **17**:14; **19**:16; **22**:20, 21

"Better Than" (κρείττων) Comparisons: Salvation in Hebrews

CHART 67

Statement in Hebrews	Reference in Hebrews
The exalted Son, Jesus, is better than the angels.	1:4
Believers are confident of better things … that belong to salvation.	6:9
The lesser is blessed by the better (or "greater").	7:7
There is … a better access to God.	7:19
Jesus is the guarantee of a better covenant	7:22
Jesus is the mediator of a better covenant.	8:6
The copies of heavenly things needed to be cleansed … with better sacrifices.	9:23
Believers know that they have a better inheritance.	10:34
Believers desire a better *country*, that is, a heavenly one.	11:16
Believers were tortured so that they might obtain a better resurrection.	11:35
God had provided something better for believers.	11:40
Jesus is the mediator of a new covenant through his blood which speaks better than *the blood* of Abel.	12:24

Angels and Jesus Comparisons in Hebrews

CHART 68

Description of Angels in Hebrews	Comparison of Jesus to Angels in Hebrews
	superior to the angels (1:4)
	a superior name (1:4)
	God never said to an angel, "You are my Son" or "I will be a Father" (1:5)
	the radiance of God the Father's glory and the representation of his essence (1:3a)
angels worship Jesus, the divine Son (1:6)	the sustainer of all things by his powerful word (1:3b)
	accomplished redemption through the purification of sins (1:3c)
angels are changeable servants (wind and fire, 1:7)	immutability of Jesus (he remains the same) (1:12)
	addressed as "God" (1:8)
	the mediatorial agent in creation (1:10)
	seated at the right hand of God, with his enemies as his footstool (1:13)
angels are ministering spirits sent by Jesus to serve the saints (1:14)	

"Covenant" (διαθήκη) in Hebrews

CHART 69

Statements Related to "Covenant"		References in Hebrews
The Covenant is …	better.	7:22; 8:6
	founded of better promises.	8:16

	new.
	
	    (καινήν)
	
	    (νέας)
		8:8 (Jer 31:31), 8:13 (implied), 9:15
		
		12:24

	not like the covenant made with their forefathers.	8:9 (via Jer 31:32)
	prophesied for "that time."	8:10; 10:16 (via Jer 31:33)
	like a "will" in force at the death of the one who made it.	9:16, 17
	put into effect with the blood of Jesus.	9:14–20; 10:29; 13:20
	eternal.	13:20
Jesus is . .	the guarantee.	7:22
	the mediator.	8:6; 9:15; 12:24
	the one who made it (and whose death put it into effect).	9:14–17
For those who are called …	receive the promised eternal inheritance.	9:15
	are set free from sin.	10:29 (cf. 9:26; 10:12, 17)
For those who perceive the blood of Jesus as unholy …	deserve severe punishment.	10:29

Discontinuities Between the Old Covenant and the New Covenant in Jesus

CHART 70

OT Theme	Discontinuities	Reference in Hebrews
The Tabernacle	Unlike the physical tabernacle made with human hands (an anti-type, copy, or shadow; Exod 25:40) in which Aaron served … in Hebrews, Jesus serves in a heavenly sanctuary (the true tent) made by God.	8:1–2, 5; 9:11, 23–24
The Sanctuary	Unlike worshipers of the Old Testament who approached only the outer limits of the sanctuary (Lev 1:3, 5; 9:5, 23–24) and ordinary priests only the altar (Lev 9:7–8; 21:17, 21) … in Hebrews, Jesus makes it possible for all believers to approach the inner sanctuary.	4:14, 16; 10:1
The Mediators	Unlike Moses' role as mediator to obtain the Sinai covenant (Exod 19:1–25; Testament (Assumption) of Moses 1:14; 3:12) … In Hebrews, Jesus' role as mediator guarantees the new and better covenant.	7:22; 8:6; 9:15; 12:24
The Covenant	Unlike the temporal and imperfect first (old) covenant mediated via Levitical priests (Jer 31:31–34) … in Hebrews, Jesus as eternal regal priest of Melchizedek's order establishes the second (new) covenant as an eternal covenant and abolishes the first.	7:12, 18–19; 8:7, 13; 10:9
The Priesthood	Unlike the appointed high priests of Aaron's line who had to make sacrifices day after day for themselves as well as others (Lev 4:3; 16:6, 11) … in Hebrews, Jesus as God's appointed regal priest of Melchizedek's order need not make a sacrifice for himself.	5:1–10; 7:26–28; 8:3–4
The Sacrifices	Unlike ceremonial animal sacrifices offered constantly year after year as signs of external cleansing (Lev 4:3; 16:6, 11) … in Hebrews, Jesus offers himself once, secures an eternal redemption, and cleanses the conscience for service.	1:3, 13; 9:11–14, 26; 10:4, 8–14

Old and New Covenants in Contrast

CHART 71

Mount Sinai	Mount Zion
Darkness	Hope
Gloom	Joy
Terror	Comfort
Fear	Victory
Trembling	Confidence
Inaccessible	Accessible
Forbidding	Inviting
Moses as Mediator	Jesus as Mediator
Conditional Covenant	New Covenant
Law of Moses	Royal Priesthood of Jesus
Exodus 19:1–20:26	Hebrew 12:22–24

Tim Sigler, professor of Bible at Moody Bible Institute offers this set of contrasts between the Mosaic covenant in Exodus 19–20 and the New Covenant in Hebrews 12.

Understanding Hebrews
Key Covenants of God's Program

CHART 72

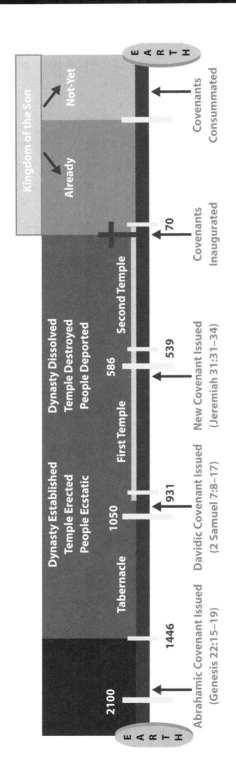

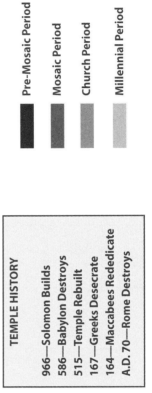

TEMPLE HISTORY

966—Solomon Builds
586—Babylon Destroys
515—Temple Rebuilt
167—Greeks Desecrate
164—Maccabees Rededicate
A.D. 70—Rome Destroys

"Once for All" (ἅπαξ, ἐφάπαξ) in Hebrews

CHART 73

"Once for all"	Contextual Appearance of "Once for All"	References in Hebrews
"once for all" (ἅπαξ)	νυνὶ δὲ **ἅπαξ** ἐπὶ συντελείᾳ τῶν αἰώνων εἰς ἀθέτησιν [τῆς] ἁμαρτίας διὰ τῆς θυσίας αὐτοῦ πεφανέρωται. But now Jesus has appeared **once for all** at the consummation of the ages to remove sin by his sacrifice.	9:26
	οὕτως καὶ ὁ Χριστός, **ἅπαξ** προσενεχθεὶς εἰς τὸ πολλῶν ἀνενεγκεῖν ἁμαρτίας, ἐκ δευτέρου χωρὶς ἁμαρτίας ὀφθήσεται τοῖς αὐτὸν ἀπεκδεχομένοις εἰς σωτηρίαν. And so, after Christ was offered **once for all** to *bear the sins of many, Jesus, who is the Christ* will appear a second time, not to bear sin but to bring salvation to those who eagerly await him.	9:28
"once for all" (ἐφάπαξ)	ὃς οὐκ ἔχει καθ᾽ ἡμέραν ἀνάγκην, ὥσπερ οἱ ἀρχιερεῖς, πρότερον ὑπὲρ τῶν ἰδίων ἁμαρτιῶν θυσίας ἀναφέρειν, ἔπειτα τῶν τοῦ λαοῦ· τοῦτο γὰρ ἐποίησεν **ἐφάπαξ** ἑαυτὸν ἀνενέγκας. Jesus has no need to do every day what those priests do, to offer sacrifices first for their own sins and then for the sins of the people, since he did this in offering himself **once for all**.	7:27
	οὐδὲ δι᾽ αἵματος τράγων καὶ μόσχων διὰ δὲ τοῦ ἰδίου αἵματος, εἰσῆλθεν **ἐφάπαξ** εἰς τὰ ἅγια, αἰωνίαν λύτρωσιν εὑράμενος. and not by the blood of goats and calves but by his own blood, Jesus entered **once for all** into the most holy *place* and thus he secured an eternal redemption.	9:12
	ἐν ᾧ θελήματι ἡγιασμένοι ἐσμὲν διὰ τῆς προσφορᾶς τοῦ σώματος Ἰησοῦ Χριστοῦ **ἐφάπαξ**. by God's will we have been made holy through the offering of the body of Jesus, *who is the* Christ **once for all**.	10:10

The Future Inheritance of Believers

CHART 74

Our Anticipation	God's Promise	Reference in Hebrews
Trusting God for our ...	... entrance into a heavenly sanctuary that has been inaugurated.	10:19–20
	... reception of a lasting possession that awaits us.	10:34
	... reception of the great reward that awaits us.	10:35
	... reception of God's promise that awaits us.	10:36
Longing for ...	... the city whose architect and builder is God.	11:10
	... a country of our own, a heavenly one.	11:14–16
	... what our eyes are fixed upon, our reward.	11:26
	... our resurrection to a better life.	11:35
	... something better already prepared for us.	11:40
Seeking ...	... the city yet to come.	13:14

"Perfection" (τελειόω, τέλειος, τελειότης) in Hebrews

CHART 75

Background of the Term	Perfection of Christ in Hebrews	Perfection of Believers in Hebrews
The author's use of the language of "perfection" (τελειόω. τέλειος, τελειότης, etc.): Occurrences in verb forms: 2:10; 5:9; 7:19, 28; 9:9; 10:1, 14; 11:40; 12:23. Occurrences in other forms: 5:14; 6:1; 7:11; 9:11; 12:2. Related synonymous term: καταρτίζω (to make complete), in 10:5; 11:3; 13:21.	Hebrews applies language of perfection to Jesus three times: (1) "who is perfected through sufferings (2:10); (2) "perfected" to be the "source of eternal salvation" (5:9); (3) and "perfected forever" in contrast to the levitical priests who continued to have weakness (7:28). (4) Finally, Jesus is the "perfecter of faith" (12:2).	Perfection and maturity: believers urged to progressively advance from infancy to adulthood (perfection or maturity). 5:14: τελείων 6:1: τελειότητα
Meaning and significance for Hebrews: completeness of God's purposes, "bringing to perfection" believers, who ultimately arrive in the heavenly realm with Jesus, the intended goal.	God perfects Jesus, the "pioneer" (ἀρχηγὸν) through sufferings (2:10). Here, Hebrews contrasts ἀρχηγὸν with the term τελειῶσαι (to make perfect), signifying that Jesus begins and finishes perfection for believers during his earthly suffering, which culminates in death (2:10, cp. 10:14).	The "many sons and daughters" (πολλοὺς υἱοὺς) also attain their final state of perfection through sufferings along the path of life, following Jesus their leader (2:10, cp. 10:14).
Philosophical texts outside of the NT: the τελ- word group is employed with reference to those who have attained the goal of philosophy, the contemplation of the realm of ideas in Plato (*Republic*, V 472–83)	The contrast of Jesus' perfection with "the days of his flesh" in which he learned obedience through suffering (5:8–9). His departure from the earthly realm and return to the goal of the heavenly realm at God's right hand, enables Jesus to be the source of eternal salvation.	
In cultic contexts (pagan and Jewish), the τελ- word group is used to express "cleanness" or "wholeness," especially of "unblemished" sacrificial animals (Homer, Illiad 1.66).	As the Messiah, Jesus' "sacrificial death" (τὸ αἷμα τοῦ Χριστοῦ) brought about the cleansing of the believer's conscience from guilt (9:14a).	The believer's conscience cleansed from dead works by Christ's redemption, something the old covenant ritual system could never accomplish (9:13–14).

Charts *on the* Book *of* Hebrews

Background of the Term	Perfection of Christ in Hebrews	Perfection of Believers in Hebrews
The LXX usage: τελ- word group is found prominently in Exodus 29 (cf. Lev 4:5; 8:33; 16:32) to "ordain" or "consecrate" to priesthood.	The death of the Son of God: the fulfillment of the sacrificial ritual of the old covenant; Christ "by means of one sacrifice perfected forever those who are being made holy" (10:14).	Believers have been made holy by virtue of the "once-for-all" offering of Jesus' own body, and are thus consecrated to God (10:10).
	Jesus' experience of humiliation, suffering, and death in his sinless humanity is the divinely appointed path through which he is fitted for the priestly ministry he performs on the heavenly side as the Son (5:8–9; 7:25–26).	Believers that have been perfected (τετελείωκεν) forever by Christ's single offering, are being sanctified" (τοὺς ἁγιαζομένους) here and now, even within this realm of imperfection (10:14).
	The final goal of his suffering: the exalted Son of God to the heavenly realm (7:26–28; 12:2)	The final perfection of believers effected by Jesus in bringing many sons and daughters to glory (2:10, cp. 10:14).
	Jesus is called the "pioneer and perfecter" (ἀρχηγὸν καὶ τελειωτὴν) of faith, having endured the cross, and completed his redemptive work (12:1–3; cf. 2:14–18; 10:5–10).	The purpose of believers' perfection, "completion" in a moral sense: "that God might equip you in every good thing (καταρτίσαι ὑμᾶς ἐν παντὶ ἀγαθῷ) to do his will (13:21a).
	Cosmological/Eschatological dimension of the Son of God's exaltation: although already at God's right hand, Jesus awaits the future time when all of his enemies are placed under his feet (10:12–13)	Cosmological/Eschatological dimension of perfection: although the believer is a resident in the earthly realm, he is also resident in the divine realm. The eschatological shaking effects the final residency of a believer. Though already sanctified by Christ's death, he or she awaits final sanctification in heaven (10:10, 14).

Other Significant Theological Concepts in Hebrews: Glory, Hope, Heir, Oath, Promise, Word

CHART 76

Theological Concept	Brief Description of the Theme	Reference in Hebrews
Glory	Jesus is the radiance of God's glory.	1:3
	Jesus, through his death, was crowned with glory and honor.	2:7, 9
	Jesus is worthy of greater glory than Moses.	3:3
	Jesus is the one through whom God is bringing many sons and daughters to glory.	2:10
Hope	Believers are to remain firm in their confidence before others and their unseen hope.	3:6
	Believers are to demonstrate eagerness for their unseen hope until the final day.	6:11
	Believers are to hold fast to the unseen hope placed before them.	6:18
	There is a better unseen hope through which believers draw near to God.	7:19
	Believers are to be resolute in the unseen hope they confess.	10:23
Heirs	Jesus sends out ministering spirits to those who will inherit salvation.	1:14
	Believers are to imitate those who through faith and perseverance, inherit the promises.	6:12
	God demonstrates to the heirs of promise that his purpose is unchangeable; God did so with an oath.	6:17
	Jesus mediates the new covenant so that believers may receive the eternal inheritance God has promised.	9:15
Oath	God swore an oath to Abraham that he would have many descendants (Gen 15:13–15) and he kept that oath.	2:16; 6:13–20
	God swore an oath that Moses' generation would not enter the promised land (Ps 95:11; cp. Num 14:30) and he kept that oath.	3:11, 16–19
	God swore an oath that David's descendant would be a regal priest in the order of Melchizedek (Ps 110:4) and he kept that oath.	7:21–22, 28 (cp. 5:5–6)

Theological Concept	Brief Description of the Theme	Reference in Hebrews
Promise	God promises believers that a place of rest remains open.	4:1
	Believers are to imitate those who, through faith and perseverance, inherit the promises.	6:12
	God demonstrates to the heirs of promise that his purpose is unchangeable; God did so with an oath.	6:17
	The new covenant is enacted on better promises.	8:6
	Jesus mediates the new covenant so that believers may receive the eternal inheritance God has promised.	9:15
	Endurance is needed to do God's will and so receive what is promised.	10:36
Word	The word was the message delivered by angelic beings.	2:2
	The word was the message heard by those in the desert.	4:2
	People have partaken in the word of righteousness.	5:13
	People have partaken in the word concerning the Messiah.	6:1
	People have partaken in the word of God's oath.	7:28
	People have partaken in the word presented at Mt. Sinai.	12:19
	The word is the message delivered to the listeners by their leaders.	13:7

Jewish Concept of Rest

CHART 77

Category	Sub-Category	Description	References
Historical	Entrance into the land of Canaan	God's promise to enter Canaan was not totally revoked: Caleb, Joshua, and a second generation of exiles entered the land.	Num 14:24, 30, 38 Josh 21–23
	No more war	After Solomon was given rest from his enemies, a temple was built in Jerusalem where the ark of the covenant found its resting place.	Deut 12:10–11 1 Kgs 8:56 (cp. 6:1–38) Ps 132:8, 13–14
	No work	Cessation of all work was a feature of the Mosaic covenant that had connections with creation.	Gen 2:2 Exod 35:2 (cp. Exod 20:11)
	Sabbath celebration	Cessation of work along with a festive celebration at a specific place.	Psalm 95 (cp. Deut 12:10–12)
Eschatological	Future end-time resting place of the blessed dead	Paradise as a place of rest and delight as opposed to hell as a place of torment.	4 Ezra 7:36, 38, 121, 123; 8:52
		Rest as an end-time reward as opposed to punishment.	2 Baruch 73:1; 85:9
	Final beyond-time resting place of the soul	Rest as a place in heaven.	Joseph and Aseneth 8:9; 15:7; 22:13
	In-between-time resting place of the soul	Rest as both an intermediate temporal place and an eternal place for the blessed.	Testament of Isaac 2:6, 13
		Rest as a description of eternal mercy, light, spiritual joy.	Testament of Jacob 2:26
		Commentary on Deuteronomy 34: Death is a temporary place of rest until the resurrection.	Pseudo-Philo, *Biblical Antiquities* 19:12
		Death is defined as entering into rest/peace.	*Babylonian Talmud b Keth* 104a[25] (cp. *b Schab* 152[26])
Philosophical	Present-time reality of a contemplative life	Rest as freedom from all labor and production	Philo, *Spec. Leg.* 2:64

Eternality in Hebrews

CHART 78

Theme	Reference in Hebrews
Jesus' authority as regal king is eternal.*	1:8 (via Ps 45:6)
Jesus is a regal priest for all eternity.*	5:6 & 7:17, 21 (via Ps 110:4); 6:20
Jesus is the source of eternal salvation for all those who obey him.	5:9
Jesus is eternal.*	7:24
Jesus as regal priest is made perfect for all eternity.*	7:28
Teachings exist of an eternal judgment.	6:2
Jesus secured an eternal redemption.	9:12
The Spirit is eternal.	9:14
God promised an eternal inheritance.	9:15
Jesus is the same for all eternity.*	13:8 (cp. 1:10 via Ps 102:26–27)
The blood of Jesus secured an eternal covenant.	13:20
God is glorified for all eternity.*	13:21

* See the "Chart Comments" for the items marked with an * (asterisk).

Trusting God for the Unseen in Hebrews 11

CHART 79

Faith is believing …	Reference in Context (from the NET)	Reference in Hebrews
… with surety & conviction in the unseen.	Faith is being sure of what we hope for, being convinced of what we do not see.	11:1
… in God's creating the visible from the invisible.	By faith we understand that the worlds were set in order at God's command, so that the visible has its origin in the invisible.	11:3
… in God's existence and his giving rewards.	Now without faith it is impossible to please him, for the one who approaches God must believe that he exists and that he rewards those who seek him.	11:6
… in future events and living life until their fruition.	By faith Noah, when he was warned about things not yet seen, with reverent regard constructed an ark for the deliverance of his family. Through faith he condemned the world and became an heir of the righteousness that comes by faith.	11:7
… God and going to an unknown place.	By faith Abraham obeyed when he was called to go out to a place he would later receive as an inheritance, and he went out without understanding where he was going.	11:8
… in future events.	For he was looking forward to the city with firm foundations, whose architect and builder is God.	11:10
… in future events and living life as strangers on the earth.	These all died in faith without receiving the things promised, but they saw them in the distance and welcomed them and acknowledged that they were strangers and foreigners on the earth.	11:13
… in a future homeland.	For those who speak in such a way make it clear that they are seeking a homeland.	11:14
… in a heavenly homeland.	But as it is, they aspire to a better land, that is, a heavenly one. Therefore, God is not ashamed to be called their God, for he has prepared a city for them.	11:16
… in the future reward.	He regarded abuse suffered for Christ to be greater wealth than the treasures of Egypt, for his eyes were fixed on the reward.	11:26
… in the invisible God.	By faith he left Egypt without fearing the king's anger, for he persevered as though he could see the one who is invisible.	11:27

Named Examples of Faith in Hebrews 11

CHART 80

Description and Verse in Hebrews	Person	Summary of the OT Event	OT Reference
"offered God a better sacrifice" (v. 4)	Abel	"Abel brought fat portions from some of the firstborn of his flock. The LORD looked with favor on Abel and his offering" (NIV).	Genesis 4:2–16
"was taken up … had been commended as having pleased God" (v. 5)	Enoch	Enoch walked with God 300 years and God took him.	Genesis 5:22–24
"constructed an ark for the deliverance of his family" (v. 7)	Noah	Noah trusted and obeyed God when God spoke to him about building an ark: "he did just as God commanded him."	Genesis 6:9–22
"obeyed when he was called" (v. 8)	Abraham	Abraham trusted and obeyed God when God called to him in Sumer: "So Abram left, as the LORD had told him" (NIV).	Genesis 12:1–5
"lived as a foreigner" (v. 9–10)	Abraham	Abraham set up an altar and lived in Bethel, then moved to Mamre at Hebron (the land of the Canaanites). Later he lived between Kadesh and Shur, and then in Beersheba (the land of the Philistines). He bought a cave from the Hittites as "an alien and a stranger" in order to bury his wife Sarah.	Genesis 12:6–9; 13:1–4; 18:1; 20:1; 21:33–34; 23:1–7, 17–20; 25:7–10
"received ability to conceive" (v. 11)	Sarah	After three visitors appeared at Abraham and Sarah's tent predicting the birth of a child, Sarah conceived and gave birth the next year.	Genesis 17:15–21; 18:9–15; 21:1–7
"offered up Issac" (v. 17)	Abraham	Abraham trusted and obeyed God, when he was told to sacrifice Isaac. God provided another sacrifice, and said "I swear by myself … I will surely bless you" (NIV).	Genesis 22:1–17
"blessed Jacob and Esau" (v. 20)	Isaac	Jacob and Esau prepare Isaac's favorite food and he blessed them both.	Genesis 27:25–29, 30, 39–40

Description and Verse in Hebrews	Person	Summary of the OT Event	OT Reference
"blessed each of the sons of Joseph" (v. 21)	Jacob	As Jacob laid on his deathbed in Egypt, he called his eleven sons and two sons of Joseph and blessed them.	Genesis 48:1–49:28
"gave instructions about his burial" (v. 22)	Joseph	As Joseph laid on his deathbed before three generations of his son Ephraim, he instructed them that when the time came to take his bones out of Egypt.	Genesis 50:24–25
"hid Moses" (v. 23)	Parents of Moses	During a time of persecution in Egypt, Moses was hidden by his parents at home for three months.	Exodus 1:22–2:10
"refused to be called the son of Pharaoh's daughter" (v. 24–26)	Moses	Moses identified himself with the Jewish people and killed an Egyptian.	Exodus 2:11–14
"left Egypt" (v. 27)	Moses	Moses fled from Pharaoh.	Exodus 2:15
"kept the Passover" (v. 28)	Moses	Moses obeyed God and inaugurated the Passover in Egypt as a lasting ordinance to be observed for generations to come.	Exodus 12:1–28
"crossed the Red Sea" (v. 29)	Exodus Community	Moses trusted and obeyed God when he stretched his hand over the sea and it parted for the Exodus community in order to save them, and again when the sea flowed back onto Pharaoh's army.	Exodus 14:5–31
"marched around the walls of Jericho" (v. 30)	Wilderness Community	Joshua trusted and obeyed God when he marched around Jericho blowing horns for seven days in order to bring down the walls of the great city of Jericho.	Joshua 5:13–6:27
"escaped the destruction of the disobedient" (v. 31)	Rahab	Rahab hid two Israelite spies, who had come to spy on Jericho.	Joshua 2:1–24; 6:17, 23–25

Unnamed Examples of Faith in Hebrews 11

CHART 81

Description and Verse in Hebrews	Possible Person(s)	Possible Examples of the OT Event	OT Reference
"conquered kingdoms" (v. 33)	Gideon	Gideon defeated the Midianites.	Judg 6:11–12; 7:1–25
	Barak	Barak conquered the Canaanites.	Judg 4:6–24
	Jephthah	Jephthah defeated the Ammonites.	Judg 11:1–29; 12:1–3
	Samuel	Samuel subdues the Philistines at Mizpah.	1 Sam 7:2–14
	David	David conquered the Amalekites, Philistines, and other surrounding nations: Moab, Aram, Ammon.	1 Sam 30:1–20; 2 Sam 5:17–25; 8:1–15
"administered justice" (v. 33)	Gideon	Gideon governed Issachar.	Judg 8:22–27
	Jephthah	Jephthah governed Gilead.	Judg 12:7
	Samuel	Samuel traveled a circuit of Bethel, Gilgal, and Mizpah.	1 Sam 7:15–16
	David	David ruled over Israel.	2 Sam 5:1–5
"shut the mouths of lions" (v. 33)	Samson	The Lord's spirit empowered Samson to tear a lion in two with his bare hands.	Judg 14:5–6
	David	David would kill lions to rescue sheep in his father's flock.	1 Sam 17:34–35
	Daniel	God shut the mouths of lions to protect Daniel.	Dan 6:22
"quenched raging fire" (v. 34)	Shadrach Meshach Abednego	King Nebuchadnezzar threw three Jewish captives into a furnace for refusing to pay homage to an idol, but they survived the blazing fire.	Dan 3:13–30
"escaped the edge of the sword" (v. 34)	Elijah	Elijah escaped Jezebel's threat of murder after defeating the Baal prophets on Mt. Carmel.	1 Kgs 19:1–8
	Jeremiah	Jeremiah was spared the threat of execution from the people.	Jer 26:22–24

Description and Verse in Hebrews	Possible Person(s)	Possible Examples of the OT Event	OT Reference
"women received back their dead by resurrection" (v. 35)	Widow of Zarephath	When the widow of Zarephath scolded Elijah for her son's death, Elijah appealed to God and restored life to the boy.	1 Kgs 17:17–24
	Shunammite woman	When a Shunammite woman's son died, she scolded Elisha because the boy's birth was Elisha's fulfilled prophecy, but God restored life to the boy.	2 Kgs 4:8–37
"suffered mocking and flogging" (v. 36)	Jeremiah	Zedekiah put Jeremiah in a dungeon, then in a cistern to starve to death. He was later placed in chains and taken to Ramah.	Jer 37:16–18; 38:1–13; 40:1–6 (cp. 4 Macc 12:2)
"were stoned to death" (v. 36)	Zechariah	Energized by God's spirit, Zechariah, a priest, spoke out against Joash and his worship of the Asherah, and he was stoned to death.	2 Chr 24:17–22 (cp. Acts 7:58–59)
"were sawn in two" (v. 36)	Isaiah	Belchîrâ, a false prophet, spoke against Isaiah to Manasseh, who in turn had Isaiah arrested and with a wood-saw was sawn in two.	Martyrdom and Ascension of Isaiah 5:1–14
"were put to death by the sword" (v. 36)	Prophets	This may be a reference to Jezebel, who in her persecution of the Lord's prophets, was killing them by way of the sword (cp. 1 Kgs 18:4).	1 Kgs 19:10
"went about in sheepskins and goatskins" (v. 36)	Judas Maccabeus	When Antiochus IV arrived in Jerusalem, he put to the sword all those who came to see him, while Judas and nine others escaped to the wilderness and lived on what grew wild like wild animals.	2 Macc 5;27
"wandered in deserts, mountains, caves, and holes in the ground" (v. 38)	Jews persecuted during Antiochus' rule	The first martyrs under Antiochus IV lived in caves until captured and burned alive; others avoided capture by wandering in the mountains and caves like wild animals.	2 Macc 6:11; 10:6

Extrabiblical References
to Jewish Ancestors in Hebrews 11
CHART 82

1 Maccabees 2:51–64	Sirach 44–50	Hebrews 11
		Abel (11:4)
	Enoch (44:16)	Enoch (11:5)
	Noah (44:17–18)	Noah (11:7)
Abraham (2:52)	Abraham (44:19–21)	Abraham (11:8–19)
	Isaac (44:22)	Isaac (11:20)
	Jacob (44:23)	Jacob (11:21)
Joseph (2:53)		Joseph (11:22)
		Moses' parents (11:23)
	Moses (45:1–5)	Moses (11:24–28)
	Aaron (45:6–22, 25)	
Phinehas (2:54)	Phinehas (45:23–24)	
Joshua (2:55)	Joshua son of Nun (46:1–8)	The people (11:30)
		Rahab (11:31)
Caleb (2:56)	Caleb (46:7–10)	
	The judges (46:11–12)	Gideon (11:32)
		Barak (11:32)
		Samson (11:32)
		Jephthah (11:32)
	Samuel (46:13–20)	
	Nathan (47:1)	
David (2:57)	David (47:2-11)	David (11:32)
	Solomon (47:12–23)	
Elijah (2:58)	Elijah (48:1–11)	
	Elisha (48:12–14)	
	Hezekiah (48:17–22a)	
	Isaiah (48:22b-25)	
	Josiah (49:1–3)	
	Jeremiah (49:6b-7)	
Hananiah, Azariah, Mishael (2:59)		
Daniel (2:60–61)	Ezekiel (49:8–9)	The prophets (11:32)
	Twelve prophets (49:10)	
	Zerubbabel (49:11)	
	Jeshua son of Jozadak (49:12)	
	Nehemiah (49:13)	
	Enoch (49:14)	
	Joseph (49:15)	
	Shem, Seth and Enosh (49:16a)	
	Adam (49:16b)	
	Simon son of Onias (50:1–21)	

Words of Exhortation in Hebrews

CHART 83

Reference in Hebrews	Exhortation
2:1	We must pay closer attention to what we have heard.
3:1	Consider Jesus, the apostle and high priest of our confession.
3:12	Take care that none of you has an evil, unbelieving heart.
3:13	Exhort one another each day … that none of you become hardened by sin's deception.
4:1	Let us fear … that none of you may fail to reach God's rest.
4:14	Let us hold fast our confession.
4:16	Let us with confidence approach the throne of grace.
6:1	Let us leave the elementary doctrine of Christ and go on to maturity.
6:11	Demonstrate the same eagerness in realizing the fulfillment of hope until the end.
6:18	Seize the hope set before us.
10:22	Let us draw near.
10:23	Let us hold fast the confession of our hope.
10:24	Let us give thought of how to stir up one another to love and to do good works.
10:32	Recall the former days when you endured a harsh conflict.
10:35	Do not throw away your confidence.
12:1	Let us get rid of every weight and the sin that clings so closely to us.
12:1	Let us run with endurance the race that is set before us.
12:3	Consider him who endured opposition from sinners.
12:12	Strengthen your listless hands and your weak knees .
12:13	Make straight paths for your feet.
12:14	Pursue peace with everyone.
12:15	See to it that no one fails to obtain God's grace.

Reference in Hebrews	Exhortation
12:16	See to it that no one among you becomes an immoral person.
12:25	Take care not to refuse the one who is speaking.
12:28	Let us give thanks and offer to God acceptable worship.
13:2	Do not neglect hospitality.
13:3	Remember those in prison as though you were in prison with them.
13:7	Remember your leaders.
13:9	Do not be carried away by all sorts of strange teachings.
13:16	Do not neglect to do good and to share what you have.
13:17	Obey your leaders and submit to them.
13:17	Let them (your leaders) do this (watch over you) with joy and not with complaints.
13:18	Pray for us.
13:22	I urge you, brothers and sisters, bear with my message of exhortation .

The Dangers of Apostasy in Hebrews

CHART 84

Types of Dangers	Danger	Reference in Hebrews
Passive Dangers	Believers are encouraged not to drift away or lose sight of the message.	2:1
	Believers are encouraged not to neglect the message.	2:3
	Believers are encouraged not to fall short of the goal.	4:1
	Believers are encouraged not to lose hold of their confession.	4:14
	Believers are encouraged not to become dull in their understanding of the message.	5:11
	Believers are encouraged not to become sluggish in learning more about the message.	6:12 (cp. 5:12–14)
	Believers are encouraged not to lose their confidence.	10:19, 23
	Believers are encouraged not to lose heart.	12:3
	Believers are encouraged not to be carried away by strange teachings.	13:9
Active Dangers	Believers will develop a sinful, unbelieving heart that will turn away from the living God.	3:12
	Believers will exhibit disobedience that mirrors the Kadesh-Barnea community.	4:11 (cf. Deut 1:19–2:14)
	Believers will fall away from Jesus and hold him in contempt.	6:6
	Believers will neglect to meet together.	10:25
	Believers will persist, willfully, in sin and profane the blood of Jesus.	10:26
	Believers will reject God who speaks from heaven.	12:25
External Dangers	Believers will fall away due to the assaults that test their faith.	2:18; 4:16
	Believers will turn away due to their suffering through persecution.	10:32–35; 12:4
	Believers will reject the message due to the threat of torture and imprisonment.	10:33–34; 13:3 (cf. 10:28–9)

Concerns of Apostasy in the Warning Passages

CHART 85

Hebrews 2:1–4				
Real Exhortation	Real Concern	Historical Precedent	Dire Consequence	Desired Consequence
Pay attention to the message about the Son (1:1–14, 2:4).	There is a concern about slipping away or forgetting the message about the Son (2:1). There is a concern about ignoring, rejecting, or disregarding the message of salvation (2:3).	The author points to the wilderness community at Mount Sinai (cf. 3:7–11).	Judgment of the Sinai community in the wilderness versus no escape from some sort of future judgment (2:2).	Believe the message of salvation (2:1).

Hebrews 3:7–4:16				
Real Exhortation	Real Concern	Historical Precedent	Dire Consequence	Desired Consequence
Be watchful (3:12). Encourage one another (3:13). Let us fear failure to enter God's rest (4:1a). Be diligent to enter God's rest (4:11a). Maintain your confession of faith (4:14). Approach God with confidence (4:16).	There is a concern about turning away from God (3:12). There is a concern about becoming hardened by sin's deception (3:13). There is a concern about falling short of entering God's place of rest (4:1b). There is a concern about disobedience (3:18; 4:6, 11b).	The author points to the distrust and disobedience of the wilderness community at Kadesh-Barnea (3:16–18; 4:2b, 6).	Whereas the disobedient are denied entrance into Canaan and condemned to die in the desert (3:17–18), the disobedient in Hebrews are denied opportunities to experience God in his heavenly place of rest (4:1, 11).	Obey God (3:15, 4:7). Enter into God's place of rest (4:10–11). Participate in God's Sabbath rest/celebration (4:9).

Hebrews 5:11–6:12				
Real Exhortation	Real Concern	Historical Precedent	Dire Consequence	Desired Consequence
Leave the elementary doctrine of Christ and press on to maturity (6:1). Demonstrate the same eagerness in realizing the fulfillment of hope until the end (6:11). Seize the hope set before you (6:18).	There is a concern about immaturity (5:12, 14). There is concern about falling away (6:6). There is a concern about being productive (6:7). There is a concern about becoming lazy in faith (6:12).	The author may be alluding to the Kadesh Barnea event (6:4–6). The author provides an agricultural image that may allude to the blessing and cursing for Israel (6:7–8).	No repentance or hope for restoration (6:6). Future judgment of God (6:8).	Believers are to show diligence to the very end so to secure their hope (6:11). Believers are to imitate those who inherit what is promised (6:12b).

Hebrews 10:19–39				
Real Exhortation	Real Concern	Historical Precedent	Dire Consequence	Desired Consequence
Approach God with confidence (10:22). Maintain confession of faith (10:23). Encourage one another (10:24). Remember former days of harsh conflict (10:32). Do not throw away your confidence with its reward (10:35).	There is a concern about deliberate sin (10:26). There is a concern about rejecting the sacrifice of Jesus (10:28–29). There is concern about treating the new covenant as unholy (10:29). There is a concern about treating the Spirit with contempt (10:29). There is a concern about throwing away their confidence (10:35).	The author alludes to the disobedience of the wilderness community at Kadesh (10:26–28). The author alludes to the disobedience of the old covenant "Law of Moses" (10:28).	Whereas there was a sacrifice under the old covenant, there is no more sacrifice under the new in Hebrews (10:26). Whereas the disobedient suffered physical death (10:28), the disobedient in Hebrews will suffer greater punishment before a vengeful God (10:27, 29, 30–31).	Obey God (10:28–29). Be watchful of the Son's return (10:25). Persevere (10:36). Receive your reward (10:35). Live by faith (10:37–38).

147

Hebrews 12:14–29				
Real Exhortation	Real Concern	Historical Precedent	Dire Consequence	Desired Consequence
Pursue peace and holiness with everyone (12:14). Do not fall short of God's grace (12:15). Do not allow immoral practices in the community (12:16). Do not refuse the Son's message from heaven (12:25). Be thankful and worship God (12:28).	There is a concern about falling short of God's grace (12:15a). There is a concern about becoming bitter (12:15b). There is a concern about becoming involved in a godless and immoral lifestyle (12:16). There is a concern about refusing the Son (12:25a). There is a concern about turning away from God (12:25b).	The author points to the wilderness community at Mount Sinai (12:26).	Judgment of the Sinai community in the wilderness versus no escape from some future judgment (12:25).	Continue in belief (12:25). Believers are receiving an unshakable kingdom (12:28).

Identifying the Warning Passages in Hebrews

CHART 86

Commentator	Source	Suggested Divisions
Bruce, F. F.	*The Epistle to the Hebrews* in The New International Commentary on the New Testament. Grand Rapids: Eerdmans, revised edition, 1990.	Admonition #1 = 2:1–4 Admonition #2 = 3:7–19 Admonition #3 = 5:11–14 Admonition #4 = 10:26–31 Pay Heed = 12:25–29
Guthrie, George H.	*The Structure of Hebrews: A Text-Linguistic Analysis.* Grand Rapids: Baker, 1998 (p. 135).	Warning #1 = 2:1–4 Warning #2 = 4:12–13 Warning #3 = 6:4–8 Warning #4 = 10:26–31 Warning #5 = 12:25–29
Koester, Craig R.	*Hebrews* in The Anchor Bible. New York: Doubleday, 2001 (pp. 84–85).	Warning/Encouragement #1 = 5:11–6:20 Warning/Encouragement #2 = 10:26–39 Warning/Encouragement #3 = 12:25–27
Lane, William L.	*Hebrews 1–8* in Word Biblical Commentary. Waco: Word, 1991 (pp. 33, 80, 128). *Hebrews 9–13* in Word Biblical Commentary. Waco: Word, 1991 (pp. 271, 435).	Warning #1 = 2:1–4 Warning #2 = 3:7–19 Warning #3 = 5:11–6:12 Warning #4 = 10:19–39 Warning #5 = 12:14–29
O'Brien, Peter T.	*The Letter to the Hebrews.* The Pillar New Testament Commentary. Grand Rapids: Eerdmans, 2010 (p. 82).	Warning #1 = 2:1–4 Warning #2 = 3:7–19 Warning #3 = 5:11–6:12 Warning #4 = 10:26–39 Warning #5 = 12:25–29
Phillips, John	*Exploring Hebrews: An Expository Commentary* in The John Phillips Commentary Series. Grand Rapids: Kregel, revised edition, 1977, 1988 (pp. 12–14).	Warning #1 = 2:1–4 Warning #2 = 3:7–4:13 Warning #3 = 5:11–6:20 Warning #4 = 10:26–31 Warning #5 = 12:14–29
Bateman, Herbert	*Four Views on the Warning Passages in Hebrews.* Grand Rapids: Kregel, 2007 (p. 27).	Warning #1 = 2:1–4 Warning #2 = 3:7–4:13 Warning #3 = 5:11–6:12 Warning #4 = 10:19–39 Warning #5 = 12:14–29

Positions on the Warning Passages in Hebrews

CHART 87

Salvation Status of the Recipients	Author's Primary Concern	Expansion of Author's Concern	Advocates
Real Christians	Loss of salvation	Persevere; there is no repentance	Osborn, "A Classical Arminian View" in *Four Views on the Warning Passages in Hebrews*, (2007).
Real Christians	Loss of faith or relationship	Persevere; there may be restoration available	McKnight, "The Warning Passages of Hebrews" in *Trinity Journal* (1992). Perhaps: I. Howard Marshall, *Kept by the Power of God* (1969).
Real Christians	Loss of opportunity for service and/or Loss of heavenly reward	Persevere to avoid eternal regret of losing your rewards	Allen, *Hebrews*. The New American Commentary (2010). Gleason, "A Moderate Reformed View" in *Four Views on the Warning Passages in Hebrews*. Hodges, "Hebrews." *Bible Knowledge Commentary* (1983).
Real Christians	Loss of confidence	Be assured that believers will persevere	Fanning, "A Classical Reformed View" in *Four Views on the Warning Passages in Hebrews*. G. Guthrie, *Hebrews*. The NIV Application Commentary (1998).
Professing and not real Christians	Loss of opportunity to become a believer	Professing believers will renounce Jesus	Hughes, *A Commentary on the Epistle to the Hebrews* (1977). Revised Scofield Reference Bible (1967). Scofield Reference Bible (1909, 1945).
Real Christians	Hypothetically speaking, the loss of salvation	Wake up! Come out of your slumber!	Ryrie Study Bible (1976). D. Guthrie, *Hebrews*. Tyndale New Testament Series (1983). Hewett, *The Epistle to the Hebrews*. Tyndale New Testament Commentaries (1960).

Part Four

EXEGETICAL MATTERS
IN HEBREWS

Pentateuch Citations Compared in Hebrews

CHART 88

English: Genesis 2:2

Hebrew	Septuagint	Hebrews 4:4
אֱלֹהִים֙ . . . וַיִּשְׁבֹּת֙ בַּיּ֣וֹם הַשְּׁבִיעִ֔י מִכָּל־מְלַאכְתּ֖וֹ אֲשֶׁ֥ר עָשָֽׂה	. . . καὶ κατέπαυσεν τῇ ἡμέρᾳ τῇ ἑβδόμῃ ἀπὸ πάντων τῶν ἔργων αὐτοῦ, ὧν ἐποίησεν . . .	Καὶ κατέπαυσεν ὁ θεὸς ἐν τῇ ἡμέρᾳ τῇ ἑβδόμῃ ἀπὸ πάντων τῶν ἔργων αὐτοῦ·

English: Genesis 21:12

Hebrew	Septuagint	Hebrews 11:18
כִּ֣י בְיִצְחָ֔ק יִקָּרֵ֥א לְךָ֖ זָֽרַע	. . . ὅτι ἐν Ισαακ κληθήσεταί σοι σπέρμα.	ὅτι Ἐν Ἰσαὰκ κληθήσεταί σοι σπέρμα,

English: Genesis 22:17

Hebrew	Septuagint	Hebrews 6:14
כִּֽי־בָרֵ֣ךְ אֲבָרֶכְךָ֗ וְהַרְבָּ֨ה אַרְבֶּ֤ה אֶֽת־זַרְעֲךָ֙	. . . ἦ μὴν εὐλογῶν εὐλογήσω σε καὶ πληθύνων πληθυνῶ τὸ σπέρμα σου . . .	Εἰ μὴν εὐλογῶν εὐλογήσω σε καὶ πληθύνων πληθυνῶ σε

English: Exodus 19:12–13		
Hebrew	**Septuagint**	**Hebrews 12:20**
וְהִגְבַּלְתָּ אֶת־הָעָם סָבִיב 12 לֵאמֹר הִשָּׁמְרוּ לָכֶם עֲלוֹת בָּהָר וּנְגֹעַ בְּקָצֵהוּ כָּל־הַנֹּגֵעַ בָּהָר מוֹת יוּמָת: לֹא־תִגַּע בּוֹ יָד כִּי־סָקוֹל 13 יִסָּקֵל אוֹ־יָרֹה יִיָּרֶה אִם־בְּהֵמָה אִם־אִישׁ לֹא יִחְיֶה	... Προσέχετε ἑαυτοῖς τοῦ ἀναβῆναι εἰς τὸ ὄρος καὶ θιγεῖν τι αὐτοῦ· πᾶς ὁ ἁψάμενος τοῦ ὄρους θανάτῳ τελευτήσει. 13 οὐχ ἅψεται αὐτοῦ χείρ· ἐν γὰρ λίθοις λιθοβοληθήσεται ἢ βολίδι κατατοξευθήσεται· ἐάν τε κτῆνος ἐάν τε ἄνθρωπος, οὐ ζήσεται. ὅταν αἱ φωναὶ καὶ αἱ σάλπιγγες καὶ ἡ νεφέλη ἀπέλθῃ ἀπὸ τοῦ ὄρους, ἐκεῖνοι ἀναβήσονται ἐπὶ τὸ ὄρος.	*Κἂν θηρίον θίγῃ τοῦ ὄρους, λιθοβοληθήσεται·*

English: Exodus 24:8		
Hebrew	**Septuagint**	**Hebrews 9:20**
דַּם־הַבְּרִית אֲשֶׁר כָּרַת יְהוָה עִמָּכֶם עַל כָּל־הַדְּבָרִים הָאֵלֶּה:	... Ἰδοὺ τὸ αἷμα τῆς διαθήκης, ἧς διέθετο κύριος πρὸς ὑμᾶς ...	*Τοῦτο τὸ αἷμα τῆς διαθήκης ἧς ἐνετείλατο πρὸς ὑμᾶς ὁ θεός·*

English: Exodus 25:40		
Hebrew	**Septuagint**	**Hebrews 8:5**
וּרְאֵה וַעֲשֵׂה בְּתַבְנִיתָם אֲשֶׁר־אַתָּה מָרְאֶה בָּהָר:	ὅρα ποιήσεις κατὰ τὸν τύπον τὸν δεδειγμένον σοι ἐν τῷ ὄρει.	*Ὅρα γάρ φησίν, ποιήσεις πάντα κατὰ τὸν τύπον τὸν δειχθέντα σοι ἐν τῷ ὄρει·*

English: Deuteronomy 4:24		
Hebrew	**Septuagint**	**Hebrews 12:29**
כִּי יְהוָה אֱלֹהֶיךָ אֵשׁ אֹכְלָה הוּא	… ὅτι κύριος ὁ θεός σου πῦρ καταναλίσκον ἐστίν	καὶ γὰρ ὁ θεὸς ἡμῶν πῦρ καταναλίσκον

English: Deuteronomy 31:6		
Hebrew	**Septuagint**	**Hebrews 13:5**
לֹא יַרְפְּךָ וְלֹא יַעַזְבֶךָּ׃	… οὐ μή σε ἀνῇ οὔτε μή σε ἐγκαταλίπῃ.	Οὐ μή σε ἀνῶ οὐδ' οὐ μή σε ἐγκαταλίπω·

English: Deuteronomy 32:35		
Hebrew	**Septuagint**	**Hebrews 10:30a**
לִי נָקָם וְשִׁלֵּם	… ἐν ἡμέρᾳ ἐκδικήσεως ἀνταποδώσω …	Ἐμοὶ ἐκδίκησις, ἐγὼ ἀνταποδώσω

English: Deuteronomy 32:36		
Hebrew	**Septuagint**	**Hebrews 10:30b**
כִּי־יָדִין יְהוָה עַמּוֹ	… ὅτι κρινεῖ κύριος τὸν λαὸν αὐτοῦ …	Κρινεῖ κύριος τὸν λαὸν αὐτοῦ.

English: Deuteronomy 32:43		
Hebrew	**Septuagint**	**Hebrews 1:6**
הַרְנִינוּ גוֹיִם עַמּוֹ	… καὶ προσκυνησάτωσαν αὐτῷ πάντες υἱοὶ θεοῦ·	Καὶ προσκυνησάτωσαν αὐτῷ πάντες ἄγγελοι θεοῦ.

Prophetic Citations Compared: Hebrew, LXX, Hebrews

CHART 89

English: 2 Samuel 7:14a		
Hebrew	**Septuagint**	**Hebrews 1:5**
אֲנִי אֶהְיֶה־לּוֹ לְאָב וְהוּא יִהְיֶה־לִּי לְבֵן	ἐγὼ ἔσομαι αὐτῷ εἰς πατέρα, καὶ αὐτὸς ἔσται μοι εἰς υἱόν·	Ἐγὼ ἔσομαι αὐτῷ εἰς πατέρα, καὶ αὐτὸς ἔσται μοι εἰς υἱόν

English: Isaiah 8:17–18		
Hebrew	**Septuagint**	**Hebrews 2:13**
17 וְחִכִּיתִי לַיהוָה הַמַּסְתִּיר פָּנָיו מִבֵּית יַעֲקֹב וְקִוֵּיתִי־לוֹ: 18 הִנֵּה אָנֹכִי וְהַיְלָדִים אֲשֶׁר נָתַן־לִי יְהוָה לְאֹתוֹת וּלְמוֹפְתִים בְּיִשְׂרָאֵל מֵעִם יְהוָה צְבָאוֹת הַשֹּׁכֵן בְּהַר צִיּוֹן:	17 καὶ ἐρεῖ Μενῶ τὸν θεὸν τὸν ἀποστρέψαντα τὸ πρόσωπον αὐτοῦ ἀπὸ τοῦ οἴκου Ιακωβ καὶ πεποιθὼς ἔσομαι ἐπ' αὐτῷ. 18 ἰδοὺ ἐγὼ καὶ τὰ παιδία, ἅ μοι ἔδωκεν ὁ θεός, καὶ ἔσται εἰς σημεῖα καὶ τέρατα ἐν τῷ οἴκῳ Ισραηλ παρὰ κυρίου σαβαωθ, ὃς κατοικεῖ ἐν τῷ ὄρει Σιων.	Ἐγὼ ἔσομαι πεποιθὼς ἐπ' αὐτῷ· καὶ πάλιν, Ἰδοὺ ἐγὼ καὶ τὰ παιδία ἅ μοι ἔδωκεν ὁ θεός.

English: Jeremiah 31:31–34		
Hebrew (31:31–34)	**Septuagint (38:31–34)**	**Hebrews 8:8–12**
31 הִנֵּה יָמִים בָּאִים נְאֻם־יְהֹוָה וְכָרַתִּי אֶת־בֵּית יִשְׂרָאֵל וְאֶת־בֵּית יְהוּדָה בְּרִית חֲדָשָׁה: 32 לֹא כַבְּרִית אֲשֶׁר כָּרַתִּי אֶת־אֲבוֹתָם בְּיוֹם הֶחֱזִיקִי בְיָדָם לְהוֹצִיאָם מֵאֶרֶץ מִצְרָיִם אֲשֶׁר־הֵמָּה הֵפֵרוּ אֶת־בְּרִיתִי וְאָנֹכִי בָּעַלְתִּי בָם נְאֻם־יְהֹוָה:	31 Ἰδοὺ ἡμέραι ἔρχονται, φησὶν κύριος, καὶ διαθήσομαι τῷ οἴκῳ Ἰσραηλ καὶ τῷ οἴκῳ Ιουδα διαθήκην καινήν, 32 οὐ κατὰ τὴν διαθήκην, ἣν διεθέμην τοῖς πατράσιν αὐτῶν ἐν ἡμέρᾳ ἐπιλαβομένου μου τῆς χειρὸς αὐτῶν ἐξαγαγεῖν αὐτοὺς ἐκ γῆς Αἰγύπτου, ὅτι αὐτοὶ οὐκ ἐνέμειναν ἐν τῇ διαθήκῃ μου, καὶ ἐγὼ ἠμέλησα αὐτῶν, φησὶν κύριος· 33 ὅτι αὕτη ἡ διαθήκη, ἣν διαθήσομαι τῷ οἴκῳ Ἰσραηλ μετὰ τὰς ἡμέρας ἐκείνας, φησὶν κύριος Διδοὺς δώσω νόμους μου εἰς τὴν διάνοιαν αὐτῶν καὶ ἐπὶ	Ἰδοὺ ἡμέραι ἔρχονται, λέγει κύριος, καὶ συντελέσω ἐπὶ τὸν οἶκον Ἰσραὴλ καὶ ἐπὶ τὸν οἶκον Ἰούδα διαθήκην καινήν, 9 οὐ κατὰ τὴν διαθήκην ἣν ἐποίησα τοῖς πατράσιν αὐτῶν ἐν ἡμέρᾳ ἐπιλαβομένου μου τῆς χειρὸς αὐτῶν ἐξαγαγεῖν αὐτοὺς ἐκ γῆς Αἰγύπτου, ὅτι αὐτοὶ οὐκ ἐνέμειναν ἐν τῇ διαθήκῃ μου, κἀγὼ ἠμέλησα αὐτῶν, λέγει κύριος. 10 ὅτι αὕτη ἡ διαθήκη ἣν διαθήσομαι τῷ οἴκῳ Ἰσραὴλ μετὰ τὰς ἡμέρας ἐκείνας, λέγει κύριος, διδοὺς νόμους μου εἰς
33 כִּי זֹאת הַבְּרִית אֲשֶׁר אֶכְרֹת אֶת־בֵּית יִשְׂרָאֵל אַחֲרֵי הַיָּמִים הָהֵם נְאֻם־יְהֹוָה נָתַתִּי אֶת־תּוֹרָתִי בְּקִרְבָּם וְעַל־לִבָּם אֶכְתֲּבֶנָּה וְהָיִיתִי לָהֶם לֵאלֹהִים וְהֵמָּה יִהְיוּ־לִי לְעָם: 34 וְלֹא יְלַמְּדוּ עוֹד אִישׁ אֶת־רֵעֵהוּ וְאִישׁ אֶת־אָחִיו לֵאמֹר דְּעוּ אֶת־יְהֹוָה כִּי־כוּלָּם יֵדְעוּ אוֹתִי לְמִקְטַנָּם וְעַד־גְּדוֹלָם נְאֻם־יְהֹוָה כִּי אֶסְלַח לַעֲוֹנָם וּלְחַטָּאתָם לֹא אֶזְכָּר־עוֹד:	καρδίας αὐτῶν γράψω αὐτούς· καὶ ἔσομαι αὐτοῖς εἰς θεόν, καὶ αὐτοὶ ἔσονταί μοι εἰς λαόν· 34 καὶ οὐ μὴ διδάξωσιν ἕκαστος τὸν πολίτην αὐτοῦ καὶ ἕκαστος τὸν ἀδελφὸν αὐτοῦ λέγων Γνῶθι τὸν κύριον· ὅτι πάντες εἰδήσουσίν με ἀπὸ μικροῦ αὐτῶν καὶ ἕως μεγάλου αὐτῶν, ὅτι ἵλεως ἔσομαι ταῖς ἀδικίαις αὐτῶν καὶ τῶν ἁμαρτιῶν αὐτῶν οὐ μὴ μνησθῶ ἔτι.	τὴν διάνοιαν αὐτῶν, καὶ ἐπὶ καρδίας αὐτῶν ἐπιγράψω αὐτούς, καὶ ἔσομαι αὐτοῖς εἰς θεὸν καὶ αὐτοὶ ἔσονταί μοι εἰς λαόν. 11 καὶ οὐ μὴ διδάξωσιν ἕκαστος τὸν πολίτην αὐτοῦ καὶ ἕκαστος τὸν ἀδελφὸν αὐτοῦ, λέγων, Γνῶθι τὸν κύριον, ὅτι πάντες εἰδήσουσίν με ἀπὸ μικροῦ ἕως μεγάλου αὐτῶν. 12 ὅτι ἵλεως ἔσομαι ταῖς ἀδικίαις αὐτῶν, καὶ τῶν ἁμαρτιῶν αὐτῶν οὐ μὴ μνησθῶ ἔτι.

	English: Jeremiah 31:33–34	
Hebrew (31:33–34)	**Septuagint (38:33–34)**	**Hebrews 10:16–17**
33 כִּי זֹאת הַבְּרִית אֲשֶׁר אֶכְרֹת אֶת־בֵּית יִשְׂרָאֵל אַחֲרֵי הַיָּמִים הָהֵם נְאֻם־יְהוָה נָתַתִּי אֶת־תּוֹרָתִי בְּקִרְבָּם וְעַל־לִבָּם אֶכְתֲּבֶנָּה וְהָיִיתִי לָהֶם לֵאלֹהִים וְהֵמָּה יִהְיוּ־לִי לְעָם׃ 34 וְלֹא יְלַמְּדוּ עוֹד אִישׁ אֶת־רֵעֵהוּ וְאִישׁ אֶת־אָחִיו לֵאמֹר דְּעוּ אֶת־יְהוָה כִּי־כוּלָּם יֵדְעוּ אוֹתִי לְמִקְטַנָּם וְעַד־גְּדוֹלָם נְאֻם־יְהוָה כִּי אֶסְלַח לַעֲוֹנָם וּלְחַטָּאתָם לֹא אֶזְכָּר־עוֹד׃	33 ὅτι αὕτη ἡ διαθήκη, ἣν διαθήσομαι τῷ οἴκῳ Ισραηλ μετὰ τὰς ἡμέρας ἐκείνας, φησὶν κύριος Διδοὺς δώσω νόμους μου εἰς τὴν διάνοιαν αὐτῶν καὶ ἐπὶ καρδίας αὐτῶν γράψω αὐτούς· καὶ ἔσομαι αὐτοῖς εἰς θεόν, καὶ αὐτοὶ ἔσονταί μοι εἰς λαόν· 34 καὶ οὐ μὴ διδάξωσιν ἕκαστος τὸν πολίτην αὐτοῦ καὶ ἕκαστος τὸν ἀδελφὸν αὐτοῦ λέγων Γνῶθι τὸν κύριον· ὅτι πάντες εἰδήσουσίν με ἀπὸ μικροῦ αὐτῶν καὶ ἕως μεγάλου αὐτῶν, ὅτι ἵλεως ἔσομαι ταῖς ἀδικίαις αὐτῶν καὶ τῶν ἁμαρτιῶν αὐτῶν οὐ μὴ μνησθῶ ἔτι.	16 Αὕτη ἡ διαθήκη ἣν διαθήσομαι πρὸς αὐτοὺς μετὰ τὰς ἡμέρας ἐκείνας, λέγει κύριος, διδοὺς νόμους μου ἐπὶ καρδίας αὐτῶν, καὶ ἐπὶ τὴν διάνοιαν αὐτῶν ἐπιγράψω αὐτούς, 17 καὶ τῶν ἁμαρτιῶν αὐτῶν καὶ τῶν ἀνομιῶν αὐτῶν οὐ μὴ μνησθήσομαι ἔτι.

	English: Habakkuk 2:3–4	
Hebrew	**Septuagint**	**Hebrews 10:37–38**
3 כִּי עוֹד חָזוֹן לַמּוֹעֵד וְיָפֵחַ לַקֵּץ וְלֹא יְכַזֵּב אִם־יִתְמַהְמָהּ חַכֵּה־לוֹ כִּי־בֹא יָבֹא לֹא יְאַחֵר׃ 4 הִנֵּה עֻפְּלָה לֹא־יָשְׁרָה נַפְשׁוֹ בּוֹ וְצַדִּיק בֶּאֱמוּנָתוֹ יִחְיֶה׃	3 διότι ἔτι ὅρασις εἰς καιρὸν καὶ ἀνατελεῖ εἰς πέρας καὶ οὐκ εἰς κενόν· ἐὰν ὑστερήσῃ, ὑπόμεινον αὐτόν, ὅτι ἐρχόμενος ἥξει καὶ οὐ μὴ χρονίσῃ. 4 ἐὰν ὑποστείληται, οὐκ εὐδοκεῖ ἡ ψυχή μου ἐν αὐτῷ· ὁ δὲ δίκαιος ἐκ πίστεώς μου ζήσεται.	37 ἔτι γὰρ μικρὸν ὅσον ὅσον, ὁ ἐρχόμενος ἥξει καὶ οὐ χρονίσει· 38 ὁ δὲ δίκαιός μου ἐκ πίστεως ζήσεται, καὶ ἐὰν ὑποστείληται, οὐκ εὐδοκεῖ ἡ ψυχή μου ἐν αὐτῷ..

Poetic Citations Compared: Hebrew, LXX, Hebrews

CHART 90

English: Psalm 2:7b

Hebrew	Septuagint	Hebrews 1:5, 5:5
אָמַר אֵלַי בְּנִי אַתָּה אֲנִי הַיּוֹם יְלִדְתִּיךָ	Κύριος εἶπεν πρός με Υἱός μου εἶ σύ, ἐγὼ σήμερον γεγέννηκά σε·	Υἱός μου εἶ σύ, ἐγὼ σήμερον γεγέννηκά σε Υἱός μου εἶ σύ, ἐγὼ σήμερον γεγέννηκά σε

English: Psalm 8:4–6

Hebrew: 8:5–7	Septuagint: 8:5–7	Hebrews 2:6b-8
5 מָה־אֱנוֹשׁ כִּי־תִזְכְּרֶנּוּ וּבֶן־ אָדָם כִּי תִפְקְדֶנּוּ׃ 6 וַתְּחַסְּרֵהוּ מְּעַט מֵאֱלֹהִים וְכָבוֹד וְהָדָר תְּעַטְּרֵהוּ׃ 7 תַּמְשִׁילֵהוּ בְּמַעֲשֵׂי יָדֶיךָ כֹּל שַׁתָּה תַחַת־רַגְלָיו׃	5 τί ἐστιν ἄνθρωπος, ὅτι μιμνήσκῃ αὐτοῦ, ἢ υἱὸς ἀνθρώπου, ὅτι ἐπισκέπτῃ αὐτόν; 6 ἠλάττωσας αὐτὸν βραχύ τι παρ' ἀγγέλους, δόξῃ καὶ τιμῇ ἐστεφάνωσας αὐτόν· 7 καὶ κατέστησας αὐτὸν ἐπὶ τὰ ἔργα τῶν χειρῶν σου, πάντα ὑπέταξας ὑποκάτω τῶν ποδῶν αὐτοῦ,	6 διεμαρτύρατο δέ πού τις λέγων, Τί ἐστιν ἄνθρωπος ὅτι μιμνήσκῃ αὐτοῦ, ἢ υἱὸς ἀνθρώπου ὅτι ἐπισκέπτῃ αὐτόν; 7 ἠλάττωσας αὐτὸν βραχύ τι παρ' ἀγγέλους, δόξῃ καὶ τιμῇ ἐστεφάνωσας αὐτόν, 8 πάντα ὑπέταξας ὑποκάτω τῶν ποδῶν αὐτοῦ. ἐν τῷ γὰρ ὑποτάξαι [αὐτῷ] τὰ πάντα οὐδὲν ἀφῆκεν αὐτῷ ἀνυπότακτον. νῦν δὲ οὔπω ὁρῶμεν αὐτῷ τὰ πάντα ὑποτεταγμένα·

English: Psalm 22:22

Hebrew: 22:23	Septuagint: 21:23	Hebrews 2:12
אֲסַפְּרָה שִׁמְךָ לְאֶחָי בְּתוֹךְ קָהָל אֲהַלְלֶךָּ׃	διηγήσομαι τὸ ὄνομά σου τοῖς ἀδελφοῖς μου, ἐν μέσῳ ἐκκλησίας ὑμνήσω σε	λέγων, Ἀπαγγελῶ τὸ ὄνομά σου τοῖς ἀδελφοῖς μου, ἐν μέσῳ ἐκκλησίας ὑμνήσω σε·

English: Psalm 40:6–8		
Hebrew: 40:7-9	**Septuagint: 39:7-9**	**Hebrews 10:5-7**
7 זֶבַח וּמִנְחָה ׀ לֹא־חָפַצְתָּ אָזְנַיִם כָּרִיתָ לִּי עוֹלָה וַחֲטָאָה לֹא שָׁאָלְתָּ׃ 8 אָז אָמַרְתִּי הִנֵּה־בָאתִי בִּמְגִלַּת־סֵפֶר כָּתוּב עָלָי׃ 9 לַעֲשׂוֹת־רְצוֹנְךָ אֱלֹהַי חָפָצְתִּי	7 θυσίαν καὶ προσφορὰν οὐκ ἠθέλησας, ὠτία δὲ κατηρτίσω μοι· ὁλοκαύτωμα καὶ περὶ ἁμαρτίας οὐκ ᾔτησας. 8 τότε εἶπον Ἰδοὺ ἥκω, ἐν κεφαλίδι βιβλίου γέγραπται περὶ ἐμοῦ· 9 τοῦ ποιῆσαι τὸ θέλημά σου, ὁ θεός μου, ἐβουλήθην καὶ τὸν νόμον σου ἐν μέσῳ τῆς κοιλίας μου.	5 Διὸ εἰσερχόμενος εἰς τὸν κόσμον λέγει, Θυσίαν καὶ προσφορὰν οὐκ ἠθέλησας, σῶμα δὲ κατηρτίσω μοι· 6 ὁλοκαυτώματα καὶ περὶ ἁμαρτίας οὐκ εὐδόκησας. 7 τότε εἶπον, Ἰδοὺ ἥκω, ἐν κεφαλίδι βιβλίου γέγραπται περὶ ἐμοῦ, τοῦ ποιῆσαι, ὁ θεός, τὸ θέλημά σου.

English: Psalm 45:6–7		
Hebrew: 45:7-8	**Septuagint: 44:7-8**	**Hebrews 1:8-9**
7 כִּסְאֲךָ אֱלֹהִים עוֹלָם וָעֶד שֵׁבֶט מִישֹׁר שֵׁבֶט מַלְכוּתֶךָ׃ 8 אָהַבְתָּ צֶּדֶק וַתִּשְׂנָא רֶשַׁע עַל־כֵּן ׀ מְשָׁחֲךָ אֱלֹהִים אֱלֹהֶיךָ שֶׁמֶן שָׂשׂוֹן מֵחֲבֵרֶיךָ׃	7 ὁ θρόνος σου, ὁ θεός, εἰς τὸν αἰῶνα τοῦ αἰῶνος, ῥάβδος εὐθύτητος ἡ ῥάβδος τῆς βασιλείας σου. 8 ἠγάπησας δικαιοσύνην καὶ ἐμίσησας ἀνομίαν· διὰ τοῦτο ἔχρισέν σε ὁ θεὸς ὁ θεός σου ἔλαιον ἀγαλλιάσεως παρὰ τοὺς μετόχους σου.	8 πρὸς δὲ τὸν υἱόν, Ὁ θρόνος σου, ὁ θεός, εἰς τὸν αἰῶνα τοῦ αἰῶνος, καὶ ἡ ῥάβδος τῆς εὐθύτητος ῥάβδος τῆς βασι λείας σου. 9 ἠγάπησας δικαιοσύνην καὶ ἐμίσησας ἀνομίαν· διὰ τοῦτο ἔχρισέν σε ὁ θεός, ὁ θεός σου, ἔλαιον ἀγαλλιάσεως παρὰ τοὺς μετόχους σου·

English: Psalm 95:7–11		
Hebrew: 95:7b-11	**Septuagint: 94:7b-11**	**Hebrews 3:7-11**
7b הַיּוֹם אִם־בְּקֹלוֹ תִשְׁמָעוּ׃ 8 אַל־תַּקְשׁוּ לְבַבְכֶם כִּמְרִיבָה כְּיוֹם מַסָּה בַּמִּדְבָּר׃	7b σήμερον, ἐὰν τῆς φωνῆς αὐτοῦ ἀκούσητε, 8 μὴ σκληρύνητε τὰς καρδίας ὑμῶν ὡς ἐν τῷ παραπικρασμῷ κατὰ τὴν ἡμέραν τοῦ πειρασμοῦ ἐν τῇ ἐρήμῳ,	7 Διό, καθὼς λέγει τὸ πνεῦμα τὸ ἅγιον, Σήμερον ἐὰν τῆς φωνῆς αὐτοῦ ἀκούσητε, 8 μὴ σκληρύνητε τὰς καρδίας ὑμῶν ὡς ἐν τῷ παρα πικρασμῷ, κατὰ τὴν ἡμέραν τοῦ πειρασμοῦ ἐν τῇ ἐρήμῳ,

English: Psalm 95:7–11

Hebrew: 95:7b-11	Septuagint: 94:7b-11	Hebrews 3:7–11
9 אֲשֶׁר נִסּוּנִי אֲבוֹתֵיכֶם בְּחָנוּנִי גַּם־רָאוּ פָעֳלִי׃ 10 אַרְבָּעִים שָׁנָה ׀ אָקוּט בְּדוֹר וָאֹמַר עַם תֹּעֵי לֵבָב הֵם וְהֵם לֹא־יָדְעוּ דְרָכָי׃ 11 אֲשֶׁר־נִשְׁבַּעְתִּי בְאַפִּי אִם־יְבֹאוּן אֶל־מְנוּחָתִי׃	9 οὗ ἐπείρασαν οἱ πατέρες ὑμῶν, ἐδοκίμασαν καὶ εἴδοσαν τὰ ἔργα μου. 10 τεσσαράκοντα ἔτη προσώχθισα τῇ γενεᾷ ἐκείνῃ καὶ εἶπα Ἀεὶ πλανῶνται τῇ καρδίᾳ καὶ αὐτοὶ οὐκ ἔγνωσαν τὰς ὁδούς μου, 11 ὡς ὤμοσα ἐν τῇ ὀργῇ μου· Εἰ εἰσελεύσονται εἰς τὴν κατάπαυσίν μου.	9 οὗ ἐπείρασαν οἱ πατέρες ὑμῶν ἐν δοκιμασίᾳ καὶ εἶδον τὰ ἔργα μου 10 τεσσαράκοντα ἔτη· διὸ προσώχθισα τῇ γενεᾷ ταύτῃ καὶ εἶπον, Ἀεὶ πλανῶνται τῇ καρδίᾳ· αὐτοὶ δὲ οὐκ ἔγνωσαν τὰς ὁδούς μου· 11 ὡς ὤμοσα ἐν τῇ ὀργῇ μου· Εἰ εἰσελεύσονται εἰς τὴν κατάπαυσίν μου.

English: Psalm 102:25–27

Hebrew: 102:26–28	Septuagint: 101:26–28	Hebrews 1:10–12
26 לְפָנִים הָאָרֶץ יָסַדְתָּ וּמַעֲשֵׂה יָדֶיךָ שָׁמָיִם׃ 27 הֵמָּה ׀ יֹאבֵדוּ וְאַתָּה תַעֲמֹד וְכֻלָּם כַּבֶּגֶד יִבְלוּ כַּלְּבוּשׁ תַּחֲלִיפֵם וְיַחֲלֹפוּ׃ 28 וְאַתָּה־הוּא וּשְׁנוֹתֶיךָ לֹא יִתָּמּוּ׃	26 κατ᾽ ἀρχὰς σύ, κύριε, τὴν γῆν ἐθεμελίωσας, καὶ ἔργα τῶν χειρῶν σού εἰσιν οἱ οὐρανοί· 27 αὐτοὶ ἀπολοῦνται, σὺ δὲ διαμενεῖς, καὶ πάντες ὡς ἱμάτιον παλαιωθήσονται, καὶ ὡσεὶ περιβόλαιον ἀλλάξεις αὐτούς, καὶ ἀλλαγήσονται· 28 σὺ δὲ ὁ αὐτὸς εἶ, καὶ τὰ ἔτη σου οὐκ ἐκλείψουσιν.	10 καί, Σὺ κατ᾽ ἀρχάς, κύριε, τὴν γῆν ἐθεμελίωσας, καὶ ἔργα τῶν χειρῶν σού εἰσιν οἱ οὐρανοί· 11 αὐτοὶ ἀπολοῦνται, σὺ δὲ διαμένεις· καὶ πάντες ὡς ἱμάτιον παλαιωθήσονται, 12 καὶ ὡσεὶ περιβόλαιον ἑλίξεις αὐτούς, ὡς ἱμάτιον καὶ ἀλλαγήσονται· σὺ δὲ ὁ αὐτὸς εἶ καὶ τὰ ἔτη σου οὐκ ἐκλείψουσιν.

English: Psalm 110:1

Hebrew: 110:1b	Septuagint: 109:1b	Hebrews 1:13
נְאֻם יְהוָה ׀ לַאדֹנִי שֵׁב לִימִינִי עַד־אָשִׁית אֹיְבֶיךָ הֲדֹם לְרַגְלֶיךָ׃	Εἶπεν ὁ κύριος τῷ κυρίῳ μου Κάθου ἐκ δεξιῶν μου, ἕως ἂν θῶ τοὺς ἐχθρούς σου ὑποπόδιον τῶν ποδῶν σου.	1:13 Κάθου ἐκ δεξιῶν μου ἕως ἂν θῶ τοὺς ἐχθρούς σου ὑποπόδιον τῶν ποδῶν σου

English: Psalm 110:4		
Hebrew: 110:4	**Septuagint: 109:4**	**Hebrews 5:6; 7:17, 21**
נִשְׁבַּע יְהוָה ׀ וְלֹא יִנָּחֵם אַתָּה־כֹהֵן לְעוֹלָם עַל־דִּבְרָתִי מַלְכִּי־צֶדֶק׃	ὤμοσεν κύριος καὶ οὐ μεταμεληθήσεται Σὺ εἶ ἱερεὺς εἰς τὸν αἰῶνα κατὰ τὴν τάξιν Μελχισέδεκ.	*5:6 Σὺ ἱερεὺς εἰς τὸν αἰῶνα κατὰ τὴν τάξιν Μελχισέδεκ* *7:17 Σὺ ἱερεὺς εἰς τὸν αἰῶνα κατὰ τὴν τάξιν Μελχισέδεκ* *7:21 ὤμοσεν κύριος καὶ οὐ μεταμεληθήσεται· Σὺ ἱερεὺς εἰς τὸν αἰῶνα*

English: Psalm 118:6		
Hebrew: 118:6	**Septuagint: 117:6**	**Hebrews 13:6**
יְהוָה לִי לֹא אִירָא מַה־יַּעֲשֶׂה לִי אָדָם׃	κύριος ἐμοὶ βοηθός, οὐ φοβηθήσομαι τί ποιήσει μοι ἄνθρωπος.	*ὥστε θαρροῦντας ἡμᾶς λέγειν, Κύριος ἐμοὶ βοηθός, [καὶ] οὐ φοβηθήσομαι· τί ποιήσει μοι ἄνθρωπος;*

English: Psalm 135:14		
Hebrew: 135:14	**Septuagint: 134:14**	**Hebrews 10:30**
כִּי־יָדִין יְהוָה עַמּוֹ וְעַל־עֲבָדָיו יִתְנֶחָם׃	ὅτι κρινεῖ κύριος τὸν λαὸν αὐτοῦ καὶ ἐπὶ τοῖς δούλοις αὐτοῦ παρακληθήσεται.	*ὥστε θαρροῦντας ἡμᾶς λέγειν, Κύριος ἐμοὶ βοηθός, [καὶ] οὐ φοβηθήσομαι· τί ποιήσει μοι ἄνθρωπος;*

English: Proverbs 3:11–12		
Hebrew: 3:11–12	**Septuagint: 3:11–12**	**Hebrews 12:5–6**
11 מוּסַר יְהוָה בְּנִי אַל־תִּמְאָס וְאַל־תָּקֹץ בְּתוֹכַחְתּוֹ׃ 12 כִּי אֶת אֲשֶׁר יֶאֱהַב יְהוָה יוֹכִיחַ וּכְאָב אֶת־בֵּן יִרְצֶה׃	11 Υἱέ, μὴ ὀλιγώρει παιδείας κυρίου μηδὲ ἐκλύου ὑπ' αὐτοῦ ἐλεγχόμενος· 12 ὃν γὰρ ἀγαπᾷ κύριος παιδεύει, μαστιγοῖ δὲ πάντα υἱὸν ὃν παραδέχεται.	*5 καὶ ἐκλέλησθε τῆς παρακλήσεως, ἥτις ὑμῖν ὡς υἱοῖς διαλέγεται, Υἱέ μου, μὴ ὀλιγώρει παιδείας κυρίου, μηδὲ ἐκλύου ὑπ' αὐτοῦ ἐλεγχόμενος·* *6 ὃν γὰρ ἀγαπᾷ κύριος παιδεύει, μαστιγοῖ δὲ πάντα υἱὸν ὃν παραδέχεται.*

Examples of Jewish Exegesis in Hebrews

CHART 91

Qal Wahomer

Qal wahomer is an argument of logic. Arguments begin with a less significant situation and progress to something more significant. Thus, what applies in a less important case will certainly apply in a more important case.

Identified in Hebrews	Lesser	Greater
2:1–4 πῶς ἡμεῖς ἐκφευξόμεθα "how shall we escape"	Physical punishment for violating God's message spoken through angels at Sinai	Eternal punishment for ignoring God's message spoken through his Son, Jesus Point: God's message, spoken through Jesus is greater.
9:13–14 πόσῳ μᾶλλον τὸ αἷμα τοῦ Χριστοῦ "how much more the blood of Christ"	Cleansing the flesh with the blood of goats and bulls	Cleansing the conscience with the blood of Jesus Point: The blood of Jesus is greater.
10:28–30 πόσῳ ... χείρονος... τιμωρίασ "How much ... worse ... punishment"	Physical punishment for the person who rejected the law of Moses	Eternal punishment for the person who spurns Jesus and profanes the blood of the covenant Point: Jesus' sacrifice and new covenant are greater.
12:9 μᾶλλον ὑποταγησόμεθα τῷ πατρὶ τῶν πνευμάτων "submit ourselves all the more to the Father of spirits"	Children respect discipline (penal and educational) from human fathers	God's children receive discipline (penal and educational) from their heavenly Father Point: God's penal and educational discipline deserves greater submission.

Qal Wahomer		
12:25 πολὺ μᾶλλον ἡμεῖς οἱ τὸν ἀπ᾽ οὐρανῶν ἀποστρεφόμενοι "how much less *will we escape* if we turn away from the *one who warns* in heaven"	People of the exodus who ignored the one who warned them on earth did not escape physical punishment.	Followers of Jesus who ignore the one who warns from heaven will not escape eternal punishment. Point: Warnings from Jesus in heaven are greater than earthly warnings from prophets.

Gezerah Shavah		
Gezerah shavah is a verbal analogy that joins one verse of the Old Testament to another which contains the same words. Even though the contexts might be different, what applies in one verse applies in the other and, by extension, can be applied in a new situation.		

Identified in Hebrews	Word	OT Citation
1:5	Son	Psalm 2:7 linked to 2 Samuel 7:14
1:6–7	Angels	Deut 32:43 (LXX) linked to Psalm 104:4
4:3–4	Rest	Psalm 95:11 Linked to Genesis 2:2
7:1, 17, 22	Priest	Genesis 14:18–20 linked to Psalm 110:4

Kelal u-ferat		
Kelal u-ferat is when a general principle may be restricted by a particularization of it in another verse; or conversely, a particular rule may be extended into a general principle. Thus one verse of Scripture is presented as a general statement followed by another to draw a particular conclusion.		

Identified in Hebrews	General Statement	Particular Conclusion
7:1–10	Genesis 14:18–20 makes a general statement about Melchizedek.	Genesis 14:20 introduces the author's particular conclusion, that Abraham as well as Levi (the inferior) paid tithes and received a blessing from someone greater (the superior). Thus Melchizedek's priesthood is superior to Levi's.

Kayose bo bemaqom aher		

Kayose bo bemaqom aher means "as is found in another place." This rule involves the comparing of texts that have points of general, though not necessarily, verbal exactness (as expected with *gezerah shavah*). Thus one verse of Scripture is linked to another based upon conceptual similarities or parallels and is thereby applicable to a new situation.

Identified in Hebrews	Conceptual Linking	OT Citation
1:7 and 1:10	In 1:7, "he makes (creates) his angels spirits" is conceptually parallel to "you founded (created) the earth" in 1:10.	Conceptual similarities of creator link Ps 104:4 with Ps 102:25.
1:8, 1:9 and 1:10	In 1:8 and 1:9, "O God" and "God" are conceptually synonymous to "Lord" in 1:10.	Conceptual similarities of divine titles link Ps 45:6-7 with Ps 102:24-25.
1:8 and 1:13	In 1:8–9, "your throne" and "scepter" are conceptually similar to "sit at my right hand" in 1:13.	Conceptual symbols of royal power link Ps 45:6 with Ps 110:1
1:5, 1:9 and 1:13	Parallel concepts exist in 1:5 when God says, "You are my son," in 1:9, "God has anointed," and in 1:13 God says, "Sit at my right hand."	Conceptual language for enthronement of a king links Pss 2:7, 45:6, and 110:1.
2:12 and 2:13	In 2:12, "I will proclaim your name to my brothers" is conceptually similar to "Here I am with your children God has given me" 2:13.	Conceptual language used for kinship links Ps 22:22 with Isa 8:17–18.
5:5 and 5:6	In 5:5, "you are my son" is conceptually parallel to "you are a priest forever in the order of Melchizedek" in 5:6 (cp. 7:17, 21).	Conceptual similarities of royalty in Ps 2:7 link with Melchizedek's royal priesthood in Ps 110:4.
10:30	In 10:30, "vengeance is mine" is conceptually parallel with "The Lord will judge."	Conceptual similarities of divine punishment in Deut 32:35-36 link with those in Ps 135:14.
13:5 and 13:6	In 13:5, "I will never abandon you" is conceptually similar to "the Lord is my helper" in 13:6.	Conceptual similarities of divine help in Deut 31:6, 8 link with those in Ps 118:6–7 (117:6 LXX).

Dabar halamed me-ʿinyano		
Dabar halamed me-ʿinyano means "a meaning established by its context." This rule is used when an interpreter explains the meaning of an OT passage based upon its context and then applies its meaning to a new situation.		
Identified in Hebrews	**OT Citation**	**Questions Answered Contextually**
2:6b–8a (quotation) 2:8b–18 (interpretation)	Psalm 8:6-8	What does it mean that God "put all things under his control?"
3:7a-11 (quotation) 3:12–19 (interpretation)	Psalm 95:7b-11	What happens to people who "harden" their hearts? Who enters, where is, and what occurs during "God's rest?"
8:8b-12 (quotation) 8:13–9:28 (interpretation)	Jeremiah 31:31–34	How does the "new covenant" affect the "old covenant?"
10:5b-7 (quotation) 10:8–18 (interpretation)	Psalm 40:6–8	What does it mean that God did not desire sacrifice?

Examples of Chiasm in Hebrews 1
CHART 92

Hebrews 1:1–4

A   The Son's superiority: The Son is superior to former prophets (1:1–2a)

   B   The Son's appointment: He is heir of all things (1:2b)

      C   The Son's relationship with the universe: He created the created order (1:2c)

        D   The Son's relationship with God: He is the reflection of God's glory (1:3a)

      C^1 The Son's relationship with the universe: He sustains the created order (1:3b)

   B^1 The Son's appointment: He is exalted (enthroned) at God's right hand (1:3c)

A^1 The Son's superiority: The Son is superior to angels (1:4)

Hebrews 1:5–13

A   The Son's status as Davidic king: He is the heir of promise in Ps 2:7; 2 Sam 7:14 (1:5)

   B   The Son's status as divine: Creation honors him in Deut 32:43 (LXX) and serves him in Ps 104:4 (1:6–7)

      C   The Son's status as divine Davidic king: His epithet and rulership is the same as God's in Ps 45:6–7 (1:8–9)

   B^1 The Son's status as divine: He is Creator-King in Ps 102:25–27 (1:10–12)

A^1 The Son's status as Davidic king: He is exalted (enthroned) at God's right hand (Ps 110:1) (1:13)

Emphasis of the Chiastic Structures

The focus of the first chiastic structure in Hebrews 1:1–4 is 1:3a (letter "D"), and the focus of the second in Heb 1:5–13 is 1:8-9 (letter "C").

The Son's designation as divine is not necessarily an ontological statement, but rather a statement of activities that identify him as God.

Example of Chiasm in Hebrews 11

CHART 93

A   Introduction (11:1–3)

   B   Abel's example of suffering on account of faith (11:4)

     C   Enoch's example of triumph through faith (11:5)

       D   Principle of faith: Impossible to please God without faith (11:6)

         E   Example of faith as seen through Noah (11:7)

           F   Abraham's faith in obeying God's calling (11:8–10)

             G   Sarah's example of faith in conceiving Isaac (11:11–12)

               H   Middle section: Interim comment (11:13–16)

             G^1 Abraham's example of faith in offering up Isaac (11:17–19)

           F^1 Other examples of faith from Isaac, Jacob, and Joseph (11:20–22)

         E^1 Other examples of faith during the Mosaic era (11:23–29)

       D^1 Other examples of faith in conquering Jericho (11:30–31)

     C^1 Other examples of those who triumphed through faith (11:32–35a)

   B^1 Other examples of those who suffered on account of faith (11:35b-38)

A^1 Conclusion (11:39–40)

The aspect of faith in Hebrews 11:13–16 is both present and future oriented (the already and the not yet). The thrust of Hebrews as whole has both a present and future orientation (e.g. 2:8; 10:13).

Manuscript Evidence for Hebrews

CHART 94

Papyri			
Text	**Date**	**Family**	**Portions of Hebrews**
p^{12}	3rd Century	Alexandrian	1:1
p^{13}	3rd – 4th Century	Alexandrian	2:14–5:5; 10:8–22; 10:29–11:13; 11:28–12:17
p^{17}	4th Century	Alexandrian	9:12–19
p^{46}	200 C.E.	Alexandrian	1:1–9:16; 9:18–10:20, 22–30; 10:32–13:25
p^{79}	7th Century	Alexandrian	10:10–12, 28–30
p^{89}	4th Century	Alexandrian	6:7–9, 15–17

Uncials			
Text	**Date**	**Family**	**Portions of Hebrews**
aleph (01)	4th Century	Alexandrian	Complete
A (02)	5th Century	Alexandrian	Complete
B (03)	4th Century	Alexandrian	1:1–9:13
C (04)	5th Century	Alexandrian	2:5–7:25; 9:16–10:23; 12:16–13:25
D (06)	6th Century	Western	Complete
E^{p} \ D^{absl}	9th Century	Western	Copy of D
H (015)	6th Century	Independent	1:3–8; 2:11–16; 3:13–18; 4:12–15; 10:1–7, 32–38; 12:10–15; 13:24–25

Uncials			
Text	**Date**	**Family**	**Portions of Hebrews**
I (016)	5th Century	Alexandrian	1:1–3, 9–12; 2:4–7, 12–14; 3:4–6, 14–16; 4:3–6, 12–14; 5:5–7; 6:1–3, 10–13; 6:20–7:2, 7–11, 18–20; 7:27–8:1, 7–9; 9:1–4, 9–11, 16–19, 25–27; 10:5–8, 16–18, 26–29, 35–38; 11:6–7, 12–15, 22–24, 31–33; 11:38–12:1, 7–9, 16–18, 25–27; 13:7–9, 16–18, 23–25
K (018)	9th Century	Byzantine	Complete
L (020)	9th Century	Byzantine	1:1–13:9
P (025)	9th Century	Independent	Complete
Psi (044)	9th–10th Century	Independent	1:1–8:10; 9:20–13:25
048	5th Century	Alexandrian	11:32–38; 12:3–13:4
0121b	10th Century	Independent	1:1–4:3; 12:20–13:25
0122	9th Century	Independent	5:8–6:10
0227	5th Century	Independent	11:18–19, 29
0228	4th Century	Independent	12:19–25
0252	5th Century	Independent	6:2–4, 6–7

Consistently Cited Manuscript Witnesses for Hebrews

CHART 95

Consistently Cited Witnesses of the First Order			
Type	**Manuscript**	**Date**	**Family**
Papyri	p^{12}	3rd century	Alexandrian
	p^{13}	3rd / 4th century	Alexandrian
	p^{17}	4th century	Alexandrian
	p^{46}	200 C.E.	Alexandrian
	p^{79}	7th century	Alexandrian
	p^{89}	4th century	Alexandrian
Uncials	*aleph* ℵ (01)	4th century	Alexandrian
	A (02)	5th century	Alexandrian
	B (03)	4th century	Alexandrian
	C (04)	5th century	Alexandrian
	D (06)	6th century	Western
	H (015)	6th century	Independent
	I (016)	5th century	Alexandrian
	044	8th / 9th century	Alexandrian
	048	5th century	Alexandrian
	0122	9th century	Independent
	0227	5th century	Independent
	0243	10th century	Alexandrian
	0252	5th century	Independent
	0278	(Date unknown)	(Unknown Family)
	0285	(Date unknown)	(Unknown Family)
Minuscules	33	9th century	Alexandrian
	1739	10th century	Alexandrian
	1881	14th century	Alexandrian

Consistently Cited Witnesses of the Second Order			
Type	**Manuscript**	**Date**	**Family**
Papyri			
Uncials	K (018)	9th century	Byzantine
	L (020)	9th century	Byzantine
	P (025)	9th century	Independent
Minuscules	81	9th century	Alexandrian
	104	1044	Independent
	365	13th century	Western
	630	14th century	Independent
	1175	11th century	Alexandrian
	1241	12th century	Alexandrian
	1505	1084	Independent
	1506	1320	Independent
	2464	10th century	Alexandrian

Frequently Cited Witnesses			
Type	**Manuscript**	**Date**	**Family**
Papyri			
Uncials			
Minuscules	6	13th century	Independent
	323	11th century	Alexandrian
	326	12th century	Independent
	424	11th century	Independent
	614	13th century	Independent
	629	14th century	Independent
	945	11th century	Independent
	2495	14th / 15th century	Independent

Classifications and Dates of Manuscript Evidence for Hebrews

CHART 96

Alexandrian Family

Aland's Category I: These manuscripts are of a very special quality because they represent texts of a very early period and thereby are always considered important for establishing the original text.

Papyri	Uncials		Minuscules	
P[12] (3rd century)	01 ℵ	(4th century)	33	(9th century)
P[13] (3rd 4th century)	A 02	(5th century)	1175	(11th century)
P[46] (200 C.E.)	B 03	(4th century)	1739	(10th century)
			2464	(10th century)

Aland's Category II: These manuscripts are also of special quality, but they show some non-Alexandrian influences. Nevertheless, they are important for establishing the original text.

P[17] (4th century)	C 04	(5th century)	81	(1044)
P[79] (7th century)	I 016	(5th century)	323	(11th century)
	044	(8th / 9th century)	1241	(12th century)
	048	(5th century)	1881	(14th century)
	0243	(10th century	1962	(11th century)
	2464	(10th century)	2127	(12th century)

Versions	Church Fathers
Co = represents all Coptic versions extant for a particular Greek reading. Bohairic and Sahidic are dialect variations of Coptic (3rd to 5th centuries).	Ath = Athanasius (373)
	Cl = Clement of Alexandria (215)
Bo = Bohairic dialect of Lower Egypt (around the delta region), ca. 4th to 5th centuries	Cl[lat] = Clement of Alexandria (540)
	Cyr = Cyril of Alexandria (d. 444)
Bo[ms] = One Bohairic witness supports a particular reading	Did = Didymus of Alexandria (398)
	Hes = Hesychius (451)
Bo[mss] = Two to four Bohairic witnesses support a particular reading	Or = Origen (254)
	Or[lat] = Origen, Latin translation
Bo[pt] = Five or more Bohairic witnesses	Or[s] = Origen, Supplement
Sa = Sahidic dialect of Upper Egypt (from Thebes to the south), ca. 3rd to 4th centuries	
Sa[ms] = One Sahidic witness supports a particular reading	
Sa[mss] = Two or more Sahidic witness supports a particular reading	

Western Family

Aland's Category IV: These manuscripts are of D (06) Codex Claromontanus.

Papyri	Uncials		Minuscules
None	D (06)	(6th century)	365 (13th century)
	E^p or D^{absl}	(9th century)	

Versions	Church Fathers
it = Itala represents the majority of Old Latin witnesses as a group.	Ambr = Ambrose (397)
it^{ar} (9th century); it^c (12–13th century); it^d (5th century); it^{dem} (13th century); it^{div} (13th century); it^f (9th century); it^{gig} (13th century); it^r (6th century); it^t (11th century); it^v (ca 800); it^x (9th century); it^z (8th century).	Aug = Augustine (430)
	Hier = Jerome (420)
	Hil = Hilary (367)
latt = represents the entire Latin tradition in support of the same Greek reading (9th to 13th centuries).	Ir^{lat} = Irenaeus (395)
	Tert = Tertullian (220)
lat = support of the Vulgate and part of the Old Latin.	
vg = Vulgata represents agreement of the most important editions of the Vulgate in support of the same Greek reading.	
vg^{cl} Editio Clementina (1592).	
vg^{ms} indicates individual Vulgate manuscripts with independent readings.	
vg^{ww} Wordsworth and White (1889–1954).	

Byzantine Family

Aland's Category V: These manuscripts are purely or predominately Byzantine.

Papyri	Uncials		Minuscules
None	K (018)	(9th century)	596 (11th century)
	L (020)	(9th century)	2144 (11th century)
	M (021)	(9th century)	
	049	(9th century)	
	056	(10th century)	
	0142	(10th century)	
	0151	(9th century)	

Versions	Church Fathers
Sy = Syriac Version (This seems to be the place for Syriac).	Eus = Eusebius of Caesarea (339–340)
Sy^p = The *Peshitta* (most widely accepted of the Syriac Versions, *circa* 4th to 5th century).	Chr = Chrysostom (407)
	CyrJ = Cyril of Jerusalem (386)
Sy^h = *Harklensis* (version by Thomas of Harkel in 615/616).	Fulg = Fulgentius (532)
Sy^{hmg} = A marginal reading of the Harklensis based on a Greek reading.	
Sy^{h**} = Reading of the Harklean text enclosed with critical signs.	

Independent Character Aland's Category III: These manuscripts are of a distinctive character with an independent text, helpful for establishing the original.		
Papyri	Uncials	Minuscules
	H (015) (6th century)	1 (12th century)
	P (025) (9th century)	69 (15th century)
	Psi (044) (9th-10th century)	88 (12th century)
	0121b (10th century)	104 1087
	0122 (9th century)	181 (11th century)
	0127 (5th century)	326 (12th century)
	0128 (4th century)	330 (12th century)
	0150 (9th century)	365 (13th century)
	0252 (5th century)	424 (11th century)
		436 (11th century)
		451 (11th century)
		630 (14th century)
		917 (12th century)
		1448 (11th century)
		1506 1320

Major Textual Issues in Hebrews

CHART 97

Ref.		Conflicting Readings	Significance & Explanation
1:3	txt	καθαρισμὸν τῶν ἁμαρτιῶν ποιησάμενος he made purification for sins (cp. ASV, ESV, NASB, NET, NIV, NRSV)	Grammatical Issue: The phrase δι᾿ ἑαυτοῦ (or δι᾿ αὐτοῦ) appears to have been added to clarify the meaning of the ambiguous middle voice of ποιησάμενος. *Txt* is preferred (Metzger, *A Textual Commentary*, 592).
	var	**δι᾿ ἑαυτοῦ** καθαρισμὸν τῶν ἁμαρτιῶν ποιησάμενος **through himself** he made purification for sins (cp. KJV)	
1:4	txt	τοσούτῳ κρείττων γενόμενος **τῶν** ἀγγέλων by becoming so much better than **the** angels (cp. ASV, KJV, NET, NIV, NRSV)	Stylistic Issue: Although the *var* has minimal manuscript support (p[46] B), whenever ἄγγελος is used in the body of the text, it is anarthrous (2:2, 5, 16; 12:22; 13:2). Only when introducing OT quotes does the author use an article (1:5, 7, 13). It seems a scribe added the article due to the similar appearances in the immediate context. *Var* is preferred (Bateman, *Jewish*, 215–16).
	var	τοσούτῳ κρείττων γενόμενος ἀγγέλων by becoming so much better than angels (cp. ESV, NRSV)	
1:8	txt	καὶ ἡ ῥάβδος τῆς εὐθύτητος ῥάβδος τῆς βασιλείας **σου** and the righteous scepter is the scepter of **your** kingdom (cp. ASV, ESV, KJV, NET, NIV, NRSV)	Theological/Exegetical Issue: Moving beyond the manuscript support (p[46] ℵ B), αὐτοῦ appears to be the last of several deliberate interpretive changes to Ps 44:8 (LXX) by the author of Hebrews, and it is the more difficult reading (Bateman, *Jewish*, 130–35). Furthermore, in Heb 2:7, 3:2, 8:11 and 9:19; a scribe appears to have altered the text to bring it into conformity with the LXX. Although most translations prefer the *txt* (cf. Heb 11:4 and 12:3, below), there is strong evidence for favoring the *var*.
	var	καὶ ἡ ῥάβδος τῆς εὐθύτητος ῥάβδος τῆς βασιλείας **αὐτοῦ** and the righteous scepter is the scepter of **his** kingdom (cp. NASB)	
1:12	txt	**ὡς ἱμάτιον** καὶ ἀλλαγήσονται and **like clothing** they will be changed (cp. ASV, ESV, KJV, NASB, NET, NIV, NRSV)	Exegetical Issue: As in verse 8, the author made an interpretive change to Ps 44:8 (LXX) to both balance and heighten the transitory character of creation in contrast to the Son. *Txt* is preferred (Metzger, *A Textual Commentary*, 593).
	var	καὶ ἀλλαγήσονται and they will be changed	
2:6	txt	**τί** ἐστιν ἄνθρωπος ὅτι μιμνῄσκῃ αὐτοῦ **what** is man that you take thought for him (cp. ASV, ESV, KJV, NASB, NET, NIV, NRSV)	Theological/Exegetical Issue: Manuscript support is strong for the *txt* (p[46] C* P 81 104 1881). It seems more likely that a scribe would have changed the text to bring into agreement with the LXX (Lane, *Hebrews 1–8*, 42).
	var	**τίς** ἐστιν ἄνθρωπος ὅτι μιμνῄσκῃ αὐτοῦ **who** is man that you take thought for him	

Ref.		Conflicting Readings	Significance & Explanation
2:7	txt	δόξῃ καὶ τιμῇ ἐστεφάνωσας αὐτόν you crowned him with glory and honor (cp. ASV, ESV, KJV, NET, NIV, NRSV)	Theological/Exegetical Issue: The additional material was probably a scribe's desire to complete the quotation from Ps 8:7 (LXX). The shorter reading of the *txt* is preferred.
	var	δόξῃ καὶ τιμῇ ἐστεφάνωσας αὐτόν, **καὶ κατέστησας αὐτόν ἐπὶ τὰ ἔργα τῶν χειρῶν σου** you crowned him with glory and honor, **and you set him over the works of your hands** (cp. NASB)	
2:9	txt	ὅπως **χάριτι** θεοῦ ὑπὲρ παντὸς γεύσηται θανάτου so that **by the grace** of God he might taste death for everyone (cp. ASV, ESV, KJV, NASB, NET, NIV, NRSV)	Theological Issue: The appearance of χωρίς may be due to a scribe's misreading of χάριτι, or it may reflect a theological point that expresses the spatial distance of Jesus from God due to his now being lower than the angels. *Txt* is preferred (Metzger, *A Textual Commentary*, 594).
	var	ὅπως **χωρὶς** θεοῦ ὑπὲρ παντὸς γεύσηται θανάτου so that **without** God he might taste death for everyone	
3:2	txt	ὡς καὶ Μωϋσῆς ἐν **ὅλῳ** τῷ οἴκῳ αὐτοῦ just as Moses also was faithful in **all** God's [his] house (cp. ASV, ESV, KJV, NASB, NIV, NRSV)	Exegetical Issue: External evidence (p[13] B) supports the omission of ὅλῳ. Yet, a scribe may have deliberately added ὅλῳ to conform more closely with Num 12:17 (LXX), which the author quotes directly in Heb 3:5. *Var* is preferred (see NET note).
	var	ὡς καὶ Μωϋσῆς ἐν τῷ οἴκῳ αὐτοῦ just as Moses also was faithful in God's house (cp. NET)	
3:6a	txt	**οὗ** οἶκός ἐσμεν ἡμεῖς **whose** house we are (cp. ASV, ESV, KJV, NASB, NET, NIV, NRSV)	Theological Issue: Manuscript support is strong for both readings: *txt* (p[13] ℵ A B C I K P 044 0278 33 81 1881) and *var* (p[46] D* 0121b 0243 6 88 1739). A scribe may have altered the text from οὗ to ὅς to affirm more exactly that Christians are God's house and not Christ's house. *Txt* is preferred (Metzger, *A Textual Commentary*, 595).
	var	**ὅς** οἶκός ἐσμεν ἡμεῖς **which** house we are	
3:6b	txt	ἐὰν τὴν παρρησίαν καὶ τὸ καύχημα τῆς ἐλπίδος κατάσχωμεν if we hold fast the confidence and the pride of hope (cp. ASV, ESV, KJV, NET, NIV, NRSV)	Theological/Exegetical Issue: Although the majority of manuscripts support the longer reading (ℵ A B C D K P 044 0243 0278 33 81 629 1739 1881 *Byz*), it appears reasonable to suspect a scribe inserted μέχρι τέλυος βέβαιαν to imitate Heb 3:14. The lack of concord between βεβαίαν and καύχημα may further support the preferred *txt* rendering (p[13] [46] B).
	var	ἐὰν τὴν παρρησίαν καὶ τὸ καύχημα τῆς ἐλπίδος **μέχρι τέλυος βεβαίαν** κατάσχωμεν if we hold fast the confidence and the pride of hope **until the end** (cp. NASB)	

Ref.		Conflicting Readings	Significance & Explanation
4:2	txt	μὴ **συγκεκερασμένους** τῇ πίστει τοῖς ἀκούσασιν because **they were not united** by faith with those who listened (cp. ASV, ESV, KJV, NASB, NET, NRSV)	Exegetical Issue: Both the manuscript evidence (p¹³ ⁴⁶ A B C D* 0243 0278 33 81 1739 2464) and the possibility that a scribe altered the case ending from ους to ος strongly supports the *txt* rendering and thereby draws attention to Kadesh-Barnea and the community's unwillingness to listen to Joshua and Caleb.
	var	μὴ **συγκεκερασμένος** τῇ πίστει τοῖς ἀκούσασιν because those who heard did **not combine it** with faith (cp. NIV)	
4:3	txt	εἰσερχόμεθα **γὰρ** εἰς [τὴν] κατάπαυσιν οἱ πιστεύσαντες **for** we who have believed enter that rest (cp. ASV, ESV, KJV, NASB, NET, NIV, NRSV)	Syntax Issue: Both the manuscript evidence (p¹³ ⁴⁶ B D K P 044 33 614) and the consecutive use of γάρ in the immediate context (Heb 4:2, 3, 4) support the *txt* rendering. The *var* may be an unintentional error due to verses nearby that use οὖν (Heb 4:1, 11, 16). *Txt* is preferred (Metzger, *A Textual Commentary*, 595–96).
	var	εἰσερχόμεθα **οὖν** εἰς [τὴν] κατάπαυσιν οἱ πιστεύσαντες **therefore** we who have believed enter that rest	
5:12	txt	πάλιν χρείαν ἔχετε τοῦ διδάσκειν ὑμᾶς **τινὰ** τὰ στοιχεῖα τῆς ἀρχῆς τῶν λογίων τοῦ θεοῦ you need **someone** to teach you again the basic elements of the oracles of God (cp. ESV, NASB, NET, NIV, NRSV)	Grammatical Issue: The difficulty of this issue surrounds the lack of accents in the earliest manuscripts. Consequently, contemporary translators discern, based upon context, which is the more appropriate form. Thus the editorial committee felt τινά gives a more accurate contrast: a teacher versus a set of teachings. *Txt* is preferred (Metzger, *A Textual Commentary*, 596).
	var	πάλιν χρείαν ἔχετε τοῦ διδάσκειν ὑμᾶς **τίνα** τὰ στοιχεῖα τῆς ἀρχῆς τῶν λογίων τοῦ θεοῦ you have need that one teach you again **which** are the basic elements of the oracles of God (cp. KJV, ASV)	
6:2	txt	βαπτισμῶν **διδαχῆς**, ἐπιθέσεώς τε χειρῶν **of instruction** about baptisms, of laying on of hands (cp. ASV, KJV, NASB)	Stylistic/Theological Issue: Although support for the *txt* (ℵ A C I K P 33 81 614 1739) and the *var* is strong (p⁴⁶ B 0150), a scribe may have changed διδαχήν (acc) to διδαχῆς (gen) to *agree* with the series of genitives in the text, or he changed διδαχῆς (gen) to διδαχήν (acc) to *avoid* the string of genitives. Yet agreement of διδαχήν with θεμέλιον (v. 1) has theological significance. *Var* is preferred (Lane, *Hebrews 1–8*, 132).
	var	βαπτισμῶν **διδαχὴν**, ἐπιθέσεώς τε χειρῶν **instruction** about baptisms, of laying on of hands (cp. ESV, NET, NIV, NRSV)	

Ref.		Conflicting Readings	Significance & Explanation
6:3	*txt*	καὶ τοῦτο **ποιήσομεν** and **we will do** this (cp. ASV, ESV, KJV, NASB, NET, NIV, NRSV)	Grammatical Issue: Manuscript support (p⁴⁶ ℵ B I K L 0122 0278 6 33 88 614 629 630 1241 1739 1881) and flow of thought to the subsequent phrase "if God permits" argues for the *txt*. Yet, it is also easy to explain a scribe's orthographic confusion between ο and ω. *Txt* is preferred (Metzger, *A Textual Commentary*, 596).
	var	καὶ τοῦτο **ποιήσωμεν** and **let us do** this	
7:13	*txt*	ἀφ᾽ ἧς οὐδεὶς **προσέσχηκεν** τῷ θυσιαστηρίῳ from which no one **has ever served** at the altar (cp. ASV, ESV, NASB, NET, NIV, NRSV)	Literary Issue: Manuscript support is strong for both readings: *txt* (ℵ B D 044 0278 1881) and *var* (p⁴⁶ A C 33 81 1739). The wordplay in Heb 7:3 between μετέσχηκεν (1ˢᵗ clause) and προσέσχηκεν (2ⁿᵈ clause) appears to support the author's style for phonetic effectiveness evident in Heb 1:1. *Txt* is preferred (Lane, *Hebrews 1–8*, 174; Towner, 99).
	var	ἀφ᾽ ἧς οὐδεὶς **προσέσχεν** τῷ θυσιαστηρίῳ from which no one ever **served** at the altar (cp. KJV)	
8:8	*txt*	μεμφόμενος γὰρ **αὐτοὺς** λέγει for when he found fault **with them**, he said (cp. ASV, ESV, KJV, NASB, NIV, NRSV)	Syntax Issue: Manuscript support is strong for both readings: *txt* (ℵ* A D* I K P 044 33 81 326 365 1505 2464) and *var* (p⁴⁶ B 0278 614 1739 1881 Byz). Txt is preferred by Metzger, var by Lane (see Lane, *Hebrews 1–8*, 202; Metzger, *A Textual Commentary*, 597).
	var	μεμφόμενος γὰρ **αὐτοῖς** λέγει for when he found fault, he said **to them** (cp. NET)	
8:11	*txt*	καὶ οὐ μὴ διδάξωσιν ἕκαστος τὸν **πολίτην** αὐτοῦ and each one shall not teach his **fellow citizen** (cp. ASV, NASB, NET, NRSV)	Lexical/Exegetical Issue: Moving beyond the manuscript support for the *txt* (p⁴⁶ ℵ A B D K L 0278 33 1739 1881), it seems a scribe may have altered the reading to bring the verse into conformity to the LXX (Jer 38:31–34). *Txt* is preferred.
	var	καὶ οὐ μὴ διδάξωσιν ἕκαστος τὸν **πλησίον** αὐτοῦ and each one shall not teach his **neighbor** (cp. ESV, KJV, NIV)	
9:1	*txt*	Εἶχε μὲν οὖν **[καὶ]** ἡ πρώτη δικαιώματα λατρείας τό τε ἅγιον κοσμικόν Now **even** the first covenant had regulations for worship and an earthly sanctuary. (cp. ASV, ESV, NASB, NRSV)	Stylistic Issue: Manuscript support is strong for both readings: *txt* (ℵ A D 0278 0285 33) and *var* (p⁴⁶ B 6 629 1739 1881). Yet the use of μὲν οὖν without the καί is in keeping with the author's style (cp. 7:11; 8:4). A scribe may have added καί to parallel the old and new order when in fact the author wishes to contrast the two. *Var* is preferred (cp. Lane, *Hebrews 9–13*, 214 with Metzger, *A Textual Commentary*, 597–98).
	var	Εἶχε μὲν οὖν ἡ πρώτη δικαιώματα λατρείας τό τε ἅγιον κοσμικόν Now the first covenant had regulations for worship and an earthly sanctuary (cp. KJV, NET, NIV)	

Ref.		Conflicting Readings	Significance & Explanation
9:2	*txt*	καὶ ἡ πρόθεσις τῶν ἄρτων and the bread of presence (cp. ASV, ESV, KJV, NASB, NET, NIV, NRSV)	Theological Issue: A few manuscripts (like B) add καὶ τὸ χρυσοῦν θυμιατήριον to 9:2 and remove χρυσοῦν θυμιατήριον from 9:4 to remove the difficulty concerning the location of the golden altar of incense in the tabernacle (cf. Exod 30:1–6). *Txt* is preferred (Metzger, *A Textual Commentary*, 598).
	var	καὶ ἡ πρόθεσις τῶν ἄρτων **καὶ τὸ χρυσοῦν θυμιατήριον** and the bread of presence **and the golden altar of incense**	
9:10	*txt*	καὶ διαφόροις βαπτισμοῖς, **δικαιώματα** σαρκὸς μέχρι καιροῦ διορθώσεως ἐπικείμενα and various baptisms, **regulations** for the body imposed until the time comes to set things right (cp. ESV, NASB, NET, NRSV)	Grammatical Issue: Moving beyond the manuscript evidence (p[46] ℵ* A I P 0278 33 81 104 1739 1881 2464), a scribe may have changed the txt from a nominative δικαιώματα to a dative δικαιώμασιν and inserted a καί because of the string of datives that presided (βρώμασιν καὶ πόμασιν καὶ διαφόροις βαπτισμοῖς, "food and drink and ceremonial baptisms"). *Txt* is preferred (Metzger, *A Textual Commentary*, 598).
	var	καὶ διαφόροις βαπτισμοῖς, **καὶ δικαιώμασιν** σαρκὸς μέχρι καιροῦ διορθώσεως ἐπικείμενα and various baptisms, **and regulations** for the body imposed until the time comes to set things right (cp. KJV, NIV?)	
9:11	*txt*	ἀρχιερεὺς τῶν **γενομένων** ἀγαθῶν a high priest of the good things **that have come** (cp. ESV, NIV, NRSV)	Theological Issue: Manuscript support exists for both readings: *txt* (p[46] B D* 1611 1739 2005) and *var* (ℵ A K L P 0142 0278 33 1881). Yet it appears a scribe may have adjusted the text here so that there would be agreement with 10:1 (τῶν μελλόντων ἀγαθῶν). (See Lane, *Hebrews 9–13*, 229; Metzger, *A Textual Commentary*, 598).
	var	ἀρχιερεὺς τῶν **μελλόντων** ἀγαθῶν a high priest of the good things **to come** (cp. ASV, KJV, NET, NASB)	
9:14	*txt*	τὴν συνείδησιν **ἡμῶν** **our** conscience (cp. ESV, NET, NIV, NASV)	Stylistic/Exegetical Issue: Manuscript support exists for both readings: *txt* (A D* K P 365 1739*) and *var* (ℵ 0278 33 1881). The use of direct address seems equally mixed in the hortatory sections (cp. 3:7–19; 10:32–36 with 2:1–4; 4:1–14; as well as 5:11–6:12; 12:25–29), though most commentators prefer the *txt*.
	var	τὴν συνείδησιν **ὑμῶν** **your** conscience (ASV, KJV, NASB)	
9:19	*txt*	τὸ αἷμα τῶν μόσχων [**καὶ τῶν τράγων**] the blood of calves **and goats** (cp. ASV, ESV, KJV, NASB, NET, NRSV)	Exegetical Issue: Manuscript support exists for both readings: *txt* (A C D P) and *var* (p[46] K L 044 0278 81 1241 1505 1739 1881). Yet, the *var* manuscript evidence is more strongly attested and it seems the shorter *var* reading would have been expanded to conform to Exod 24:5. *Var* is preferred (Lane, *Hebrews 9–13*, 232).
	var	τὸ αἷμα τῶν μόσχων the blood of calves (NIV)	

Ref.	Conflicting Readings		Significance & Explanation
10:1a	*txt*	<u>οὐκ αὐτὴν</u> τὴν εἰκόνα τῶν πραγμάτων <u>**not the true**</u> form of these realities (NRSV; cp ASV, ESV, KJV, NASB, NET, NIV)	Theological/Exegetical Issue: Support of the *txt* among the manuscripts (א C 044 1739 1881) overwhelms the *var's* support (p⁴⁶). The *var* treats σκιά ("house") and εἰκόνα ("image") as complementary terms rather than contrasting and perhaps reflects a scribe's having been influenced by a traditional Platonic concept (Lane, *Hebrews 9–13*, 254). *Txt* is preferred by translators.
	var	<u>**καὶ**</u> τὴν εἰκόνα τῶν πραγμάτων <u>**and**</u> the form of these realities	
10:1b	*txt*	<u>**οὐδέποτε δύναται**</u> τοὺς προσερχομένους τελειῶσαι <u>**it can never make**</u> perfect those who approach (cp. ASV, ESV, KJV, NASB, NET, NIV, NRSV)	Grammatical Issue: Support for the *var* is strong (א A C P 0278 33 81 104 614 1241 1505), but the lack of concord between δύνανται (plural) and νόμος (singular) argues against it. *Txt* is preferred by most translators (p⁴⁶ D* H K 0285 326 365 629 630 17391881; see Lane, *Hebrews 9–13*, 254).
	var	οὐδέποτε <u>**δύνανται**</u> τοὺς προσερχομένους τελειῶσαι <u>**they can never make**</u> perfect those who approach	
10:11	*txt*	καὶ πᾶς μὲν ἱερεὺς ἕστηκεν καθ' ἡμέραν and every priest stands day after day (cp. ASV, ESV, KJV, NASB, NET, NIV, NRSV)	Literary/Exegetical Issue: Manuscript support exists for both readings: *txt* (p¹³ ⁴⁶ א D K P 044 33 81 1739 1881) and *var* (A C P 88 104 365 614 630). Yet, the *var* may have been a scribal addition and a desire to create literary conformity with Heb 5:1 and 8:3. *Txt* is preferred (Lane, *Hebrews 9–13*, 254; Metzger, *A Textual Commentary*, 600).
	var	καὶ πᾶς μὲν <u>**ἀρχιερεὺς**</u> ἱερεὺς ἕστηκεν καθ' ἡμέραν and every <u>**high**</u> priest stands day after day	
10:34a	*txt*	καὶ γὰρ τοῖς <u>**δεσμίοις**</u> συνεπαθήσατε for you also had compassion for those who were in <u>**prison**</u> (cp. ASV, ESV, NASB, NET, NIV, NRSV)	Exegetical Issue: Manuscript support exists for both readings. Yet it appears a scribe unintentionally omitted the first iota from δεσμίοις (p⁴⁶ 044 104 1739), which in turn led to subsequent scribes to add μου (א K P 88 614 1881). *Txt* is preferred (A 33 1739; see Lane, *Hebrews 9–13*, 278; Metzger, *A Textual Commentary*, 600).
	var	καὶ γὰρ τοῖς <u>**δεσμοῖς μου**</u> συνεπαθήσατε for you also had compassion for <u>**my chains**</u> (KJV)	
10:34b	*txt*	γινώσκοντες ἔχειν <u>**ἑαυτοὺς**</u> κρείττονα ὕπαρξιν καὶ μένουσαν knowing that you <u>**yourselves**</u> possessed something better and more lasting (cp. ESV, NASB, NET, NIV, NRSV)	Manuscript support exists for both readings. Yet it appears the *txt* was altered from ἑαυτούς (p¹³ ⁴⁶ א A H 044 6 33 81 365 1505 1739) to ἑαυτοῖς (D K 614 *Byz*), which led a subsequent scribe to add the preposition ἐν (1 467 489 1881). *Txt* is preferred (Metzger, *A Textual Commentary*, 601).
	var	γινώσκοντες ἔχειν <u>**ἐν ἑαυτοῖς**</u> κρείττονα ὕπαρξιν καὶ μένουσαν knowing that you possessed <u>**among yourselves**</u> something better and more lasting (ASV, KJV)	

Ref.		Conflicting Readings	Significance & Explanation
10:38	*txt*	ὁ δὲ δίκαιός **μου** ἐκ πίστεως ζήσεται but **my** righteous one will live by faith (cp. ASV, ESV, NASB, NET, NIV, NRSV)	Exegetical Issue: Perhaps the scribe of p[13] omitted so to bring the Hab 2:4 quote in line with Paul (Rom 1:17; Gal 3:11), which led subsequent scribes to follow (p[13] K P 044 81 614). Yet older and reliable texts support the appearance of μου after δίκαιός (p[46] ℵ A H* 104 257 383 1175 1739 1831 1875). *Txt* is preferred (Metzger, *A Textual Commentary*, 601).
	var	ὁ δὲ δίκαιός ἐκ πίστεως ζήσεται but the righteous one will live by faith (KJV)	
11:4	*txt*	πίστει πλείονα θυσίαν Ἄβελ παρὰ Κάϊν προσήνεγκεν **τῷ θεῷ** by faith Abel offered **to God** a more acceptable sacrifice than Cain (cp. ASV, ESV, KJV, NASB, NET, NIV, NRSV)	Exegetical Issue: Manuscript evidence strongly supports the *txt* (p[13* 46] 044 0285 1739 1881). Elsewhere in Hebrews προσφέρω ("I offer") is not followed by τῷ θεῷ (5:1, 3, 7; 8:3, 4; 9:7, 9, 25, 28; 10:1, 2, 8, 11, 12; 11:27; 12:7). Thus the early manuscript supporting the *var*, p[13], may represent an orginal reading. The *txt* is preferred, *but* as with Heb 1:8, there is strong evidence for questioning the decision and for favoring the *var*.
	var	πίστει πλείονα θυσίαν Ἄβελ παρὰ Κάϊν προσήνεγκεν by faith Abel offered a more acceptable sacrifice than Cain	
11:11	*txt*	πίστει – καὶ αὐτὴ Σάρρα **στεῖρα** – δύναμιν εἰς καταβολὴν σπέρματος ἔλαβεν by faith – even though Sarah herself **the barren one** – he/she received power to conceive	Cultural/Exegetical Issue: Problems abound with this variant. First, ἔλαβεν could be translated as either "he" or "she." Thus "he" (Abraham) became a "father" (σπέρματος; NIV, NRSV, NET). Or "she" (Sarah) became "pregnant" (σπέρματος; ASV, ESV, KJV, NASB). Second, was στεῖρα added (p[46] P 044 81 88 1739)? It seems more probable that στεῖρα dropped out of subsequent manuscripts (ℵ A 33 614). *Txt* is preferred (Lane, *Hebrews 9–13*, 344; Metzger, *A Textual Commentary*, 602).
	var	πίστει – καὶ αὐτὴ Σάρρα – δύναμιν εἰς καταβολὴν σπέρματος ἔλαβεν by faith – even though Sarah herself – he/she received power to conceive	
11:37	*txt*	ἐλιθάσθησαν, ἐπρίσθησαν they were stoned to death, they were sawn in two (cp. ESV, NET, NIV, NRSV)	Exegetical Issue: Although minimally supported (p[46] 1241 1984), the *txt* is preferred. It appears ἐπειράσθησαν was a scribal addtion, primarily because "they were tempted" does not fit among the string of violent deaths enumerated in context (see Lane, *Hebrews 9–13*, 381; Metzger, *A Textual Commentary*, 604).
	var	ἐλιθάσθησαν, ἐπρίσθησαν, **ἐπειράσθησαν** they were stoned to death, they were sawn in two, **they were tempted** (cp. ASV, KJV, NASB)	
12:1	*txt*	καὶ τὴν **εὐπερίστατον** ἁμαρτίαν and the sin that **clings so closely** (cp. ESV, NET, NRSV)	Theological/Exegetical Issue: With minimal support (p[46] 1739), most translations appear to favor the variant. It's been suggested the *var* is evidence of a palaeographic error or a deliberate modification of εὐπερίστατον (cp. Lane, *Hebrews 9–13*, 398–99 with Metzger, *A Textual Commentary*, 604).
	var	καὶ τὴν **εὐπερίσπαστον** ἁμαρτίαν and the sin that **so easily distracts** (cp. ASV, KJV, NASB, NIV)	

Ref.		Conflicting Readings	Significance & Explanation
12:3	*txt*	εἰς ἑαυτόν against himself (cp. ASV, ESV, KJV, NASB, NET, NRSV)	Exegetical Issue: Manuscripts appear to favor the *var* (p¹³ ⁴⁶ 1739 33 044 ℵ) over the *txt* (A P 104 326 1241). The *txt* is preferred because it is difficult to make sense out of the plural. But as with Heb 1:8 and 11:4, there is evidence for questioning the decision and for favoring the *var* (cp. Lane, *Hebrews 9–13*, 400 with Metzger, *A Textual Commentary*, 604–05).
	var	εἰς ἑαυτούς (or) εἰς αὐτούς against themselves (cp. NIV)	
12:18	*txt*	οὐ γὰρ προσεληλύθατε ψηλαφωμένῳ for you have not come to what may be touched (cp. ESV, NET, NRSV)	Exegetical Issue: Although many follow the *var* (D K P 044 88 614 1739 1881 *Byz*), manuscript evidence supports strongly the *txt* (p⁴⁶ ℵ A C 048 33 81 1175). Furthermore, there appears to be a scribal assimilation with Heb 12:22 where Mt. Zion contrasts verse 18. *Txt* is preferred (Lane, *Hebrews 9–13*, 441; Metzger, *A Textual Commentary*, 605).
	var	οὐ γὰρ προσεληλύθατε ψηλαφωμένῳ **[ὄρει]** for you have not come **to a mountain** that can be touched (cp. ASV, KJV, NASB, NIV, NRSV)	
13:6	*txt*	Κύριος ἐμοὶ βοηθός, **[καὶ]** οὐ φοβηθήσομαι The Lord is my helper **and** I will not be afraid (cp. KJV, NET)	Grammatical/Exegetical Issue: Manuscript support exists for both readings: *txt* (p⁴⁶ A D 044 0121b 0243 1881) and *var* (ℵ* C* P 33 1175 1739). A scribe wishing to bring the quote into conformity with the LXX may have added καί. Its absence may be the author's deliberate alteration of the LXX for emphasis. *Var* is preferred (Lane, *Hebrews 9–13*, 509).
	var	Κύριος ἐμοὶ βοηθός; οὐ φοβηθήσομαι The Lord is my helper; I will not be afraid (cp. ASV, ESV, NASB, NIV, NRSV)	
13:15	*txt*	δι' αὐτοῦ **οὖν** ἀναφέρωμεν θυσίαν αἰνέσεως through him, **therefore,** let us offer the sacrifice of praise (cp. ASV, ESV, KJV, NASB, NET, NIV, NRSV)	Style/Syntax Issue: Manuscript support exists for both readings: *txt* (A C K 056 0121b 0142 0243 0285 81 88 614 1739) and *var* (p⁴⁶ ℵ* D* P 044). It seems easier to explain a scribe's desire to add οὖν because it's a natural place for a conclusion, though one might argue it was inadvertently omitted. Yet οὖν's use in Hebrews is infrequent (2:14; 4:1, 6, 11, 16; 7:11; 8:4; 9:1, 23; 10:19, 35). *Var* is preferred (cp. Lane, *Hebrews 9–13*, 524).
	var	δι' αὐτοῦ ἀναφέρωμεν θυσίαν αἰνέσεως through him let us offer the sacrifice of praise	
13:21a	*txt*	ἐν παντὶ ἀγαθῷ with everything good (cp. ESV, NIV, NRSV with NASB, NET)	Theological Issue: Though manscripts support the *var* (C K M P 0243 0285 33 1739 1881 *Byz*), the *txt* is preferred (p⁴⁶ ℵ D* 044). Perhaps there is an intentional addition made to align Heb 13:21 with 2 Thess 2:17 (see Lane, *Hebrews 9–13*, 559; Metzger, *A Textual Commentary*, 605).
	var	ἐν παντὶ **ἔργῳ** ἀγαθῷ in every good **work** (cp. ASV, KJV)	

Ref.		Conflicting Readings	Significance & Explanation
13:21b	*txt*	ποιῶν ἐν **ἡμῖν** τὸ εὐάρεστον ἐνώπιον αὐτοῦ working in **us** that which is pleasing in his sight (cp. ASV, ESV, NASB, NIV, NRSV)	Exegetical Issue: Manuscript support exists for both readings: *txt* (p⁴⁶ ℵ A K M 0243 0285 33 81 104 326 1175 1241 1739 1881) and *var* (C P 044 6 88 629* 630 1505). Perhaps a scribe altered the text due to the preceding ὑμῖν. *Txt* is preferred (Lane, *Hebrews 9–13*, 559; Metzger, *A Textual Commentary*, 606).
	var	ποιῶν ἐν **ὑμῖν** τὸ εὐάρεστον ἐνώπιον αὐτοῦ working in **you** that which is pleasing in his sight (cp. KJV, NET)	
13:21c	*txt*	ᾧ ἡ δόξα εἰς τοὺς αἰῶνας [**τῶν αἰώνων**]. ἀμήν. to whom be glory forever **and ever**. Amen. (cp. ASV, ESV, KJV, NASB, NIV, NRSV)	Exegetical Issue: Manuscript support exists for both readings: *txt* (ℵ A C* K P 0243 0285 33 1739 1881) and *var* (p⁴⁶ D 044 6 104 365 1241). Perhaps a scribe lengthened the text to agree with similar doxologies in 1 Tim 1:17; 2 Tim 4:18. In Heb 5:6; 6:2; 7:17, 21, the short form occurs, εἰς τὸν αἰῶνα. *Var* is preferred (cp. Lane, *Hebrews 9–13*, 559 with NET note and Metzger, *A Textual Commentary*, 606).
	var	ᾧ ἡ δόξα εἰς τοὺς αἰῶνας. ἀμήν. to whom be glory forever. Amen. (cp. NET)	
13:25	*txt*	ἡ χάρις μετὰ πάντων ὑμῶν Grace be with you all. (cp. ESV, NASB, NET, NIV, NRSV)	Exegetical Issue: Manuscript support exists for both readings: *txt* (p⁴⁶ ℵ*) and *var* (A C D H K P 044 0121b 0243 81 1739 1881). It seems almost impossible for a scribe to resist placing ἀμήν at the conclusion of this sermonic letter. *Txt* is preferred (Lane, *Hebrews 9–13*, 567; Metzger, *A Textual Commentary*, 607)
	var	ἡ χάρις μετὰ πάντων ὑμῶν. **ἀμήν.** Grace be with you all. **Amen!** (cp. ASV, KJV)	

Figures of Speech Categorized, Defined, and Identified

CHART 98

Figures of Speech Involving Omission

Category	Figure	Definition	Reference in Hebrews
When Omissions Affect Words	Ellipsis	The omission of a word (or words) that makes a sentence "ungrammatical"—yet the sentence is usually understood in context. Occurs frequently in Hebrews.	2:3, 11; 5:3; 7:4, 26; 8:1; 9:18; 10:25; 11:7; 13:25
	Asyndeton	A string of statements that omits the use of many "ands."	11:32–38
When Omissions Affect Sense	Meiosis	A belittling of one thing to magnify another or an affirming of something by negating its contrary (also called *litotes* or understatement).	4:14–15; 9:12–13; 13:17
	Tapeinosis	The lessening of a thing in order to increase it.	11:16; 13:2

Figures of Speech Involving Addition

Category	Figure	Definition	Reference in Hebrews
When Additions Affect Words	Alliteration	The repetition of the same letter or syllable at the commencement of successive words.	1:1; 7:3; 11:28; 12:11
	Anaphora	The repetition of a word or phrase at the beginning of successive clauses or sentences.	11:3, 4, 5, 7, 8, 9, 11, 17, 20, 21, 22, 24, 27, 28, 29, 30, 31
	Polysyndeton	The repetition of the conjunction "and."	13:8
	Polyptoton	The repetition of the same word in different inflections.	6:14
	Antanaclasis	The repetition of the same word in the same sentence, but each having a different meaning.	2:14
	Paregmenon	The repetition of words from the same root that have a similar sound, but a different sense.	10:34
	Paranomasia	The repetition of words similar in sound, but not necessarily in sense.	5:8

Figures of Speech Involving Addition			
Category	**Figure**	**Definition**	**Reference in Hebrews**
When Additions Affect Sense	Inclusio	The repetition of a phrase, line or concept at the beginning and end of a unit of text to enclose it.	1:3 & 13; 3:12 & 19; 4:14 & 5:10; 8:7 & 10:16
	Chiasm	A form of parallelism in which there is an inversion of terms in the second half of a unit of text.	1:1–4; 1:5; 1:5–13; 11:1–40; 12:14–29
	Periphrasis	Using a description or an attribute of a thing (or person) in place of its name.	1:14
	Hyperbole	When more is said than is literally meant.	11:12
	Epithet	When an adjective or a noun is used to add some attribute, character, or quality to that which it describes.	1:2, 5, 8; 11:31

Figures of Speech Involving Change			
Category	**Figure**	**Definition**	**Reference in Hebrews**
When Change Affects Words	Antimereia	The substitution of one part of speech for another.	2:15; 6:17; 12:9
	Metonymy	The change of a word naming an object for another word closely associated with it.	
		a. When the cause is stated but the effect is intended (instrument for product).	11:15
		b. When the effect is stated but the cause is intended (reverse of the above).	9:28; 13:4
		c. When the subject is stated for an attribute or adjunct of it (metonymy of subject).	1:8; 9:14; 11:7; 13:10
		d. When two metonymies (double metonymy) are contained in a single word.	9:14
		e. When the attribute or adjunct that pertains to the subject is put for the subject (opposite of metonymy of subject).	1:2; 11:13; 12:1

Figures of Speech Involving Change			
Category	**Figure**	**Definition**	**Reference in Hebrews**
When Change Affects Words (cont.)	Synecdoche	The exchange of one idea for another associated idea (metonymy deals with nouns, synecdoche with closely related ideas). a. The genus is put for the species (general for specific). b. The species is put for the genus (specific for the general). c. The whole is put for the part (this may be a lexical consideration). d. The part is put for the whole.	2:9; 13:4 1:2; 1:7; 9:12; 11:5; 13:9 11:13 2:14; 10:7; 10:19
	Hendiadys	When two words—one of them defining the other—are used to express a single concept.	5:2
	Catachresis	Misuse of a word (sometimes deliberate to create a paradox).	13:15
When Change Affects Arrangement of Words	Hyperbaton	The placing of a word or a phrase out of its usual order in the sentence for the sake of emphasis or heightened effect.	2:9; 7:4; 10:30
	Hysteron-Proteron	When words or ideas are arranged in what might be considered a reverse order.	3:8; 4:2
	Hysteresis	A narration of a prior event providing more details.	9:19; 11:12
When Change Affects Application of Words	Simile	A comparison of two unlike things using "like" or "as."	3:15; 9:27–28; 11:12
	Metaphor	An analogy/implied comparison between two unlike things without using "like" or "as."	5:12–14; 12:7–11; 13:20
	Hypocatastasis	A declaration that implies a comparison between two things.	4:12
	Parabola (Parable)	An extended simile.	12:5–6
	Allegory	A continued comparison by representation or implication.	7:3, 17

Figures of Speech Involving Change

Category	Figure	Definition	Reference in Hebrews
When Change Affects Application of Words (cont.)	Proverb	A commonly used saying to illustrate a truth of life.	11:12; 12:5–6
	Type	A prefigured illustration or example of a corresponding reality.	8:5; 10:1
	Gnome	The quotation of short, well-known maxims or sayings without citing the author's name.	3:7; 5:5–6; 10:15
	Idiom	A fixed expression that cannot be understood grammatically from its component parts, but it has an understood and set meaning.	1:3, 13; 8:1; 10:20
	Anthropomorphism	The representation of God with human attributes, such as feelings, actions and physical characteristics.	1:3, 5, 12; 3:18; 4:13; 5:7; 6:13; 8:10; 10:38; 11:10; 12:2, 29; 13:20
	Association	When the author associates himself with his readers.	3:6; 10:23–24
	Metabasis	Transition to another subject.	6:1–3
	Eleutheria	Candor, particularly in regard to criticism, with neither desire, nor fear, for causing offense.	4:16; 10:19
	Erotesis	The asking of questions without waiting for answers; rhetorical questions.	1:5; 1:13; 2:3, 6; 3:16; 9:14; 10:29; 11:32; 12:7

Literary Devices of Omission Used in Hebrews

CHART 99

	When Omissions Affect Words and Sense
Ellipsis	Hebrews 2:3 "it was confirmed to us by those who heard *him*" (The pronoun "him" is omitted but understood to be God in the context.)
	Hebrews 2:11 "For indeed he who makes holy and those being made holy are all from one *Father*" (The noun "Father" is omitted; perhaps: 5:7; 9:16–17.)
	Hebrews 5:3 "and for this reason he is obligated to make *sacrifices* for sin for himself as well as for the people" (The noun "sacrifices" is omitted.)
	Hebrews 7:4 "But see how great he *must be* (*was*), to whom Abraham, the patriarch gave …" (The verb "must be" [NET] or "was" [NASB] is omitted)
	Hebrews 8:1 "Now the main point of what we are saying *is this*" (The verb and demonstrative pronoun are omitted; cp. 7:26.)
	Hebrews 9:18 "Therefore even the first *covenant* was inaugurated with blood" (The noun "covenant" is omitted; cf. 9:1.)
	Hebrews 10:25 "but encouraging *one another*" (The direct object "one another" is omitted.)
	Hebrews 11:7 "By faith Noah, being warned *by God*" (The prepositional phrase is omitted.)
	Hebrews 12:25 "if we turn away from *the one who warns* from heaven?" (The participle "the one who warns" is omitted but understood due to the previous clause.)
	Hebrews 13:25 "Grace *of God be* with you all" (Prepositional phrase and verb are omitted.)
Asyndeton	Hebrews 11:32–38 "And what more shall I say? For time will fail me if I tell of Gideon, …
	Through faith they conquered kingdoms, administered justice, gained what was promised, shut the mouths of lions, quenched raging fire, escaped the edge of the sword, gained strength in weakness, became mighty in battle, put foreign armies to flight, and women received back their dead... And others experienced mocking and flogging, and even chains and imprisonment. They were stoned, sawed apart, murdered with the sword; they went about in sheepskins and goatskins; they were destitute, afflicted ill-treated … they wandered in deserts … (NET)

	When Omissions Affect Words and Sense
Meiosis	Hebrews 4:14–15 "Therefore since we have a great high priest who has passed through the heavens, Jesus the Son of God, let us hold fast to our confession. For we do not have a high priest incapable of sympathizing with our weaknesses, but one who has been tempted in every way just as we are, yet without sin." Hebrews 9:12, 13 "if the blood of goats and bulls and the ashes of a young cow sprinkled … how much more will the blood of Christ" Christ's sacrifice diminishes the importance of sacrifices offered under the law. This is also a lesser-to-greater form of argument known as *qal wahomer* (Chart 91). Hebrews 13:17 "Obey your leaders and submit to them, for they keep watch over your souls and will give an account for their work. Let them do this with joy and not with complaints, *for this would be no advantage for you.*" The concluding statement is an understatement given the negative consequences that can arise from disobedience.
Tapeinosis	Hebrews 11:16 "God is not ashamed to be called their God, for he has prepared a city for them." (God is not embarrassed to be their God, which is apparent by the future he has for them.) Hebrews 13:2 "Do not neglect to show hospitality to strangers" (NASB). (Be alert, or be on the lookout, for opportunities to help strangers.)

Literary Devices of Addition Used in Hebrews

CHART 100

When Additions Affect Words

Alliteration	Hebrews 1:1 "God spoke long ago in *various portions* and in *various ways*" The word "πολυμερῶς" (various portions) and "πολυτρόπως" (various ways) both begin with πολυ and end with ως. Hebrews 7:3 "Without father, without mother, without genealogy" ἀπάτωρ (father), ἀμήτωρ (mother), and ἀγενεαλόγητος (genealogy) with their "α" prefixes, may be considered a form of alliteration (perhaps also 11:28 and 12:11.)
Anaphora	Hebrews 11:3, 4, 5, 7, 8, 9, 11, 17, 20, 21, 22, 24, 27, 28, 29, 30, 31 "By faith we understand … By faith Abel offered to God … By faith Enoch was taken up … By faith Noah …By faith Abraham … By faith he lived … By faith even Sarah … By faith Abraham … By faith Isaac … By faith Jacob … By faith Joseph … By faith Moses … By faith Moses …" etc. The repeated use of πίστει (by faith) at the beginning of numerous lines throughout Hebrews 11:3–17 provides emphasis and is an excellent example of anaphora.
Polysyndeton	Hebrews 13:8 "Jesus Christ is the same *yesterday* *and* today *and* forever"
Polyptoton	Hebrews 6:14 "Surely I will *bless* (εὐλογῶν εὐλογήσω) you greatly and *multiply* (πληθύνων πληθυνῶ) your descendants *abundantly*" (NET). When used together, the present participle and future indicative of εὐλογέω and πληθύνω are translated "bless" and "multiply," respectively. The English translation captures the emphasis of these polyptotons by adding the adverbs "greatly" and "abundantly."
Antanaclasis	Hebrews 2:14 "through death he could nullify the one who holds the power of death (that is, the devil)" (NET) The use of the first "death" is a synecdoche for the atoning works of Jesus, the second use of "death" may be physical death.
Paregmenon	Hebrews 10:34 "you … accepted joyfully the seizure of your property (ὑπαρχόντων), knowing that you have for yourselves a better and a lasting possession (ὕπαρξιν)" Both ὑπάρχω (property) and ὕπαρξις (possession) come from the same root, ἄρχω.
Paranomasia	Hebrews 5:8 "Although he was a son, he learned (ἔμαθεν) obedience through the things he suffered (ἔπαθεν)." ἔμαθεν (he learned) and ἔπαθεν (he suffered) both end with θεν and thereby have similar sounding inflections.

When Additions Affect Sense

Inclusio	**Some Units of Thought:**	
	Hebrews 1:3 and 1:13	= the Son at the right hand of God
	Hebrews 3:12 and 3:19	= the unfaithfulness of the wilderness generation
	Hebrews 4:14 and 5:10	= Jesus as regal priest
	Hebrews 8:7 and 10:16–17	= the new covenant
	Two Major Sections:	
	Hebrews 1:1 and 4:13	= the similar periodic sentence on God's Son and the periodic sentence on God's word
	Hebrews 4:14 and 10:23	= exhortation to hold fast

Chiasm

Hebrews 1:5

    A   You are my Son

        B   today I have become your Father

        B^1 I will be his Father

    A^1 and he will be my Son

Hebrews 12:14–29

    A   Exhortation: Do not fail to obtain the grace of God (12:14–17)

        B   Exposition: You have not come to Mount Sinai (12:18–21)

        B^1 Exposition: You have come to Mount Zion (12:22–24)

    A^1 Exhortation: Do not refuse him who is speaking (12:25–29)

For other chiastic structures in Hebrews see Charts 23, 92 and 93.

Periphrasis

Hebrews 1:14 "… sent out to serve those who will inherit salvation"

By "those who will inherit salvation" the author is speaking of people who are saved.

Hyperbole

Hebrews 11:12 *"like the number of stars in the sky and like the innumerable grains of sand on the seashore."*

Describing Abraham's descendants to be as numerous as stars and innumerable as grains of sand is an exaggeration that expresses more than what is meant literally.

Epithet

Hebrews 1:5 *"You are my Son!"*

Hebrews 1:8 "but of the *Son* he says"

The term "Son" is an epithet for Davidic king, but a king who is greater than any previous Davidite known to have ruled (cp. 1:2, 3; see Chart 50).

Hebrews 11:31 "The *harlot* Rahab"

The term "harlot" is as an epithet that provides information about Rahab's character.

Literary Devices of Change Used in Hebrews

CHART 101

	When Change Affects Words
Antimereia	Hebrews 2:15 "and set free those who were held in slavery all their *lives* (ζῆν) by their fear of death." The infinitive of the verb ζάω is used instead of a noun and is translated "lives" instead of "to live" (cf. 6:1). Hebrews 6:17 "to show to the heirs of the promise the *unchangeableness* of His purpose" The adjective ἀμετάθετον (unchanging) is used as a noun. Hebrews 12:9 "we had *earthly* fathers" The article and noun in the genitive case (τῆς σαρκός), which literally mean "of the flesh," are used adjectivally to describe "fathers" in a way that attracts the attention of readers (cp. 9:10).

Metonymy	a. Hebrews 11:15 "if they had *remembered* the country that they had left"
	     The Greek text supplies only the verb for "remembered" (the cause). What was being remembered (the effect) must be supplied by the reader.
	
	b. Hebrews 9:28 "after Christ was offered once *to bear the sins of many*"
	     "*To bear the sins*" is the effect substituted for "punishment/death," the cause.
	
	     Hebrews 13:4 "sexually immoral people and adulterers God *will judge.*"
	     The verb "judge" (effect) is substituted for punish or condemn (cause).
	
	c. Hebrews 1:8 "and a righteous *scepter* is the *scepter* of his kingdom."
	     The subject "scepter" is used for the attribute of "power" or "authority."
	
	     Hebrews 9:14 "purify our consciences from *dead works.*"
	     The subject "dead works" is substituted for the attribute "old nature."
	
	     Hebrews 11:7 "constructed an ark for the deliverance of his *house.*"
	     The subject "house" is substituted for "family."
	
	     Hebrews 13:10 "We have an *altar* that those who serve in the tabernacle have no right to eat from."
	     The subject "altar" is put for "sacrifice" or "sin-offering."
	
	d. Hebrews 9:14 "how much more will the *blood* of Christ"
	     The noun "blood" serves as a double metonymy: "physical death" and "atoning sacrifice of Jesus" (see also 9:12; 10:19; 12:24; 13:12).
	
	e. Hebrews 1:2 "and through whom he created *the ages* (τοὺς αἰῶνας)."
	     A period of time, "ages," is put for the subject, "world." (cp. perhaps 11:13).
	
	     Hebrews 12:1 "and run with endurance the *race* set out for us"
	     The "race" is put for a specific course, which is run throughout life.

When Change Affects Words

Synecdoche	a.	Hebrews 2:9 "by God's grace he would experience death on behalf of *everyone*." Hebrews 13:4 "Marriage must be honored among *all*." The general "everyone" and "all" is put for the specific—in this case "people."
	b.	Hebrews 1:2 "whom *he placed* (ἔθηκεν) heir of all things" The verb "he placed" is given a broader meaning of "appointed" (NASB, NET).
		Hebrews 1:7 *"the one who makes* (ὁ ποιῶν) his angels spirits and his ministers a flame of fire." Perhaps the participle "the one who makes" has the broader meaning of "creating" the angels.
		Hebrews 9:12 "he himself *having found* (εὑράμενος) eternal redemption for us" The verb "having found" is given a broader meaning of either "obtain" (NASB) or "secured" (NET).
		Hebrews 11:5 "he was not to be *found* because God took him up" The verb "found" is given a broader meaning of "presence."
		Hebrews 13:9 "not by *foods* (βρώμασιν) which have never benefited" Perhaps "foods" has a broader meaning for all kinds of ritual doctrinal practices or taboos.
	c.	Hebrews 11:13 "These *all died* in faith without receiving the things promised" "All died" is put for those particular people mentioned in chapter 11 (with the exception of Enoch).
	d.	Hebrews 2:14 "since the children share in *flesh and blood*, he likewise shared in their humanity" The part, i.e., "flesh and blood" is put for the whole, i.e. "human body."
		Hebrews 2:14 "so that through *death* he could destroy" Perhaps the part, i.e., "death" is put for the whole, i.e., atonement and its results: victory over death, devil, sin, etc.
		Hebrews 10:7 "it is written of me in *the scroll* of the book" The part is "κεφαλίδι," literally, "the head" which refers to the knob on the end of a book roll. It is substituted for the whole, i.e., "the scroll."
		Hebrews 10:19 "we have confidence to enter the holy place by the *blood* of Jesus" The part, i.e., "blood" is put for the whole, i.e., Jesus' sacrificial, atoning death.
Hendiadys		Hebrews 5:2 "those who are ignorant and erring" (NET) The two words ἀγνοοῦσιν (ignorant) and πλανωμένοις (erring) are coordinate words expressing a single concept or a single group of people, "those who ignorantly go astray" (cp. Lev 4:2; 5:17–18 and Num 15:22–31).

When Change Affects Words

Catachresis	Hebrews 13:15 "let us lift up a *sacrifice* (θυσίαν) of praise to God…the fruit of lips that *confess* (ὁμολογούντων) his name" Given the focus on ritual sacrifice in Hebrews, the phrase "sacrifice of praise" is unexpected and strikingly different. Similarly, "confession" seems incongruous with "praise" or "celebration."

When Change Affects Arrangement of Words

Hyperbaton	Hebrews 2:9 "we see Jesus, who was made **lower than the angels for a little while**, now crowned with glory and honor because he suffered death" (NET).
	    In Greek, the word order places "for a little while" first, followed by "made lower than the angels," then "we see Jesus because he suffered death now crowned with glory and honor." Emphasis is first placed on Jesus' being lower than the angels only for a little while, then his suffering and death is emphasized as the reason for his attaining glory and honor.
	
	Hebrews 7:4 "But see how great he must be (was), even Abraham *the patriarch* gave him a tithe of his plunder."
	    In Greek, "the patriarch" is withheld to the very end of the sentence to emphasize that Melchizedek was greater than Abraham.
	
	Hebrews 10:30 "Vengeance is mine, *I myself* will repay,"
	    In Greek, using the pronoun "I" with a first person singular verb adds emphasis to the "I."

Hysteron-Proeron	Hebrews 3:8 "Do not harden your hearts as in the rebellion, in the day of testing in the wilderness" (NET)
	    Although the testing occurred first, the provocation of God is described first to emphasize what believers are not supposed to do.
	
	Hebrews 4:2 "For we had good news proclaimed to us just as they did" (NET)
	    The order of time is reversed.

Hysteresis	Hebrews 9:19 "he took the blood of calves and goats with water and scarlet wool and hyssop and *sprinkled both the book* itself and all the people" (NET).
	    The "sprinkled both the book " is supplemental material not mentioned in Exodus 24.
	
	Hebrews 11:21 "By faith Jacob, as he was dying, blessed each of the sons of Joseph and *worshiped as he leaned on his staff*" (NET).
	    The "worshiped as he leaned on his staff" is supplemental material not mentioned in Genesis 47:31-48:20.
	
	Hebrews 12:20 "For they could not bear what was commanded: 'If even an animal touches the mountain, it must be stoned"
	    "If even an animal touches the mountain, it must be stoned" is supplemental material not mentioned in Exodus 19:12–13.

When Change Affects the Application of Words	

Simile	Hebrews 3:15 "Do not harden your hearts *as* in the rebellion."
	    A warning given not to harden one's heart like the people of Kadesh Barnea.
	
	Hebrews 9:27, 28 "*just as* people are appointed to die once … *so also*, after Christ was offered once …"
	    As a person dies once *so* Jesus offered his life once.
	
	Hebrews 11:12 "and him as good as dead at that, as many descendants as the stars in heaven…innumerable as grains of sand"
	    The first simile declares Abraham virtually incapable of fathering children to emphasize the miraculous power of God in providing him with offspring as illustrated by the two similes that follow.

Metaphor	Hebrews 5:12–14 "For though you should in fact be teachers by this time, you need someone to teach you the beginning elements of God's utterances. You have gone back to needing milk, not solid food. For everyone who lives on milk is inexperienced in the message of righteousness, because he is an infant. But solid food is for the mature, whose perceptions are trained by practice to discern both good and evil."
	    The author of Hebrews uses this extended metaphor to rebuke his audience, calling them spiritual infants who still need to be fed milk, rather than spiritually mature adults. The same kind of metaphor appears in some of Philo's work (cf. *Agr* 9; *Congr* 19) in relation to teaching students.
	
	Hebrews 12:7–11 "Endure your suffering as discipline; God is treating you as sons. For what son is there that a father does not discipline? But if you do not experience discipline … then you are illegitimate and are not sons. Besides, we have experienced discipline from our earthly fathers and we respected them" (NET)
	    The idea of "discipline…as sons" is a metaphor for our relationship with God and how God disciplines us (cp. Prov 1:8; 4:1–4; Wis 7:11–12).
	
	Hebrews 13:20 "the great *shepherd* of the *sheep*, our Lord Jesus Christ"
	    The shepherd is a metaphor representing one who guides and protects.

Hypocatastasis	Hebrews 4:12 "the *word of God* is living and active and sharper than any double-edged sword, piercing even to the point of dividing soul from spirit, and joints from marrow; it is able to judge the desires and thoughts of the heart" (NET). In this example of hypocatastasis, "the word of God" is not only compared to a sword by declaration, it is personified and given divine attributes: it is a "life–breathing" or "living power" (NLT) capable of probing the human soul.
Parabola (Parable)	Hebrews 12:5–6 "And have you forgotten the exhortation addressed to you as sons? 'My son, do not scorn the Lord's discipline or give up when he corrects you. For the Lord disciplines the one he loves and chastises every son he accepts'" (NET). This quote from Proverbs 3:12 may be considered either a parable or proverb.

When Change Affects the Application of Words	
Allegory	Hebrews 7:3, 17 "Without father, without mother, without genealogy, he has neither beginning of days nor end of life but is like the son of God, and he remains a priest for all time … . For here is the testimony about him: "You are a priest forever in the order of Melchizedek" (NET). Perhaps the incorporation of Gen 14:18–20 within Ps 110:4 may be a mild allegorical/etymological treatment of the Genesis narrative.

Proverb	Hebrews 11:12 "children were fathered by one man … *like the number of stars in the sky and like the innumerable grains of sand on the seashore*" (NET).
	    This is proverbial way to illustrate an infinite number.
	
	Hebrews 12:5–6 "My son, do not scorn the Lord's discipline or give up when he corrects you. For the Lord disciplines the one he loves and chastises every son he accepts" (NET).
	    Here, the author of Hebrews quotes Prov 3:11–12.

Type	Hebrews 5:5–6 "So also Christ did not glorify himself in becoming high priest, but the one who glorified him was God, who said to him, "**You are my Son! Today I have fathered you**," as also in another place God says, "**You are a priest forever in the order of Melchizedek**" (NET).
	    The regal priest, Melchizedek, of Gen 14:18–24 (cp. Ps 110:4) serves as a type after which Jesus is patterned as regal priest throughout Hebrews (cp. 5:9–10; 6:20).
	
	Hebrews 8:5 "they serve as a sketch and shadow of the heavenly sanctuary" (NET).
	    Perhaps the use of ὑποδείγματι (example/sketch) or σκιᾷ (shadow), points to the concept of a type.
	
	Hebrews 10:1 "For the law possesses *a shadow* of the good things to come but not the reality itself" (NET).
	    Again, the use of σκιὰν, "a shadow," suggests the concept of a type.

Gnome	Hebrews 3:7–10 "Therefore, as the Holy Spirit says, '*Oh, that today you would listen … Do not harden your hearts as in the rebellion … your fathers tested me …Therefore, I became provoked … and they have not known my ways*'" (NET). This citation is credited to the Holy Spirit without citing Ps 95:7–8 (cp. Heb 10:15). Hebrews 5:5–6 is an example of two brief citations without quoting the author or text.

When Change Affects the Application of Words	
Idiom	Hebrews 1:3, 13; 8:1 "he sat down *at the right hand* of the Majesty on high" The expression "right hand" may be considered by some to be an idiomatic expression for ruling authority. Hebrews 10:20 "by the fresh and *living way* that he inaugurated" The expression "living way" is idiomatic for "excellent way."
Anthropomorphism	Hebrews 1:3 "he sat down at the right *hand* of the Majesty on high" (Ps 110:1 quote; cp. 1:13; 8:1) God has *hands*. Hebrews 1:5 "You are my son! Today I have *fathered* you" God "*fathers*" a son. Hebrews 1:12 "and like a robe you will fold them up and like a garment they will be changed, but you are the same and *your years* will never run out" (NET). From Ps 102:24 where human years are attributed to God, and here attributed to God's Son (cp. 13:8). Hebrews 3:18 "And to whom did He *swear* that they would not enter His rest, but to those who were disobedient?" (NET, cp. 6:13). God *swears*. Hebrews 4:13 "no creature is hidden from God's *sight*" God has *eyes* to see. Hebrews 5:7 "he offered up prayers…and he was *heard*" God can *hear*. Hebrews 8:10 "and I will *write* them on their hearts" God *writes* his laws. Hebrews 10:38 "if he shrinks back, *my soul* has no pleasure in him." God has a *soul*. Hebrews 11:10 "whose *architect* and *builder* is God." God can *design* and *build*. Hebrews 12:29 "For our God is a *consuming fire*" God as *fire* via Deut 4:24 conveys the emotions of anger and jealousy. Hebrews 13:20 "the great *shepherd* of the sheep, our Lord Jesus Christ" (NET). Jesus is both human and divine, but he is a shepherd metaphorically—just as God is depicted in Psalm 23.

When Change Affects the Application of Words

Association	Hebrews 3:6 "*We* are of his house, if in fact *we* hold firmly to our confidence and the hope *we* take pride in" (NET).
	Hebrews 10:23–24 "And *let us* hold unwaveringly to the hope that *we* confess… And *let us* take thought of how to spur one another on to love and good works" (NET).
	Here are just two examples where the author clearly associates himself with his readers.
Metabasis	Hebrews 6:1–3 "Therefore we must progress beyond *the elementary principles…* teaching about baptisms, laying on of hands, resurrection of the dead, and eternal judgment. And this is what we intend to do, if God permits" (NET).
	The principles are mentioned briefly in order to get to the next point.
Eleutheria	Hebrews 5:11b–13 "you have become dull of hearing. …you…need milk and not solid food. …everyone who partakes *only* of milk is…an infant" (NASB).
	Hebrews 6:6b–8 "since they again crucify to themselves the Son of God and put Him to open shame. For ground that drinks the rain…and brings for vegetation useful…receives a blessing from God; but if it yields thorns and thistles, it is worthless and close to being cursed, and it ends up being burned" (NASB).
	The author of Hebrews is speaking candidly to his audience, as he admits in 6:9. (cf. Heb 5:14, 6:4-6a).
Erotesis	Hebrews 1:5 "For to which of the angels did He ever say…?"
	Hebrews 1:13 "But to which of the angels has He ever said…?"
	Hebrews 1:14 "Are they not all ministering spirits, sent out to render service for the sake of those who will inherit salvation?"
	Hebrews 2:3 "How will we escape if we neglect such a great salvation?"
	Hebrews 2:6 "What is man, that you remember him; or the son of man, that you are concerned about him?"
	Hebrews 3:16 "For which ones heard and rebelled? Was it not all who came out of Egypt under Moses' leadership?"
	Hebrews 9:14 "How much more will the blood of Christ … cleanse your conscience from dead works to serve the living God?"
	Hebrews 10:29 "How much severer punishment do you think he will deserve who has trampled under foot the Son of God … by which he was sanctified, and has insulted the Spirit of grace?"
	Hebrews 11:32 "And what more shall I say?"
	Hebrews 12:7 "for what son is there whom *his* father does not discipline?"

Words Used Frequently in Hebrews

CHART 102

Word	Hebrews	New Testament
Abraham	10	73
Angel	13	175
Holy	19	233
Blood	21	97
Age, world	15	123
Sin	25	173
Earth	11	248
Covenant	17	33
To enter into	17	192
Promise	14	52
To live	12	140
Today	18	388
Death	10	120
Sacrifice, offering	15	28
Priest	14	31
Heart	11	156
Better, preferable	13	19
To speak	16	298
To receive, take	17	259
People	13	141
Word	12	331
Moses	11	79
Once	8	14
Law	14	191
House	11	112
Heaven	10	272
Faith	32	243
To do, make	19	565
To bring, offer	20	47
Tent, tabernacle	10	20
To complete, fulfill	9	23
Son	24	375
Apart from, separately	13	41
High Priest	17	122
To hear, listen	8	428
Harden	4	6
Unable, impossible	4	10

Alphabetical Listing of Greek Words Unique to Hebrews

CHART 103

Greek Word	Reference in Hebrews	English Version and Translation	
ἀγενεαλόγητος	7:3	KJV	without descent
		NLT	any of his ancestors
		ESV, NASB, NRSV, NIV, NET, TNIV	without genealogy
ἀγνόημα	9:7	ESV	unintentional sins
		KJV	errors
		NRSV	sins committed unintentionally
		NLT, TNIV, NIV, NET, NASB	sins committed in ignorance
ἀθέτησις	7:18	KJV	a disannulling
		NASB	a setting aside
		NRSV	the abrogation of
		ESV, NET, NIV, NLT, TNIV	set aside
	9:26	ESV, KJV, NASB, NET	put away
		NLT, NRSV	remove
		NIV, TNIV	do away
ἄθλησις	10:32	ESV	hard struggle
		KJV	fight
		NASB, NET, TNIV	conflict
		NRSV	struggle
		NIV	contest
		NLT	terrible (suffering)
αἴγειος	11:37	TNIV, NIV, NASB, NET	goat skins
		ESV, KJV, NRSV, NLT	goats
αἱματεκχυσία	9:22	All	shedding of blood
αἴνεσις	13:15	All	praise
ἀκατάλυτος	7:16	KJV	endless
		NLT	cannot be destroyed

		ESV, NASB, NRSV, NIV, NET, TNIV	indestructible
ἀκλινής	10:23	NIV, TNIV	unswervingly
		NET	unwaveringly
		ESV, KJV, NASB, NRSV, NLT	without wavering
ἀκροθίνιον	7:4	ESV, KJV, NRSV	spoils
		NASB	choicest spoils
		NIV, NET, TNIV	plunder
		NLT	what he had taken in battle
ἀλυσιτελής	13:17	KJV, NASB	unprofitable
		NRSV	harmful
		ESV, NIV, NET	no advantage
		NLT	not be for your benefit
		TNIV	no benefit
ἀμετάθετος	6:17	KJV	immutability
		NASB	unchangeableness
		ESV, NRSV, NET	unchangeable
		NIV, TNIV	unchanging
		NLT	never change
ἀμετάθετος	6:18	KJV	immutable
		ESV, NASB, NRSV, NIV, NET, NLT, TNIV	unchangeable
ἀμήτωρ	7:3	NLT	no record of his mother
		KJV, NASB, NRSV, ESV, NIV, NET, TNIV	without mother
ἀνακαινίζω	6:6	NIV, TNIV	brought back
		NLT	bring…back
		KJV, NASB, NET	renew
		ESV, NRSV	restore
ἀναλογίζομαι	12:3	NET, NLT	think of
		ESV, KJV, NASB, NIV NRSV, TNIV	consider
ἀνασταυρόω	6:6	NLT	nailing…to the cross
		ESV, KJV, NASB, NIV, TNIV, NRSV, NET	crucify
ἀνταγωνίζομαι	12:4	KJV, NASB	striving

		ESV, NRSV, NIV, NET, NLT, TNIV	struggle
ἀντικαθίστημι	12:4	NLT	given your lives
		KJV, NASB, NET, ESV, TNIV, NRSV, NIV	resisted
ἀπαράβατος	7:24	KJV	unchangeable
		NLT	lasts forever
		NIV, TNIV	permanent
		ESV, NASB, NRSV, NET	permanently
ἀπάτωρ	7:3	NLT	no record of his father
		ESV, KJV, NRSV, NASB, TNIV, NET, NIV	without father
ἀπαύγασμα	1:3	KJV	brightness
		NRSV	reflection
		NLT	radiates
		ESV, NASB, NIV, NET, TNIV	radiance
ἄπειρος	5:13	KJV	unskillful
		ESV, NRSV	unskilled
		NASB	not accustomed
		NIV, TNIV	not acquainted
		NET	inexperienced
		NLT	doesn't know how
ἀποβλέπω	11:26	KJV	had respect unto the recompense
		ESV, NASB	was looking to
		NIV, NLT, NRSV, TNIV	was looking ahead
		NET	eyes were fixed
ἁρμός, ὁ	4:12	All	joints
ἀφανισμός, ὁ	8:13	ESV, KJV	vanish away
		NASB, NET, NIV, NLT, NRSV, TNIV	disappear
ἀφανής, ἁ	4:13	KJV	manifest
		ESV, NASB, NET, NRSV, NIV, NLT, TNIV	hidden
ἀφομοιόω	7:3	KJV, NASB	made like
		NIV, NET	like
		ESV, NLT, NRSV, TNIV	resembling

βοηθός	13:6	All	helper
βοτάνη	6:7	KJV	herbs
		NASB, NET	vegetation
		ESV, NIV, NLT, NRSV, TNIV	crop
γεωργέω	6:7	ESV, NRSV	cultivated
		KJV	dressed
		NASB	tilled
		NET	tend
		NIV, TNIV	farmed
		NLT	farmer
γνόφος	12:18	KJV	blackness
		NET, ESV, NASB, NIV, TNIV, NLT, NRSV	darkness
δάμαλις	9:13	NET, NLT	young cow
		ESV, KJV, NASB, NIV, NRSV, TNIV	heifer
δεκατόω	7:6	KJV	received tithes
		ESV	take tithes
		NASB, TNIV, NIV, NLT	collect/collected a tenth
		NRSV	collected tithes
		NET	collect a tithe
δεκατόω	7:9	TNIV, NIV	paid the tenth
		NET, NLT	paid a tithe
		KJV, ESV, NRSV, NASB	paid tithes
δέος	12:28	KJV	godly fear
		ESV, NASB, NET, NIV, NLT, NRSV, TNIV	awe
δέρμα	11:37	All	skins
δημιουργός	11:10	KJV	maker
		NLT	built by
		ESV, NASB, NET, NIV, NRSV, TNIV	builder
δήπου	2:16	KJV	verily
		NASB	assuredly
		NLT	also know

		NRSV	it is clear
		ESV, NET, NIV, TNIV	surely
διάκρισις	5:14	KJV, NASB, NET	discern
		ESV, NIV, NRSV, TNIV	distinguish
		NLT	recognize the difference
διάταγμα	11:23	KJV	commandment
		NLT	command
		ESV, NIV, NRSV, TNIV, NASB, NET	edict
διϊκνέομαι	4:12	TNIV, NIV	penetrates
		NLT	cutting
		ESV, NASB, NET, KJV, NRSV	piercing
διηνεκής	7:3	ESV	continues…forever
		KJV	continually
		NASB	perpetually
		NET	for all time
		NLT, TNIV, NRSV, NIV	forever
διηνεκής	10:1	NIV, TNIV	endlessly
		NLT	repeated again and again
		ESV, NASB, NET, NRSV, KJV	continually
διηνεκής	10:12	KJV	for ever
		ESV, NASB, NET, NIV NLT, NRSV, TNIV	for all time
διηνεκής	10:14	KJV, NIV, NLT, TNIV	for ever
		ESV, NASB, NET, NRSV	for all time
διόρθωσις	9:10	ESV, KJV, NASB	reformation
		NRSV	to set things right
		NET, NIV, TNIV	the new order
		NLT	a better system
δίστομος	4:12	NET, NIV, TNIV	double-edged
		ESV, KJV, NASB, NLT, NRSV	two-edged
δοκιμασία	3:9	KJV	proved
		NASB	testing
		ESV, NRSV	put to the test

		NLT	tested
		NET, NIV, TNIV	tried
δυσερμήνευτος	5:11	KJV	hard to be uttered
		NET, NLT	difficult to explain
		ESV, NASB, NRSV, NIV	hard to explain
		TNIV	hard to make clear
ἐάνπερ	3:6	NET	if in fact
		ESV, TNIV	if indeed
		NLT, NASB, NRSV, NIV, KJV	if
ἐάνπερ	3:14	NET	if in fact
		NRSV	if only
		ESV, TNIV	if indeed
		NIV, NASB, NLT, KJV	if
ἐάνπερ	6:3	NIV, NLT, TNIV	not translated
		ESV, KJV, NASB, NET, NRSV	if
ἔγγυος, ὁ	7:22	KJV	surety
		ESV, TNIV	guarantor
		NASB, NET, NIV	guarantee
		NRSV, NLT	guarantees
ἐγκαινίζω	9:18	ESV, NASB, NRSV, NET	inaugurated
		KJV	dedicated
		NIV, NLT, TNIV	put into effect
ἐγκαινίζω	10:20	KJV	consecrated
		NASB, NET	inaugurated
		ESV, NRSV, NIV, TNIV, NLT	opened
εἰ μήν	6:14	NLT	certainly
		ESV, KJV, NASB, NET, NIV, NRSV, TNIV	surely
ἐκβαίνω	11:15	ESV	gone out
		KJV	came out
		NASB	went out
		NLT	came from
		NIV, NET, TNIV	had left
		NRSV	had left behind

ἐκδοχή	10:27	KJV	looking for
		NRSV	prospect
		ESV, NASB, NET, NIV, TNIV, NLT	expectation
ἐκλανθάνομαι	12:5	All	forgotten
ἔλεγχος	11:1	ESV, NASB, NRSV	conviction
		KJV	evidence
		NLT	assurance
		NIV, TNIV	certain
		NET	being convinced
ἐμπαιγμός	11:36	NIV, TNIV	jeers
		NLT	jeered at
		KJV, NASB	mockings
		NET, NRSV, ESV	mocking
ἐνυβρίζω	10:29	KJV	done despite
		NET	insults
		NASB, NIV, TNIV	insulted
		ESV, NRSV	outraged
		NLT	insulted and disdained
ἐπεισαγωγή	7:19	KJV, NASB	bringing in
		NRSV	introduction of
		ESV, NET, NIV, TNIV	introduced
		NLT	now…have confidence
ἐπιλείπω	11:32	NIV, TNIV	I do not have
		NLT	take too long
		ESV, KJV, NASB, NET, NRSV	fail
ἔπος	7:9	NASB	so to speak
		NET	it could be said
		KJV	may so say
		NRSV, TNIV, ESV, NIV, NLT	might even say
ἕξις	5:14	KJV	use
		NASB, NET, NRSV, ESV	practice
		NIV, TNIV	constant use
		NLT	training
εὐαρεστέω	11:5	NASB	pleasing

		ESV, KJV, NET, NRSV, TNIV, NIV, NLT	pleased
εὐαρεστέω	11:6	All	please
εὐαρεστέω	13:16	ESV, NRSV	pleasing
		NLT	please
		KJV, NET, NIV, NASB, TNIV	is pleased
εὐαρέστως	12:28	KJV, NIV, TNIV	acceptably
		ESV, NASB, NRSV	acceptable
		NET	pleasing
		NLT	(not translated)
εὐθύτης	1:8	ESV	uprightness
		KJV, NIV	righteousness
		NASB, NRSV, NET	righteous
		NLT, TNIV	justice
εὐλάβεια	5:7	ESV	reverence
		KJV	feared
		NASB	piety
		NRSV, NIV, TNIV	reverent submission
		NET	devotion
		NLT	deep reverence
εὐλάβεια	12:28	NET	devotion
		NLT	holy fear
		ESV, KJV, NASB, NRSV, TNIV, NIV	reverence
εὐλαβέομαι	11:7	ESV	in reverent fear
		KJV	moved with fear
		NASB	in reverence
		NRSV	respected the warning
		NIV, TNIV	in holy fear
		NET	with reverent regard
		NLT	obeyed
εὐπερίστατος	12:1	ESV, NRSV, NET	clings so closely
		KJV	so easily beset
		NASB, NIV, TNIV	so easily entangles
		NLT	so easily trips up
εὐποιΐα	13:16	All	do good

θεατρίζω	10:33	KJV	gazingstock
		NASB	public spectacle
		NLT	exposed to public
		NRSV, NET, NIV, TNIV, ESV	publicly exposed
θέλησις	2:4	NLT	chose
		ESV, KJV, NASB, NET, NRSV, NIV, TNIV	will
θεράπων	3:5	All	servant
θυέλλα	12:18	ESV, KJV, NRSV	tempest
		NASB, NET, NLT	whirlwind
		NIV, TNIV	storm
θυμιατήριον	9:4	KJV	censer
		NLT	incense altar
		ESV, NASB, NET, NRSV, TNIV, NIV	altar of incense
ἱερωσύνη (ἱερος)	7:11	All	priesthood
ἱερωσύνη (ἱερος)	7:12	All	priesthood
ἱερωσύνη (ἱερος)	7:24	All	priesthood
ἱκετηρία	5:7	NIV, TNIV	petitions
		NLT	pleadings
		ESV, KJV, NASB, NET, NRSV	supplications
λειτουργικός	1:14	NRSV	divine service
		NLT	(no translation)
		ESV, NASB, NET, NIV, TNIV, KJV	ministering
καθαρότης (καθαρός)	9:13	ESV	purification
		KJV	purifying
		NASB	cleansing
		NRSV	purified
		NIV, TNIV	outwardly clean
		NET	ritual purity
		NLT	cleanse
καθώσπερ	5:4	KJV	as

		NASB	even as
		NET	as in fact
		ESV, NIV, NLT, NRSV, TNIV	just as
κακουχέω	11:37	KJV, NRSV	tormented
		NASB, NET	ill-treated
		ESV, NIV, NLT, TNIV	mistreated
	13:3	KJV	suffer adversity
		NASB, NET	ill-treated
		NRSV	tortured
		ESV, NIV, NLT, TNIV	mistreated
καρτερέω	11:27	ESV, KJV, NASB	he endured
		NLT	kept right on going
		NET, NIV, NRSV, TNIV	he persevered
καταγωνίζμαι	11:33	KJV	subdued
		NLT	overthrew
		ESV, NASB, NET, NIV, NRSV, TNIV	conquered
κατάδηλος	7:15	ESV	even more evident
		KJV	far more evident
		NASB	clearer still
		NET	even clearer
		NIV, TNIV	even more clear
		NLT	very clear
		NRSV	even more obvious
καταναλίσκω	12:29	NET, NLT	devouring
		ESV, TNIV, KJV, NASB, NIV, NRSV	consuming
καταπέτασμα	10:20	KJV, NASB	veil
		ESV, NET, NIV, NLT, NRSV, TNIV	curtain
κατασκιάζω	9:5	KJV	shadowing
		NLT	stretched out over
		ESV, NASB, NET, NIV, NRSV, TNIV	overshadowing
κατάσκοπος	11:31	All	spies
καῦσις	6:8	NLT	burn

		ESV, KJV, NASB, NET, TNIV, NRSV, NIV	burned
κεφαλίς	10:7	KJV	volume
		NLT	Scriptures
		ESV, NASB, NET, NRSV, TNIV, NIV	scroll
κοπή	7:1	ESV, KJV, NASB	slaughter
		NRSV, NET	defeating
		NIV, TNIV	defeat
		NLT	after winning a great battle
κριτικός	4:12	ESV	discerning
		KJV	discerner
		NLT	exposes
		TNIV, NIV	judges
		NASB, NET, NRSV	able to judge
κῶλον, το	3:17	KJV	carcasses
		NLT	corpses
		ESV, NASB, NET, NIV, NRSV, TNIV	bodies
μετέπειτα	12:17	NRSV, NET	later
		ESV, KJV, NASB, NIV, TNIV, NLT	afterward
μετριοπαθέω	5:2	KJV	to have compassion
		NET	deal compassionately
		ESV, NASB, NIV, NLT, NRSV, TNIV	deal gently
μεσιτεύω	6:17	KJV, NIV, TNIV	confirmed
		NASB	interposed
		ESV, NRSV	guaranteed
		NET	intervened
		NLT	bound
μερισμός, ὁ	2:4	NLT	giving
		KJV, NASB	(no translation)
		ESV, TNIV, NET, NIV, NRSV	distributed
μερισμός, ὁ	4:12	ESV, NASB	division
		NLT	cutting
		TNIV, KJV, NET, NIV	dividing

		NRSV	divides
μηδέπω	11:7	ESV, KJV, NRSV	as yet
		NASB, NET, NIV, TNIV	not yet
		NLT	never happened before
μηλωτή	11:37	ESV, NLT, NRSV	skins of sheep
		KJV, NASB, NET, NIV, TNIV	sheepskins
μισθαποδότης	11:6	KJV, NASB	rewarder
		ESV, NET, NLT, NIV, NRSV, TNIV	he rewards
μισθαποδοσία	2:2	ESV	just retribution
		KJV	recompense of reward
		NASB, NRSV, NET	just penalty
		NIV, TNIV	just punishment
		NLT	punished
μισθαποδοσία	10:35	TNIV, NIV	rewarded
		ESV, KJV, NASB, NRSV, NLT, NET	reward
μισθαποδοσία	11:26	All	reward
μυελός, ὁ	4:12	All	marrow
νέφος	12:1	NLT	huge cloud
		ESV, KJV, NASB, NRSV, TNIV, NIV, NET	great cloud
νόθος	12:8	KJV	bastards
		TNIV	not legitimate
		ESV, NASB, NET, NLT, NRSV, NIV	illegitimate
νομοθετέω	7:11	NLT	law was based
		NIV	law was given
		TNIV	law given
		KJV, NASB, NET, NRSV, ESV	received the law
νομοθετέω	8:6	KJV, TNIV	established
		NIV	founded
		NLT	based
		NASB, NRSV, NET, ESV	enacted

νωθρός	5:11	NIV	slow
		NET	sluggish
		TNIV	no longer try to understand
		ESV, KJV, NASB, NLT, NRSV	dull
νωθρός	6:12	KJV	slothful
		NLT	dull
		NIV, TNIV	lazy
		ESV, NASB, NRSV, NET	sluggish
ὄγκος	12:1	NASB	encumbrance
		NIV, TNIV	everything that hinders
		ESV, KJV, NRSV, NET, NLT	weight
ὀλιγωρέω	12:5	KJV	despise
		ESV, NASB, NRSV	regard lightly
		NLT, NIV, TNIV	make light
		NET	scorn
ὀλοθρεύω	11:28	KJV, NASB, NET	who destroyed
		ESV, NRSV, NIV, TNIV	destroyer
		NLT	angel of death
ὁμοιότης (ὁμός)	4:15	KJV	like as we are
		ESV, NASB, NRSV	as we are
		NET, TNIV	just as we are
		NLT	same…we do
ὁμοιότης (ὁμός)	7:15	KJV	similitude
		ESV, NASB, NET	likeness of
		NRSV	resembling
		NIV, NLT, TNIV	like
ὀρκωμοσία	7:20	NET	sworn affirmation
		ESV, KJV, NASB, NIV, TNIV, NLT, NRSV	oath
ὀρκωμοσία	7:21	NET	sworn affirmation
		ESV, KJV, NASB, NIV, TNIV, NLT, NRSV	oath
ὀρκωμοσία	7:28	NET	solemn affirmation
		ESV, KJV, NASB, NIV, TNIV, NLT, NRSV	oath

πανήγυρις	12:22	KJV	company
		ESV, NRSV	festal gathering
		NLT	joyful gathering
		NET	assembly
		NIV, TNIV	joyful assembly
		NASB	(no translation)
παραπλησίως	2:14	NIV, TNIV	too
		NLT	also
		ESV, KJV, NASB, NET, NRSV	likewise
παραπίπτω	6:6	KJV, NIV	fall away
		NASB, NRSV, TNIV, ESV	fallen away
		NET	committed apostasy
		NLT	turn away
παραρρέω	2:1	KJV	slip
		ESV, NASB, NET, NIV, NLT, NRSV, TNIV	drift away
παραπικρασμός, ὁ	3:8	KJV	provocation
		NASB	provoked
		NLT	rebelled
		ESV, NET, NIV, NRSV, TNIV	rebellion
παραπικρασμός, ὁ	3:15	KJV	provocation
		NASB	provoked
		NLT	rebelled
		ESV, NET, NIV, NRSV, TNIV	rebellion
παραπικραίνω	3:16	KJV, NASB	provoked
		NRSV	rebellious
		NET, NIV, NLT, ESV, TNIV	rebelled
πεῖρα	11:29	KJV	assaying to do
		ESV, NASB, NRSV	attempted
		NET, NIV, NLT, TNIV	tried
πεῖρα	11:36	KJV	had trial
		NASB, NET	experienced
		ESV, NRSV	suffered
		NIV, TNIV	faced
		NLT	were

πήγνυμι	8:2	KJV, NASB	pitched
		NLT	built
		ESV, NRSV, NET, NIV, TNIV	set up
πολυμερῶς	1:1	KJV	sundry times
		NASB	many portions
		NRSV	many ways
		NET	various portions
		ESV, NIV, NLT, TNIV	many times
πολυτρόπως	1:1	KJV	divers manners
		ESV, NASB, NLT	many ways
		NET, NIV, NRSV, TNIV	various ways
πρίζω	11:37	NET	sawed apart
		NLT	sawed in half
		NIV, TNIV	sawed in two
		KJV	sawn asunder
		NRSV, NASB, ESV	sawn in two
προβλέπω	11:40	NIV, TNIV	planned
		NLT	in mind
		KJV, NASB, NET, NRSV, ESV	provided
πρόδρομος	6:20	NIV	who went before
		NLT	already gone in there
		ESV, KJV, NASB, NET, NRSV, TNIV	forerunner
προσαγορεύω	5:10	KJV	called
		ESV, NASB, NET, NIV, NLT, NRSV, TNIV	designated
προσοχθίζω	3:10	ESV, NET	provoked
		KJV	grieve
		NASB, NIV, NLT, NRSV, TNIV	angry
προσοχθίζω	3:17	ESV, NET	provoked
		KJV	grieved
		NASB, NIV, NLT, NRSV, TNIV	angry
πρωτοτόκια	12:16	NIV, TNIV	inheritance rights

		ESV, KJV, NASB, NET, NRSV, NLT	birthright
σαββατισμός	4:9	KJV	rest
		NLT	special rest
		ESV, NASB, NET, NIV, NRSV, TNIV	Sabbath rest
στάμνος	9:4	KJV	pot
		ESV, NET, NRSV	urn
		NASB, NIV, NLT, TNIV	jar
συγκακουχέομαι	11:25	KJV	to suffer affliction
		NASB	to endure ill-treatment
		NRSV	to share ill-treatment
		ESV, NIV, TNIV	to be mistreated
		NET	to be ill-treated
		NLT	to share the oppression
συμπαθέω	4:15	KJV	touched
		NLT	understand
		TNIV	empathize
		ESV, NASB, NET, NIV, NRSV	sympathize
συμπαθέω	10:34	ESV, KJV, NRSV	compassion
		NASB	sympathy
		NIV	sympathized
		NET	shared the sufferings
		NLT, TNIV	suffered along with
συναπόλλυμαι	11:31	KJV	perished
		ESV, NASB, NRSV	perish
		NIV, TNIV	killed
		NET	escaped destruction
		NLT	not destroyed
συνδέω	13:3	KJV	bound with
		NIV	fellow prisoner
		TNIV	together with them in prison
		NRSV, ESV, NASB, NET, NLT	in prison with
τελειωτής	12:2	KJV	finisher
		NLT	perfects

		ESV, NASB, NET, NIV, NRSV, TNIV	perfecter
τιμωρία	10:29	NIV, TNIV	be punished
		ESV, KJV, NASB, NET, NRSV, NLT	punishment
τομός	4:12	All	sharper
τράγος	9:12	All	goats
τράγος	9:13	All	goats
τράγος	9:19	All	goats
τράγος	10:4	All	goats
τραχηλίζομαι	4:13	ESV, NLT, NET	exposed
		KJV	opened
		NIV, TNIV, NASB, NRSV	laid bare
τρίμηνος	11:23	All	three months
τροχιά	12:13	All	paths
τυμπανίζω	11:35	All	tortured
ὑπείκω	13:17	NLT	do what they say
		NASB, NIV, TNIV, ESV, NRSV, NET, KJV	submit
ὑποστολή	10:39	KJV	draw back
		NLT	turn away
		NRSV, TNIV, NIV, NASB, NET, ESV	shrink back
φαντάζομαι	12:21	NET	the scene
		ESV, KJV, NASB, NIV, NRSV, NLT, TNIV	the sight

φοβερός, ὁ	10:27	NASB	terrifying
		NLT	terrible
		ESV, KJV, NET, TNIV, NRSV, NIV	fearful
φοβερός, ὁ	10:31	ESV, KJV, NRSV	fearful
		NIV, TNIV	dreadful
		NASB, NET	terrifying
		NLT	terrible
φοβερός, ὁ	12:21	KJV, NASB	terrible
		NLT	frightened
		ESV, NET, NIV, NRSV, TNIV	terrifying
χαρακτήρ	1:3	KJV	express image
		NASB, NIV, TNIV	exact representation
		ESV, NRSV	exact imprint
		NET	representation
		NLT	character
Χερουβίν	9:5	All	Cherubim

Chapter Listing of Greek Words Unique to Hebrews

CHART 104

HEBREWS CHAPTER ONE

Greek Word	Hebrews	English Version and Translation	
πολυμερῶς	1:1	KJV	sundry times
		NASB	many portions
		NRSV	many ways
		NET	various portions
		ESV, NIV, NLT, TNIV	many times
πολυτρόπως	1:1	KJV	divers manners
		ESV, NASB, NLT	many ways
		NET, NIV, NRSV, TNIV	various ways
χαρακτήρ	1:3	KJV	express image
		NASB, NIV, TNIV	exact representation
		ESV, NRSV	exact imprint
		NET	representation
		NLT	character
ἀπαύγασμα	1:3	KJV	brightness
		NRSV	reflection
		NLT	radiates
		ESV, NASB, NIV, NET, TNIV	radiance
εὐθύτης	1:8	ESV	uprightness
		KJV, NIV	righteousness
		NASB, NRSV, NET	righteous
		NLT, TNIV	justice
λειτουργικός	1:14	NRSV	divine service
		NLT	(no translation)
		ESV, NASB, NET, KJV NIV, TNIV	ministering

HEBREWS CHAPTER TWO

Greek Word	Hebrews	English Version and Translation	
παραρρέω	2:1	KJV	slip

		ESV, NASB, NET, NIV, NRSV, NLT, TNIV	drift away
μισθαποδοσία	2:2	ESV	just retribution
		KJV	recompense of reward
		NASB, NRSV, NET	just penalty
		NIV, TNIV	just punishment
		NLT	punished
θέλησις	2:4	NLT	chose
		ESV, KJV, NASB, NET, NRSV, NIV, TNIV	will
μερισμός, ὁ	2:4	NLT	giving
		KJV, NASB	(no translation)
		ESV, NET, NRSV, NIV, TNIV	distributed
παραπλησίως	2:14	NIV, TNIV	too
		NLT	also
		ESV, KJV, NASB, NET, NRSV	likewise
δήπου	2:16	KJV	verily
		NASB	assuredly
		NLT	also know
		NRSV	it is clear
		ESV, NET, NIV, TNIV	surely

HEBREWS CHAPTER THREE

Greek Word	Hebrews	English Version and Translation	
θεράπων	3:5	All	servant
ἐάνπερ	3:6	NET	if in fact
		ESV, TNIV	if indeed
		NASB, NRSV, NLT, KJV, NIV	if
παραπικρασμός, ὁ	3:8	KJV	provocation
		NASB	provoked
		NLT	rebelled
		NIV, TNIV, ESV, NET, NRSV	rebellion
δοκιμασία	3:9	KJV	proved
		NASB	testing

Greek Word	Hebrews	English Version and Translation	
		ESV, NRSV	put to the test
		NLT	tested
		NET, NIV, TNIV	tried
προσοχθίζω	3:10	ESV, NET	provoked
		KJV	grieve
		NASB, NIV, NLT, NRSV, TNIV	angry
ἐάνπερ	3:14	NRSV	if only
		NET	if in fact
		ESV, TNIV	if indeed
		NIV, NASB, NLT, KJV	if
παραπικρασμός, ὁ	3:15	KJV	provocation
		NASB	provoked
		NLT	rebelled
		ESV, NET, NIV, NRSV, TNIV	rebellion
παραπικραίνω	3:16	KJV, NASB	provoked
		NRSV	rebellious
		NET, NIV, ESV, NLT, TNIV	rebelled
κῶλον, το	3:17	KJV	carcasses
		NLT	corpses
		ESV, NASB, NET NIV, NRSV, TNIV	bodies
προσοχθίζω	3:17	ESV, NET	provoked
		KJV	grieved
		NASB, NIV, NLT, NRSV, TNIV	angry

HEBREWS CHAPTER FOUR

Greek Word	Hebrews	English Version and Translation	
σαββατισμός	4:9	KJV	rest
		NLT	special rest
		ESV, NASB, NET, NIV, NRSV, TNIV	Sabbath rest
ἁρμός, ὁ	4:12	All	joints
διϊκνέομαι	4:12	NIV, TNIV	penetrates
		NLT	cutting

Greek Word	Hebrews	English Version and Translation	
		ESV, NASB, NET, KJV, NRSV	piercing
δίστομος	4:12	NET, NIV, TNIV	double-edged
		ESV, KJV, NASB, NRSV, NLT	two-edged
κριτικός	4:12	ESV	discerning
		KJV	discerner
		NLT	exposes
		TNIV, NIV	judges
		NASB, NET, NRSV	able to judge
μερισμός, ὁ	4:12	ESV, NASB	division
		NLT	cutting
		TNIV, NIV, NET, KJV	dividing
		NRSV	divides
μυελός, ὁ	4:12	All	marrow
τομός	4:12	All	sharper
ἀφανής, ἁ	4:13	KJV	manifest
		ESV, NASB, NET, TNIV, NIV, NLT	hidden
τραχηλίζομαι	4:13	ESV, NLT, NET	exposed
		NIV, TNIV, NASB, NRSV	laid bare
		KJV	opened
ὁμοιότης (ὁμός)	4:15	KJV	like as we are
		ESV, NASB, NRSV	as we are
		NET, TNIV	just as we are
		NLT	same…we do
συμπαθέω	4:15	KJV	touched
		NLT	understand
		TNIV	empathize
		ESV, NASB, NET, NIV, NRSV	sympathize

HEBREWS CHAPTER FIVE

Greek Word	Hebrews	English Version and Translation	
μετριοπαθέω	5:2	KJV	to have compassion
		NET	deal compassionately

		ESV, NASB, NIV, NLT, NRSV, TNIV	deal gently
καθώσπερ	5:4	KJV	as
		NASB	even as
		NET	as in fact
		ESV, NIV, NLT, NRSV, TNIV	just as
εὐλάβεια	5:7	ESV	reverence
		KJV	feared
		NASB	piety
		NRSV, NIV, TNIV	reverent submission
		NET	devotion
		NLT	deep reverence
ἱκετηρία	5:7	NIV, TNIV	petitions
		NLT	pleadings
		ESV, KJV, NASB, NRSV, NET	supplications
προσαγορεύω	5:10	KJV	called
		ESV, NASB, NET, NIV, NRSV, NLT, TNIV	designated
δυσερμήνευτος	5:11	KJV	hard to be uttered
		NET, NLT	difficult to explain
		ESV, NASB, NRSV, NIV	hard to explain
		TNIV	hard to make clear
νωθρός	5:11	NIV	slow
		NET	sluggish
		TNIV	no longer try to understand
		ESV, KJV, NASB, NLT, NRSV	dull
ἄπειρος	5:13	KJV	unskillful
		ESV, NRSV	unskilled
		NASB	not accustomed
		NIV, TNIV	not acquainted
		NET	inexperienced
		NLT	doesn't know how
διάκρισις	5:14	KJV, NASB, NET	discern
		ESV, NIV, NRSV, TNIV	distinguish
		NLT	recognize the difference

ἔξις	5:14	KJV	use
		NASB, NET, NRSV, ESV	practice
		NIV, TNIV	constant use
		NLT	training

HEBREWS CHAPTER SIX

Greek Word	Hebrews	English Version and Translation	
ἐάνπερ	6:3	NIV, NLT, TNIV	(not translated)
		ESV, KJV, NASB, NET, NRSV	if
ἀνακαινίζω	6:6	NIV, TNIV	brought back
		NLT	bring…back
		KJV, NASB, NET	renew
		ESV, NRSV	restore
ἀνασταυρόω	6:6	NLT	nailing…to the cross
		NIV, TNIV, KJV, ESV, NRSV, NET, NASB	crucify
παραπίπτω	6:6	KJV, NIV	fall away
		NASB, NRSV, TNIV, ESV	fallen away
		NET	committed apostasy
		NLT	turn away
βοτάνη	6:7	KJV	herbs
		NASB, NET	vegetation
		ESV, NIV, NLT, NRSV, TNIV	crop
γεωργέω	6:7	ESV, NRSV	cultivated
		KJV	dressed
		NASB	tilled
		NET	tend
		NIV, TNIV	farmed
		NLT	farmer
καῦσις	6:8	NLT	burn
		ESV, KJV, NASB, NET, TNIV, NIV, NRSV	burned
νωθρός	6:12	KJV	slothful
		NLT	dull
		NIV, TNIV	lazy

Greek Word	Hebrews	English Version and Translation	
		ESV, NASB, NRSV, NET	sluggish
εἰ μήν	6:14	NLT	certainly
		ESV, KJV, NASB, NET, NIV, NRSV, TNIV	surely
ἀμετάθετος	6:17	KJV	immutability
		NASB	unchangeableness
		ESV, NRSV, NET	unchangeable
		NIV, TNIV	unchanging
		NLT	never change
μεσιτεύω	6:17	KJV, NIV, TNIV	confirmed
		NASB	interposed
		ESV, NRSV	guaranteed
		NET	intervened
		NLT	bound
ἀμετάθετος	6:18	KJV	immutable
		ESV, NASB, NRSV, NIV, NET, NLT, TNIV	unchangeable
πρόδρομος	6:20	NIV	who went before
		NLT	already gone in there
		ESV, KJV, NASB, NET, NRSV, TNIV	forerunner

HEBREWS CHAPTER SEVEN

Greek Word	Hebrews	English Version and Translation	
κοπή	7:1	ESV, KJV, NASB	slaughter
		NRSV, NET	defeating
		NIV, TNIV	defeat
		NLT	after winning a great battle
ἀγενεαλόγητος	7:3	KJV	without descent
		NLT	any of his ancestors
		ESV, NASB, NRSV, NIV, NET, TNIV	without genealogy
ἀμήτωρ	7:3	NLT	no record of his mother
		NASB, NIV, TNIV, KJV, NRSV, ESV, NET	without mother
ἀπάτωρ	7:3	NLT	no record of his father

		ESV, KJV, NRSV, NET, NASB, TNIV, NIV	without father
ἀφομοιόω	7:3	KJV, NASB	made like
		NIV, NET	like
		ESV, NLT, NRSV, TNIV	resembling
διηνεκής	7:3	ESV	forever
		KJV	continually
		NASB	perpetually
		NET	for all time
		NLT, TNIV, NRSV, NIV	forever
ἀκροθίνιον	7:4	ESV, KJV, NRSV	spoils
		NASB	choicest spoils
		NIV, NET, TNIV	plunder
		NLT	what he had taken in battle
δεκατόω	7:6	KJV	received tithes
		ESV	take tithes
		NET	collect a tithe
		NRSV	collected tithes
		NASB, NIV, TNIV, NLT	collect/collected a tenth
δεκατόω	7:9	NIV, TNIV	paid the tenth
		NET, NLT	paid a tithe
		KJV, ESV, NRSV, NASB	paid tithes
ἔπος	7:9	NASB	so as to speak
		NET	it could be said
		KJV	may so say
		ESV, NIV, TNIV, NLT, NRSV	might even say
ἱερωσύνη (ἱερος)	7:11	All	priesthood
νομοθετέω	7:11	NLT	law was based
		NIV	law was given
		TNIV	law given
		KJV, NASB, NET, NRSV, ESV	received the law
ἱερωσύνη (ἱερος)	7:12	All	priesthood
κατάδηλος	7:15	ESV	eveN more evident
		KJV	far more evident
		NASB	clearer still

		NET	even clearer
		NIV, TNIV	even more clear
		NLT	very clear
		NRSV	even more obvious
ὁμοιότης (ὁμός)	7:15	KJV	similitude
		ESV, NASB, NET	likeness of
		NRSV	resembling
		NIV, NLT, TNIV	like
ἀκατάλυτος	7:16	KJV	endless
		NLT	cannot be destroyed
		ESV, NASB, NRSV, NIV, TNIV, NET	indestructible
ἀθέτησις	7:18	KJV	a disannulling
		NASB	a setting aside
		NRSV	the abrogation of
		ESV, NET, NIV, NLT, TNIV	set aside
ἐπεισαγωγή	7:19	KJV, NASB	bringing in
		NRSV	introduction of
		ESV, NET, NIV, TNIV	introduced
		NLT	now…have confidence
ὁρκωμοσία	7:20	NET	sworn affirmation
		ESV, KJV, NASB, NET, NLT, NRSV, TNIV	oath
ὁρκωμοσία	7:21	NET	sworn affirmation
		ESV, KJV, NASB, NIV, NRSV, NLT, TNIV	oath
ἔγγυος, ὁ	7:22	KJV	surety
		ESV, TNIV	guarantor
		NASB, NET, NIV, NRSV	guarantee
		NLT	guarantees
ἀπαράβατος	7:24	KJV	unchangeable
		NLT	lasts forever
		NIV, TNIV	permanent
		ESV, NASB, NRSV, NET	permanently
ἱερωσύνη (ἱερος)	7:24	All	priesthood
ὁρκωμοσία	7:28	NET	solemn affirmation

		ESV, KJV, NASB, NRSV, NLT, TNIV, NIV	oath

HEBREWS CHAPTER EIGHT

Greek Word	Hebrews	English Version and Translation	
πήγνυμι	8:2	KJV, NASB	pitched
		NLT	built
		ESV, NRSV, NET, TNIV, NIV	set up
νομοθετέω	8:6	KJV, TNIV	established
		NIV	founded
		NLT	based
		NASB, NRSV, NET, ESV	enacted
ἀφανισμός, ὁ	8:13	ESV, KJV	vanish away
		NASB, NET, NIV, NLT, NRSV, TNIV	disappear

HEBREWS CHAPTER NINE

Greek Word	Hebrews	English Version and Translation	
θυμιατήριον	9:4	KJV	censer
		NLT	incense altar
		ESV, NASB, NET, NIV, NRSV, TNIV	altar of incense
στάμνος	9:4	KJV	pot
		ESV, NET, NRSV	urn
		NASB, NIV, NLT, TNIV	jar
κατασκιάζω	9:5	KJV	shadowing
		NLT	stretched out over
		ESV, NASB, NET, NIV, NRSV, TNIV	overshadowing
Χερουβίν	9:5	All	Cherubim
ἀγνόημα	9:7	ESV	unintentional sins
		KJV	errors
		NRSV	sins committed unintentionally
		NLT, TNIV, NASB, NET, NIV	sins committed in ignorance

Greek Word	Hebrews	English Version and Translation	
διόρθωσις	9:10	ESV, KJV, NASB	reformation
		NRSV	to set things right
		NET, NIV, TNIV	the new order
		NLT	a better system
τράγός	9:12	All	goats
δάμαλις	9:13	NET, NLT	young cow
		ESV, KJV, NASB, NIV, NRSV, TNIV	heifer
καθαρότης (καθαρός)	9:13	ESV	purification
		KJV	purifying
		NASB	cleansing
		NRSV	purified
		NIV, TNIV	outwardly clean
		NET	ritual purity
		NLT	cleanse
τράγος	9:13	All	goats
ἐγκαινίζω	9:18	ESV, NASB, NRSV, NET	inaugurated
		KJV	dedicated
		NIV, NLT, TNIV	put into effect
τράγός	9:19	All	goats
αἱματεκχυσία	9:22	All	shedding of blood
ἀθέτησις	9:26	KJV, NASB, NET, ESV	put away
		NLT, NRSV	remove
		NIV, TNIV	do away

HEBREWS CHAPTER TEN

Greek Word	Hebrews	English Version and Translation	
διηνεκής	10:1	NIV, TNIV	endlessly
		NLT	repeated again and again
		ESV, NASB, NET, KJV, NRSV	continually
τράγός	10:4	All	goats
κεφαλίς	10:7	KJV	volume

		NLT	Scriptures
		ESV, NASB, NET, NRSV, NIV, TNIV	scroll
διηνεκής	10:12	KJV	for ever
		ESV, NASB, NET, NIV, NRSV, NLT, TNIV	for all time
διηνεκής	10:14	KJV, NIV, NLT, TNIV	for ever
		ESV, NASB, NET, NRSV	for all time
ἐγκαινίζω	10:20	KJV	consecrated
		NET, NASB	inaugurated
		NRSV, NIV, TNIV, NLT, ESV	opened
καταπέτασμα	10:20	KJV, NASB	veil
		ESV, NET, NIV, NLT, NRSV, TNIV	curtain
ἀκλινής	10:23	NIV, TNIV	unswervingly
		NET	unwaveringly
		ESV, KJV, NASB, NRSV, NLT	without wavering
ἐκδοχή	10:27	KJV	looking for
		NRSV	prospect
		ESV, NASB, NET, NLT, TNIV, NIV	expectation
φοβερός, ὁ	10:27	NASB	terrifying
		NLT	terrible
		ESV, KJV, NET, NIV, NRSV, TNIV	fearful
ἐνυβρίζω	10:29	KJV	done despite
		NET	insults
		NASB, NIV, TNIV	insulted
		ESV, NRSV	outraged
		NLT	insulted and disdained
τιμωρία	10:29	NIV, TNIV	be punished
		ESV, KJV, NASB, NET, NRSV, NLT	punishment
φοβερός, ὁ	10:31	ESV, KJV, NRSV	fearful
		NIV, TNIV	dreadful

Greek Word	Hebrews	English Version and Translation	
		NASB, NET	terrifying
		NLT	terrible
ἄθλησις	10:32	ESV	hard struggle
		KJV	fight
		NASB, NET, TNIV	conflict
		NRSV	struggle
		NIV	contest
		NLT	terrible (suffering)
θεατρίζω	10:33	KJV	gazingstock
		NASB	public spectacle
		NLT	exposed to public
		NRSV, NET, NIV, TNIV, ESV	publicly exposed
συμπαθέω	10:34	ESV, KJV, NRSV	compassion
		NASB	sympathy
		NIV	sympathized
		NET	shared the sufferings
		NLT, TNIV	suffered along with
μισθαποδοσία	10:35	TNIV, NIV	rewarded
		ESV, KJV, NASB, NLT, NRSV, NET	reward
ὑποστολή	10:39	KJV	draw back
		NLT	turn away
		NRSV, TNIV, ESV, NASB, NET, NIV	shrink back

HEBREWS CHAPTER ELEVEN

Greek Word	Hebrews	English Version and Translation	
ἔλεγχος	11:1	ESV, NASB, NRSV	conviction
		NET	being convinced
		KJV	evidence
		NLT	assurance
		NIV, TNIV	certain
εὐαρεστέω	11:5	NASB	pleasing
		ESV, KJV, NET, NIV, TNIV, NRSV, NLT	pleased
εὐαρεστέω	11:6	All	please

μισθαποδότης	11:6	KJV, NASB	rewarder
		ESV, NET, NLT, NIV, NRSV, TNIV	he rewards
εὐλαβέομαι	11:7	ESV	in reverent fear
		KJV	moved with fear
		NASB	in reverence
		NRSV	respected the warning
		NIV, TNIV	in holy fear
		NET	with reverent regard
		NLT	obeyed
μηδέπω	11:7	ESV, KJV, NRSV	as yet
		NASB, NET, NIV, TNIV	not yet
		NLT	never happened before
δημιουργός	11:10	KJV	maker
		NLT	built by
		ESV, NASB, NET, NIV, NRSV, TNIV	builder
ἐκβαίνω	11:15	ESV	gone out
		KJV	came out
		NASB	went out
		NLT	came from
		NIV, NET, TNIV	had left
		NRSV	left behind
διάταγμα	11:23	KJV	commandment
		NLT	command
		ESV, NIV, NRSV, TNIV, NET, NASB	edict
τρίμηνος	11:23	All	three months
συγκακουχέομαι	11:25	KJV	to suffer affliction
		NASB	to endure ill-treatment
		NRSV	to share ill-treatment
		ESV, NIV, TNIV	to be mistreated
		NET	to be ill-treated
		NLT	to share the oppression
ἀποβλέπω	11:26	KJV	had respect unto the recompense
		ESV, NASB	was looking to
		NIV, NLT, NRSV, TNIV	was looking ahead
		NET	eyes were fixed

μισθαποδοσία	11:26	All	reward
καρτερέω	11:27	ESV, KJV, NASB	he endured
		NLT	kept right on going
		NET, NIV, NRSV, TNIV	he persevered
ὀλοθρεύω	11:28	KJV, NASB, NET	who destroyed
		ESV, NRSV, NIV, TNIV	destroyer
		NLT	angel of death
πεῖρα	11:29	KJV	assaying to do
		ESV, NASB, NRSV	attempted
		NET, NIV, NLT, TNIV	tried
κατάσκοπος	11:31	All	spies
συναπόλλυμαι	11:31	KJV	perished
		ESV, NASB, NRSV	perish
		NIV, TNIV	killed
		NET	escaped destruction
		NLT	not destroyed
ἐπιλείπω	11:32	NIV, TNIV	I do not have
		NLT	take too long
		ESV, KJV, NASB, NET, NRSV	fail
καταγωνίζμαι	11:33	KJV	subdued
		NLT	overthrew
		ESV, NASB, NET, NIV, NRSV, TNIV	conquered
τυμπανίζω	11:35	All	tortured
ἐμπαιγμός	11:36	NIV, TNIV	jeers
		NLT	jeered at
		ESV, NET, NRSV	mocking
		KJV, NASB	mockings
πεῖρα	11:36	KJV	had trial
		NASB, NET	experienced
		ESV, NRSV	suffered
		NIV, TNIV	faced
		NLT	were
αἴγειος	11:37	TNIV, NIV, NASB, NET	goat skins

		ESV, KJV, NRSV, NLT	goats
δέρμα	11:37	All	skins
κακουχέω	11:37	KJV, NRSV	tormented
		NASB, NET	ill-treated
		ESV, NIV, NLT, TNIV	mistreated
μηλωτή	11:37	ESV, NLT, NRSV	skins of sheep
		KJV, NASB, NET, NIV, TNIV	sheepskins
πρίζω	11:37	NLT	sawed in half
		TNIV	sawed in two
		NET	sawed apart
		NIV	sawed in two
		KJV	sawn asunder
		NRSV, NASB, ESV	sawn in two
προβλέπω	11:40	NIV, TNIV	planned
		NLT	in mind
		KJV, NASB, NET, NRSV, ESV	provided

HEBREWS CHAPTER TWELVE

Greek Word	Hebrews	English Version and Translation	
εὐπερίστατος	12:1	ESV, NRSV, NET	clings so closely
		KJV	so easily beset
		NASB, NIV, TNIV	so easily entangles
		NLT	so easily trips up
νέφος	12:1	NLT	huge cloud
		NIV, TNIV, NET, NASB, NRSV, ESV, KJV	great cloud
ὄγκος	12:1	NASB	encumbrance
		NIV, TNIV	everything that hinders
		ESV, KJV, NRSV, NET, NLT	weight
τελειωτής	12:2	KJV	finisher
		NLT	perfects
		ESV, NASB, NET, NIV, NRSV, TNIV	perfecter
ἀναλογίζομαι	12:3	NET, NLT	think of

		ESV, KJV, NASB, NRSV, TNIV, NIV	consider
ἀνταγωνίζομαι	12:4	KJV, NASB	striving
		ESV, NRSV, NIV, NET, TNIV, NLT	struggle
ἀντικαθίστημι	12:4	NLT	given your lives
		KJV, NASB, NET, NRSV, NIV, TNIV, ESV	resisted
ἐκλανθάνομαι	12:5	All	forgotten
ὀλιγωρέω	12:5	KJV	despise
		ESV, NASB, NRSV	regard lightly
		NLT, NIV, TNIV	make light
		NET	scorn
νόθος	12:8	KJV	bastards
		TNIV	not legitimate
		ESV, NASB, NET, NLT, NRSV, NIV	illegitimate
τροχιά	12:13	All	paths
πρωτοτόκια	12:16	NIV, TNIV	inheritance rights
		ESV, KJV, NASB, NET, NLT, NRSV	birthright
μετέπειτα	12:17	NRSV, NET	later
		ESV, KJV, NASB, TNIV, NIV, NLT	afterward
γνόφος	12:18	KJV	blackness
		ESV, NASB, NET, NLT, NRSV, TNIV, NIV	darkness
θύελλα	12:18	ESV, KJV, NRSV	tempest
		NASB, NET, NLT	whirlwind
		NIV, TNIV	storm
φαντάζομαι	12:21	NET	the scene
		ESV, KJV, NASB, NIV, NLT, NRSV, TNIV	the sight
φοβερός, ὁ	12:21	KJV, NASB	terrible
		NLT	frightened

Greek Word	Hebrews	English Version and Translation	
		ESV, NET, NIV, NRSV, TNIV	terrifying
πανήγυρις	12:22	KJV	company
		ESV, NRSV	festal gathering
		NLT	joyful gathering
		NET	assembly
		NIV, TNIV	joyful assembly
		NASB	(no translation)
δέος	12:28	KJV	godly fear
		ESV, NASB, NET, NIV, NLT, NRSV, TNIV	awe
εὐαρέστως	12:28	KJV, NIV, TNIV	acceptably
		ESV, NASB, NRSV	acceptable
		NET	pleasing
		NLT	(not translated)
εὐλάβεια	12:28	NET	devotion
		NLT	holy fear
		ESV, KJV, NASB, NIV, NRSV, TNIV	reverence
καταναλίσκω	12:29	NET, NLT	devouring
		KJV, NASB, NIV, NRSV, ESV, TNIV	consuming

HEBREWS CHAPTER THIRTEEN

Greek Word	Hebrews	English Version and Translation	
κακουχέω	13:3	KJV	suffer adversity
		NASB, NET	ill-treated
		NRSV	tortured
		ESV, NIV, NLT, TNIV	mistreated
συνδέω	13:3	KJV	bound with
		NIV	fellow prisoner
		TNIV	together with them in prison
		ESV, NASB, NET, NLT, NRSV	in prison with
βοηθός	13:6	All	helper
αἴνεσις	13:15	All	praise

εὐαρεστέω	13:16	ESV, NRSV	pleasing
		NLT	please
		KJV, NET, NIV, TNIV, NASB	is pleased
εὐποιΐα	13:16	All	do good
ἀλυσιτελής	13:17	KJV, NASB	unprofitable
		NRSV	harmful
		ESV, NIV, NET	no advantage
		NLT	not be for your benefit
		TNIV	no benefit
ὑπείκω	13:17	NLT	do what they say
		NASB, NIV, TNIV, NET, ESV, NRSV, KJV	submit

Chart Comments

Part 1: Introductory Considerations in Hebrews

Authorship of Hebrews

1–3 THE AUTHORSHIP OF HEBREWS

From the earliest beginnings of the church, the authorship of Hebrews baffled church leaders and commentators alike. No less than 19 options have been offered in order to identify the author of this stupendous canonical work. Thus, this series of charts on the authorship of Hebrews begins with **Chart 1** that identifies when these 19 options were first put forward as a possibility. **Chart 2**, however, advances our observation to include how these various options have fared throughout the centuries: The Early Church & Church Fathers (150–600, Middle Ages (600–1500), Humanists & Reformers (1500–1750), and Critical Scholarship (1750 to present). Needless to say, Chart 2 is not exhaustive, but it does show the debate is not new, has generated many options, and continues to this day. The final chart in this series, **Chart 3**, identifies where the majority of contemporary commentators stand concerning the authorship of Hebrews. Although numerous commentators were of value here, I am indebted to these works in particular for Chart 2: Ellingworth's *The Epistle to the Hebrews* (1993), 3–21; D. Guthrie's *New Testament Introduction* (1990), 668–82; Koester's *Hebrews* (2001), 19–46.

4–7 THE DEBATED CONSIDERATIONS ABOUT THE AUTHORSHIP OF HEBREWS

This series of charts serves to identify the debated considerations of a select number of options for the authorship of Hebrews: Barnabas (**Chart 4**), Paul (**Chart 5**), Luke (**Chart 6**), and Apollos (**Chart 7**). The four charts represent what appears to be the front-running options and the pros and cons for each perspective. Once again, numerous commentators and journal articles were of value here, but I am indebted to these works in particular: Allen's *Lukan Authorship of Hebrews* (2010), 29–61; Black's "Who Wrote Hebrews? Internal and External Evidence Reexamined"; Guthrie's "The Case for Apollos as the Author of Hebrews"—the latter two found in *Faith and Mission* 18:2 (2001): 3–26, 41–56.

Destination, Recipients, and Dating of Hebrews

8–9 THE DESTINATION OF HEBREWS

Chart 8 provides five potential destinations for the book of Hebrews: Rome (and Italy), Jerusalem (and Judea), Antioch of Syria, Colossae, and the city of Cyrene. The chart also provides information about the location, founding, ethnicity, and primary sources that reference each city, which may be used to undergird any particular option. A glance at **Chart 9**, however, shows which option most current commentators choose: Rome. Various articles from the *Anchor Bible Dictionary*, and the works of Strabo and Josephus are the primary sources undergirding Chart 8. Guthrie's *New Testament Introduction* (1990), 696–701; and Koester's *Hebrews* (2001), 48–50 were also helpful resources.

10–12 The Recipients of Hebrews

These three charts describe the debate concerning the recipients of Hebrews and the positions current commentators hold. Based upon the assumption that there are two prominent views—a Jewish Christian audience or a Gentile Christian audience—**Chart 10** concentrates on the pros and cons for a Jewish Christian audience which, in turn, illuminate the pros and cons for a Gentile Christian audience. **Chart 11**, however, clearly shows the option most current commentators choose: Jewish Christians. **Chart 12** further supports the opinion that the recipients were Christians. Although numerous commentators were of value here, I am indebted to these works in particular for Chart 10: Guthrie's *New Testament Introduction* (1990), 682–87; and Koester's *Hebrews* (2001), 46–48.

The term "partner" (μέτοχος, *metochos*) from **Chart 12** is of particular significance. On the one hand, in Heb 3:1, "holy brethren" emphasizes the community's partnership with one another, people who share in spiritual realities as sons of God (2:10, 13), who are members of the same family (2:11), and who have common use of Jesus' riches (6:4; cf. *TLNT*, 490). They are, however, joined also to God due to their "heavenly calling." Thus they are "fellow–Christians," namely partners with one another due to their call from God via Jesus, the Son (cp. 2:11–12). On the other hand, in Heb 3:14, three slightly different nuances exist. (1) "We have become partakers of Christ" (KJV, NASB) and the closely related (2) "We share in Christ" (RSV, NIV, ESV, NLT) apply both to possession of, and activities with, Christ. The better rendering (3) "We have become partners with Christ" (NRSV, NET) implies that the community takes part in activities and experiences with King Jesus. The added presence of βέβαιος (*bébaios*) with μέτοχος (*metochos*) appears to emphasize an associate "partnership" with Christ in a legal sense, one that is similar to a business relationship. "Simon and the others who were in the same boat … signaled *to their associates* in the other boat that they should come help them" (Luke 5:7; cf. 2 Cor 6:14; Lane 1:87). Thus, it may be said that believers have a legally binding partnership "with Christ."

13–15 The Dating of Hebrews

These three charts unveil who potentially received this unique letter and pinpoint the view most commonly shared among commentators. **Chart 13** uncovers evidence that is most agreed upon by all commentators in determining the date of Hebrews, then moves to facts that could support either position (pre 70 or post 70 date), and finally to those debatable proofs. The chart is open-ended in that it leaves you, the reader, to make the call. In the event, however, that you would rather allow someone else to make the call, we provide **Chart 14** which discloses the various views of current commentators. **Chart 15** reveals not only the dating of Hebrews but also the dating of the entire New Testament by NT scholars. Although numerous commentators were of value here, these were of particular help: Attridge's *Hebrews* (1989), 6–9; Ellingworth's commentary on Hebrews (1993), 29–33; Guthrie's *New Testament Introduction* (1990), 701–05; and Koester's *Hebrews* (2001), 50–54.

Genre and Structure of Hebrews

16–18 The Genre of Hebrews

Chart 16 opens this series with the pros and cons of a very popular view, namely that Hebrews is a sermonic letter. **Chart 17** counters with another possibility—that Hebrews is a mixed letter of exhortation with paraenetic, admonishing, encouraging, and consolation features. Naturally, we close the series with **Chart 18** that discloses the various views of current commentators. For a more detailed overview about the genre of the General Letters see Bateman, "The Genre of the General Letters" (2013) and Stowers, *Letter Writing in Greco-Roman Antiquity* (1986), 91–151. Although numerous commentators were of value here, these were of particular help: Ellingworth's *The Epistle to the Hebrews* (1993), 59–62; and Koester's *Hebrews* (2001), 80–82. Charles Martin created Chart 17.

19–24 The Structure of Hebrews

Like the series of charts above, this series on the structure of Hebrews begins with recognizing the pros and cons for the various options put forward for the structure of Hebrews (**Chart 19**), and then identifies where the majority of contemporary commentators stand concerning the structure of Hebrews (**Chart 20**). The subsequent charts, however, name both proponents for and specific samplings of several thematic arrangements (**Chart 21**), two rhetorical arrangements (**Chart 22**), several chiastic arrangements (**Chart 23**), and one text-linguistic arrangement (**Chart 24**) for the Book of Hebrews. Of particular significance for the compiling of Chart 18 were Attridge's *Hebrews* (1989), 17–21; Koester's *Hebrews* (2001), 83–92; Lane's *Hebrews 1–8* (1991), lxxxiv–xcviii; Mitchell's *Hebrews* (2007), 17–21; and O'Brien's *The Letter to the Hebrews* (2010), 22–34.

Canonicity of Hebrews

25–29 THE CANONICITY OF HEBREWS

This series of five charts traces the acceptance of Hebrews' canonicity historically. **Chart 25** is simply a canonical overview of the New Testament from Nix and Geisler's *A General Introduction to the Bible* (1986), 295. **Chart 26** spots the placement of Hebrews within different manuscripts (not an exhaustive list), the manuscript's date, and the manuscript's geographical location/family. For these canonical placements of Hebrews, I am indebted to Metzger's *A Textual Commentary on the Greek New Testament* (1992), 591. **Chart 27** is a listing of early church leaders and the portions of Hebrews they cited in their respective writings. This is not an exhaustive list; Scripture citations can often be found in the footnotes or appendices of collections of early works. Reference numbers to the pertinent passages in the ancient text follow its name. Readers should be aware, however, that numbering systems vary, sometimes including book, chapter and line, but other times just chapter or line number. Many texts can be located using the index in Volume 3 of Jurgens's *The Faith of the Early Fathers* (1979). Church Fathers marked with an * signify readings found in Schaff's *A Select Library of the Nicene and Post–Nicene Fathers of the Christian Church* (1979). **Charts 28–29** illustrate the reality that Hebrews was sometimes included among the early church canons (**Chart 28**) and sometimes it was not (**Chart 29**). A commentary that was particularly helpful was Ellingworth's *The Epistle to the Hebrews* (1993), 34.

Part 2: Old Testament and Second Temple Influences in Hebrews

Old Testament Quotes and Allusions

30–34 THE OLD TESTAMENT IN HEBREWS

This series of charts lists both direct quotations and allusions found in Hebrews. When addressing direct quotations, it is helpful to note that 54 out of 303 verses contain direct quotations from the Old Testament. (Bateman, *Early Jewish Hermeneutics and Hebrews* 1:5–13 (1997), 247.) Thus, eighteen percent of Hebrews consists of direct quotations from the Old Testament. On the one hand, **Chart 30** lists 36 Old Testament quotes that occur in Hebrews. On the other hand, **Chart 31** categorizes the quotations by way of Old Testament divisions: Pentateuch, Historical and Prophetic Books, and Poetic Books. Similarly, **Chart 32** lists 28 different allusions from the Old Testament, and **Chart 33** categorizes the allusions by way of OT divisions: Pentateuch, Historical and Prophetic Books, and Poetic Books. All four charts note where they can be found in the Hebrew Bible, Septuagint and the Book of Hebrews. The series closes with **Chart 34**. It cites all the people from the Old Testament named in Hebrews, Old Testament references, the event for which they are known, and where exactly they are named in Hebrews. Charts 88–91 are technical companions to these five charts.

Jewish Cultic System

35–38 THE TABERNACLE

This series of charts both illustrates and identifies biblical references for the tabernacle as mentioned in both the Pentateuch and Hebrews 9. The concept for this series of charts arose from Koester's diagram that compared the tabernacle of the Old Testament with the one in Hebrews (*Hebrews*, 2001, 403). **Chart 35** points us to the beginning when in the Book of Exodus God directed Moses concerning both the structure and furniture for the tabernacle. Naturally, the tabernacle is referenced elsewhere in the Pentateuch, which is precisely the point for **Chart 36**. It provides additional Pentateuch references to the tabernacle but with an emphasis upon the tabernacle's sanctuary. **Chart 37** shifts to Hebrews 9 where the author of Hebrews describes the tabernacle's sanctuary, particularly the placement of the tabernacle's furniture. This series of charts on the tabernacle concludes with diagrams comparing the tabernacle in Exodus with that of Hebrews in **Chart 38**. It also compares information about the tabernacle as it is found in Hebrews, Exodus, and Josephus.

The "tent" (RSV, NRSV, NET, NLT) or "tabernacle" (KJV, NASB, NIV) occurs in Hebrews 9:2, 3, 6. These three appearances of "tabernacle" speak of the earthly tabernacle proper, constructed by the Israelites in the wilderness of Sinai, which measured approximately 75 feet by 25 feet (Exod 26:1–37; 36:8–38; Josephus, *Ant.* 3.115–21). Although a single entity, the tabernacle was divided into two sections: the holy place and the holy of holies (Josephus, *Ant.* 3.124–26). The holy place, or as the author of Hebrews says in 9:2, "the first room" (NIV), "first section" (ESV), or "outer one" (NET) measured approximately 50 feet by 25 feet. It contained two pieces of furniture: *the lampstand* (Exod 25:31–40; 26:35; 37:17–24; 40:4; Josephus, *Ant.* 3.144–46; Philo, *Mos.* 2:102) and *the table* on which the consecrated bread was placed (Exod 25:23–30, 26:35; 37:10–16, 40:4; 1 Chron 28:16; 2 Chron 29:18; 1 Macc 1:22; Josephus, *Ant.* 3.139–43; Philo, *Mos.* 2:104). The holy of holies (NIV: "a room" or NET: "a tent"), which was behind a second veil or curtain, measured about 25 feet square. It too contained, according to Heb 9:3–4, two pieces of furniture: *the golden altar of incense* (different placement than Exod 30:1–10, 37:25–28; Josephus, *Ant.* 3.147–48) and the ark (Exod 25:10–22, 26:34; 37:1–9; Josephus, *Ant.* 3.134–37; Philo, *Mos.* 2:95). The ark itself contained three items: a golden urn of manna (Exod 16:33–34; Philo, *Congr.* 100), Aaron's rod that budded (Num 17:1–10), and the stone tablets of the covenant (Exod 31:18; Deut 9:9, 10:2; 1 Kgs 8:9; 2 Chron 5:10; Josephus, *Ant.* 3.138; Philo, *Mos.* 2:97). Although the author could have said more (9:5b, and we wish he had since he differs with the Exodus account at times), he belabors the description merely to emphasize the "earthly" nature of the tabernacle, as opposed to the "true tabernacle" mentioned previously in Heb 8:2, as well as to illustrate the cultic regulations that governed this tent of meeting (9:6–7).

39–40 OLD TESTAMENT FEASTS AND CELEBRATIONS, AND THE DAY OF ATONEMENT

These two charts provide information about Old Testament forms of worship, celebrations and sacrifice. In the Pentateuch, God sets forth eight feasts and celebrations for God's chosen people to practice throughout the year, as well as the observance of the Day of Atonement. Obviously, a lot of time has passed since God set forth the feasts and celebrations, yet **Chart 39** specifies three that are mentioned in Hebrews. **Chart 40** is devoted solely to the Day of Atonement as presented in Leviticus 16 answering five questions (who officiates, what is needed, what happens to the animals, who benefits, how often does the event occur), and then comparing the Day of Atonement with the presentation in the Book of Hebrews. A very helpful source for Chart 39 was Archer's *A Survey of Old Testament Introduction* (1974), 244.

In Hebrews, the author alludes to the Day of Atonement in 9:7 with "once a year," an event repeated annually in the life of a Jew (10th Tishri = Sept/Oct; cf. Exod 30:10; Lev 16:34; cp. Philo, *Legat.* 306–07; Josephus, *Ant.* 3.240). Second, and of equal importance is the term "once." Unlike other occurrences where "once" conveys a unique and unrepeatable event, in Heb 9:7 "once" conveys a numerical concept (like that of being stoned: 2 Cor 11:25). Thus once a year, during the annual Day of Atonement (also referred to as *Yom Kippur*), the high priest enters into the holy of holies (3 Macc 1:11). This is the one and only day the high priest may enter the "inner tent" of the tabernacle or "the heart of the sanctuary" (Philo, *Ebr.* 135–36). The high priest first enters to seek propitiation (to be purged of guilt) for himself and his priestly family (Lev 16:6, 11; himself alone: Josephus, *Ant.* 3.243). He then enters a third time to seek propitiation for the entire community (Lev 16:34; Josephus, *Ant.* 3.241). One of many important *symbols* of the Day of Atonement is the scapegoat that is sent into the wilderness, and with it, the sins of the community (Lev 16:7–10, 20–22; Josephus, *Ant.* 3.241). God's loving compassion must have appeared larger than life on this day, since the event needed repeating year after year. The important observation to be made here, however, is that the author contrasts the continuous priestly activities in the holy place ("outer tent": 9:6) with the high priest's activity in the holy of holies ("inner tent," 9:7). Despite the contrast, the multiple offerings and the annual atonement sacrifice merge into one big ineffective regulation (9:25, 10:1–4).

Second Temple High Priesthood

41–47 SECOND TEMPLE HIGH PRIESTHOOD

This series of charts lists all the high priests who served during the second temple period. **Chart 41** is a simple overview of four major periods in Jewish history whereby the first and last of the high priests are listed for any given period, with dates and primary sources. Subsequent charts present information about each high priest who was in power during the Persian Period (**Chart 42**), Hellenistic Period (**Chart 43**), Hasmonean Period (**Chart 45**), and the Herodian Period (**Chart 47**). Each chart presents dates, primary sources, and the historical issues that plagued each high priest. They are based primarily upon James C. VanderKam's *From Joshua to Caiaphas: High Priests After the Exile* (Minneapolis: Fortress, 2005). Interspersed between these charts are two family trees: the Hasmonean Family Tree (**Chart 44**) and the Herodian Family Tree (**Chart 46**), which are from Maier's *Josephus: The Essential Writings* (1988). The family trees are intended to help orient users of the high priest charts to when certain individuals are named. For instance, Agrippa I appointed four high priests to their positions between 37–48 C.E. (**Chart 47**). Who was Herod Agrippa I? A quick glance at the Herodian Family Tree identifies him to be the grandson of Herod the Great and a descendant from the Hasmonean dynasty (**Chart 45**). One might naturally ask, "How do these charts help in our study of Hebrews?" Quite simply, it is due to the discontentment with the high priests during both the Hasmonean and Herodian periods that messianic expectations began to peak. The concept of a combined office of king-priest began with Aristobulus and the Hasmoneans (**Chart 45**). The Old Testament system of high priests was eventually replaced with the coming of Jesus as divine royal priest after the order of Melchizedek. For a historical overview of the significance of that transition see Bateman's "Expectations of Israel's King" in *Jesus the Messiah* (2012).

Second Temple Messianic Figures

48–50 SECOND TEMPLE MESSIANIC FIGURES

This series of three charts is actually part one of a two-part series. Whereas **Charts 48–50** present multiple portraits of messiah, **Charts 51–53** draw attention to the Melchizedek figure. Here in part one, however, we address Second Temple messianic portraits. **Chart 48** lists four figures: prophet, high priest, king, and heavenly or apocalyptic figure, who are labeled "anointed ones" in both the Old Testament and extrabiblical literature. (The terms "messiah of Aaron" and "messiah of Israel" from the DSS are interpreted as high priest and king, respectively. Verse numbering in the DSS may vary slightly depending on which translation is used.) **Chart 49** identifies the numerous portraits of messiah in extrabiblical literature from the Second Temple period, which include the fact that a messiah is a human figure, an authority figure, and a relational figure in that he has a special relationship with God. **Chart 50** closes out this series with a listing of seven different messianic titles usually employed when people wrote about a messianic figure in extrabiblical literature: son, son of God, son of man, messiah, heir, Melchizedek, high priest. All of these charts appear in Bateman in "Expectations of Israel's King" in *Jesus the Messiah* (2012).

51–54 Melchizedek and Other Regal Priest Figures

This series of charts, part two of the previous series, deals with the concept of "regal priest" with particular attention to Melchizedek. **Chart 51** actually expands on Chart 48 which mentions a "Heavenly or Apocalyptic Figure" in 11QMelch (11Q13) II, 8–9, and on Chart 50 which mentions a "Melchizedek Figure," by listing where Melchizedek is mentioned in other Jewish literature. (Verse numbering in the DSS may vary slightly depending on which translation is used.) **Chart 52** goes on to compare similarities and differences concerning Melchizedek in Genesis 14, Psalm 110, 11Q13, and Heb 1–7. **Chart 53** is a description of regal priests in the Old Testament and how they measure up to Jesus in Hebrews. **Chart 54** closes the series with a description of Jesus as regal priest in Hebrews, with emphasis on his position and his character. The initial idea for this series of charts on the Melchizedek figure came from Hagner's *Encountering the Book of Hebrews* (2002), 100, 104. Chart 52 was created by Schwerdtfeger and may be found with detailed discussion in "Portraits of Melchizedek: Tracing the Development from the Old Testament to 11Q13 to Hebrews" (2010), Appendix 1.

Of particular significance to this set of charts is the momentous yet ever so brief encounter between Melchizedek and Abraham in Gen 14:18–20, which serves as our primary source of information. After defeating four kings from Mesopotamia and rescuing his nephew, Abraham meets Melchizedek, a Canaanite king and priest of Salem. (Salem was a Jebusite stronghold of old Jerusalem, see 2 Sam 5:6–10.) Unlike other regal priests, however, this Canaanite royal priest serves the "Most High God." (*El Elyon* means "one sovereign God who created the universe"). While some Jewish traditions recognize Melchizedek as a human figure in history (Josephus, *J. W.* 6.438–39; *Ant.* 1.179–181; Philo, *Abr.* 235; but allegorized in *Leg.* 3.79–82), others *elevate* him to angelic status (4QAmram[b], 4Q401; perhaps 4Q280, 4Q286, 11Q13) or an exalted priestly figure (4Q491 with 11Q13; cf. Eskola, 84). Like the former Jewish traditions, Heb 7:1–3 also accepts the humanity of Melchizedek, but with a twist. In Heb 7:1–2, the extracted portions from Gen 14:18–20 direct attention to Melchizedek's *kingship* and *priesthood* with particular stress on his priestly functions (he blesses Abraham and he receives a tithe from Abraham, cf. Heb 7:4, 6–7, 9–10). Commenting briefly on Melchizedek as king, the author interprets his name, "king of righteousness" (*melech* = Hebrew word for "king"; *zedek* = Hebrew word for "righteousness") and describes the sort of king he was, a king of righteousness. Thus selected facts about Melchizedek from Genesis 14 are restated and reapplied to advance the reader's Old Testament knowledge about what it means to be a priest "according to the order of Melchizedek," and thereby complete an OT concept. The author's advancement comes in Heb 7:3.

55 The Role of Divine Beings in Jewish Theology

Chart 55 reveals two things about angels in Jewish theology. First, it reveals the references to angels in the Old Testament and the continuity between the Old Testament and extrabiblical material. Second, it reveals the significance of angels to Jewish theology during the latter part of the Second Temple period (167 B.C.E. to 70 C.E.) and even exposes a progression in presentations of angels in extrabiblical Jewish material. (Please note that there are discrepancies in angel names in the *Enoch* texts. In addition, verse numbering in the Dead Sea Scrolls may vary slightly depending on which translation is used.) It was during the Second Temple period that Jewish angelology expanded which, in turn, underscores an emphasis upon angels. Nevertheless, a disparity of beliefs about angels is apparent in Qumran literature. For example, The Songs of the Sabbath Sacrifice (4Q400–407, 11Q17, etc.) reveals a fully developed angelology, but only some *pesharim* employ angelic terms (4Q174, 4Q177, etc.), and the Temple Scroll (11Q19) is silent on heavenly beings. Needless to say, several works were of significance in the making of this chart: Mach, "Angels" in EDSS (2000); Davidson, *Angels at Qumran* (1992); and Isaac, "1 (Ethiopic Apocalypse of) Enoch," 5–11. This chart was co-created with Charles Martin. (Chart 68 is another chart that addresses angels, namely the superiority of the Son to angelic beings.)

Part 3: Theology in Hebrews

The Godhead in Hebrews

56–59 Portraits of the Godhead in Hebrews

This series of charts provides characteristics of the godhead in Hebrews that are both unique to each member as well as shared. **Chart 56** begins the series by providing various descriptions of God as the living creator, relational, yet judging God evident throughout Hebrews. **Chart 57** moves to the presentation of Jesus as human, regal priest, and God. Of particular significance is **Chart 58** where the shared portraits of God and Jesus occur in Hebrews: creator, eternal, ruler, and worshiped to name a few. This series of charts ends with **Chart 59** in which the portrait of God's Spirit is compared with how the Spirit is portrayed in the Dead Sea Scrolls (translations are from Wise's *The Dead Sea Scrolls*) and in Hebrews. (Verse numbering in the DSS may vary slightly depending on which translation is used.) Where Charts 56–58 were influenced by Ellingworth's *The Epistle to the Hebrews* (1993), 64–68, Chart 59 was created for "Response to Nathan Holsteen's 'The Trinity in the Letter to the Hebrews'" for the God and God Incarnate Study Group (Moderator: Douglas Blount) at the Annual National Meeting of the ETS (Nov 2009).

60–64 Wisdom in Hebrews and Jesus as Wisdom

Charts 60–64 reflect discussions of Wisdom terminology, which are frequent in the New Testament. For instance, compare Matt 11:27–30 with Sir 51:23–27; John 1:1 with Wis 9:9; John 1:11, 14 with *1 En.* 42:2; 1 Cor 8:6 with Prov 3:19 and Wis 8:4–6; Col 1:15 with Prov 8:22, 25 and Wis 7:26; Col 1:17 with Sir 24:9; Heb 1:3 with Prov 8:27–30 and Wis 7:26. For Dunn, "Hellenistic Judaism of the LXX did not think of Wisdom as a 'hypostasis' or 'intermediary being' any more than did the Old Testament writers and the rabbis. Wisdom, like the name, the glory, the Spirit of Yahweh, was a way of asserting God's nearness, his involvement with his world, his concern for his people. All these words provided expressions of God's *immanence*, his active concern in creation, revelation and redemptions, while at the same time protecting his holy transcendence and wholly otherness." He further notes that "within Jewish monotheism … Wisdom never really becomes more than a personification … a way of speaking about God himself, of expressing God's active involvement with his world and his people without compromising his transcendence." Later Dunn avers, "Christ alone embodies God's Wisdom, that is God's creative, revelatory and redemption action, that what can be said of Wisdom can be said of Christ …," and continues, "the deity of Christ is the deity of Wisdom incarnate; that is, to recognize the deity of Christ is to recognize that in Christ God manifested himself, his power as Creator, his love as Saviour, in a full and final way." See Dunn, *Christology in the Making* (1980), ch. 6, esp. 176, 209, 212. For my discussion of Jesus as divine wisdom see Bateman, *Early Jewish Hermeneutics and Hebrews 1:5–13* (1997), 210–13. An abbreviated chart is in Hagner's *Encountering the Book of Hebrews* (2002), 42.

65 Titles Ascribed to Jesus in Hebrews and in the New Testament

Chart 65 is an expansion and redesign of Hagner's chart in *Encountering the Book of Hebrews* (2002), 65. It directs special attention, however, to titles ascribed to Jesus found only in Hebrews. Of particular significance are "pioneer" (ἀρχηγός) and "perfecter" (τελειωτής) for they serve as two significant titles for Jesus in Hebrews. Both titles are used exclusively for Jesus in the New Testament (Acts 3:15, 5:31; Heb 2:10, 12:2). To begin with, the noun ἀρχηγός means "pioneer." As it was in Hebrews 2:10, so it is in Hebrews 12:2. Jesus is more than merely the "author" (KJV, NRSB, NIV) of faith, he is the "pioneer" (RSV, NET) or "founder" (ESV) of our faith. This is not to say that Jesus was the first person to exhibit faith. It is, however, to say that Jesus is the first, the pioneer, who takes faith to its ultimate goal, going where no one person has gone before (Heb 11:4–38). He blazes the trail (Heb 6:20) and leads the way for many sons and daughters (2:10) to experience all of God's promises—promises never experienced by Old Testament saints (Heb 11:39–40; cp. Koester, 523. See the previous entry for 2:10. Likewise and closely related, the noun "perfecter" conveys the idea of completion.) "Perfecter" (τελειωτής) is found nowhere in Greek literature. Perhaps coined by the author of Hebrews, it is found only in a few Christian texts. The title "perfecter" in Hebrews 12:2 affirms the fact that God's ultimate goal of faith is completed or accomplished in Jesus (cf. BAGD 810c; BDAG 997a; *TDNT* 8:86).

Another significant title ascribed to Jesus found on this chart and unique to Hebrews is "apostle" (ἀπόστολος). It speaks of a person having been *sent* by someone to someone else. Apostles are messengers from God with extraordinary status (BAGD 99d 3, BDAG 122b 2). In the LXX, ἀπόστολος is the Greek rendering for the Hebrew term שָׁלוּחַ (*šālûah*). The prophet Ahijah, for example, was *sent* to deliver a divine message to the wife of King Jeroboam when she came and asked about her sick son (3 Kgdms 12:24k [1 Kgs 14:6]; cf. *TDNT*, 1:413–14, 423). Although used only once in the New Testament to speak of Jesus, the idea that Jesus was an ἀπόστολος is observed throughout the Gospels (Mark 9:37; Matt 10:40; 15:24; Luke 10:16; and John 3:17; 6:57; 7:29; 8:42; 11:42; 17:21; cf. Gal 4:4). Jesus, having been sent by God, spoke God's message (see Mark 1:21–22; Luke 4:31–32; John 3:34, 7:8) and acted with God's authority (see Mark 1:23–28; Luke 4:33–37; John 5:36–38). Thus, the author rightly speaks of Jesus as a messenger (an ἀπόστολος) who was sent by God, through whom God delivered His message (cp. Heb 1:2 with Heb 2:12's quotation of Ps 21:23 LXX [22:22]).

66 Titles Ascribed to Jesus in Hebrews and Shared in the New Testament

Chart 66 is a listing of titles ascribed to Jesus in Hebrews and other New Testament books. Yet, there are nuanced differences to take into consideration when using this chart. For instance, in the Gospels and Acts the title Lord is used from two differing perspectives. In the pre-resurrection perspective "lord" tends to be a typical designation for Messiah (Luke 2:11; John 11:27), while "Lord" in a post resurrection understanding escalates to be a title Jesus shares with God the Father (John 20:28; Acts 2:36; 10:36; Rom 10:9; 1 Cor 12:3; 2 Cor 4:5; Phil 2:11; 1 Tim 6:15; Rev 17:14; 19:16). Consequently, Paul's use of "Lord" for Jesus had to be very specific to be listed on this chart. If "Lord" could refer to either God or Jesus, it was not listed. Furthermore, the use of "Son of Man" in the Gospels differs from that in Hebrews. It is interesting to note that Paul never uses that title for Jesus. Nevertheless, these nuanced differences between a pre-resurrection and post-resurrection presentation demonstrate a progressive understanding by the early followers of Jesus as they retell the story about Jesus. Hebrews obviously tells a post-resurrection story about Jesus.

Theological Themes in Hebrews

67 Better Than (κρείττων) Comparisons in Hebrews

Chart 67 lists all the "better than" (κρείττων) statements in Hebrews. Since I could think of no way to improve this nicely designed chart, I lifted it—with permission—from Girdwood and Verkruyse's commentary *Hebrews* **(1997), 268. Chart 21 is a good companion chart. Subsequent charts expand and develop this initial listing: Chart 68** = Jesus better than the angels; **Charts 69–70** = Jesus offering a better covenant.

68 Angels and Jesus Comparisons in Hebrews

Chart 68 focuses attention on angels in the book of Hebrews, particularly as the Son is said to inherit a name "better than the angels." It is interesting that angels are described as "ministers" (λειτουργός) in Heb 1:7. The term "ministers" (λειτουργός) is part of a significant word group that speaks of someone engaged in special service on behalf of a superior person (8:2, 6; 9:21; 10:11). In keeping with Heb 1:7, angels are presented as engaged in the service of the Son, the divine Davidite. The recipients of this angelic service are believers. Thus angels are "ministers" (λειτουργός) of the Son, "ministering" (λειτουργικός) on behalf of the Son to care for all those who will receive salvation through the Son (cp. NLT). The ideas behind Charts 67–78 are grounded in Hagner's *Encountering the Book of Hebrews* (2002), 46, 101, 104–05, 122, 137.

There is yet one other reference to angels in Hebrews. Cherubim are also mentioned in Hebrews 9:5 as ornaments in the earthly tabernacle. In fact, this is the only reference to Cherubim in the New Testament. Yet, in the LXX and extrabiblical material, Cherubim (also referred to as "living creatures") are winged celestial beings of governance (cp. Ezek 1:22–28 with 10:20; *1 En.* 61:10) who appear to possess both human and animal (lion, ox and eagle) characteristics (Ezek 1:5–10; 10:8, 14, 21; cp. *Apoc. Ab.* 18:3–13). Josephus contends, however, "no one can say or imagine what they looked like" (Josephus, *Ant.* 8.73). They serve as God's guardians of the tree of life (Gen 3:24; cf. *1 En.* 20:7), as God's vehicle to move through the universe (2 Sam 22:11, Ps 18:10, cp. Ezek 10:19–20), and as God's means of departing from Jerusalem's temple before its destruction (Ezek 10:1–10). They also appear to surround God's throne (Ps 80:1, 99:1; 4Q405 20 II, 6–9; *1 En.* 14:18–20; *2 En.* 21:1; Josephus, *Ant.* 3.137). When mentioned in connection with the earthly tabernacle and the temple, they are prominent ornamental figures. Cherub figures are crafted from gold (Exod 25:18, 37:7; Josephus, *Ant.* 8.72) or of wood overlaid with gold (1 Kgs 6:23–32; 2 Chron 3:10–13), which overshadow the cover on the ark (Exod 25:19–20, 37:8–9; 1 Sam 4:4; 1 Kgs 8:6–7; 1 Chron 13:6; 2 Chron 5:7–8; Philo, *Mos.* 2.97). Cherub figures are embroidered on the curtains or veil separating the holy of holies from the holy place (Exod 26:1, 31–33, 36:35; 2 Chron 3:14; and an allusion to cherubim in Josephus, *Ant.* 3.126). Finally, carved engravings of cherubs appeared on the walls and doors of the temple (1 Kgs 6:29, 32, 34–35). In Hebrews 9:5, the author mentions the cherubim in closing his description of the earthly tabernacle and its furniture as regulations prescribed in the first covenant. The prominence of cherubim, as ornaments in the earthly tabernacle and temple, warrant their mention in Hebrews 9:5. Of course in the heavenly tabernacle, cherubim are not ornamental figures crafted, embroidered, or carved. They are real living beings.

69–71 Covenant in Hebrews

Charts 69–71 draw attention to the concept of "covenant" (διαθήκη) in Hebrews. While **Chart 69** identifies what the covenant is, who mediates it, and whom it benefits and how in Hebrews, **Chart 70** reveals the continuities and discontinuities between the old and new covenants. **Chart 71** contrasts the Mosaic covenant in Exodus 19–20 with the new covenant in Hebrews 12. (Tim Sigler of the Moody Bible Institute offers this set of contrasts between the covenants.)

Of the thirty-three New Testament occurrences of "covenant," over half appear in Hebrews (7:22; 8:6, 7, 8, 9 [twice], 10; 9:4 [twice], 15 [twice], 16, 17, 20; 10:16, 29; 12:24; 13:20). Instances also exist in Hebrews where "covenant" is merely implied and thus, various translations insert the term for clarity (8:7, 13; 9:1). The Jewish concept of covenant denotes the special kind of relationship believed to exist between the one and only God and Israel. In the LXX, "covenant" (διαθήκη) not only translates the Hebrew word *běrît* but also represents a significant development in Jewish thinking. "It is" as Philo says, "a symbol of the grace which God has set between Himself Who proffers it and man who receives it. And this is the crowning benefaction, that there is nothing between God and the soul save the virgin grace" (cf. Philo, *Mut.* 52–53). Thus "covenant" (διαθήκη) decisively makes the covenant relationship between Israel and God *asymmetrical*, in that it is initiated, implemented, and governed by God alone (cf. BAGD 183a–b 2; BDAG 228b 2; *TDNT* 2:126–29; Holmén, *Jesus & Jewish Covenant Theology*, 40–41). The author of Hebrews, likewise, speaks of God's initiated and implemented covenants. The theme of covenant runs throughout all of Hebrews. The Davidic (2 Kgdms [2 Sam] 7:14 in Heb 1:5), the Abrahamic (Gen 22:16 in Heb 6:13) and the new covenant (Jer 38 LXX [31]: 31–34 in Heb 8:8–12) are all part of the author's argument, namely that God has begun to fulfill his covenant promises through the Son, namely Jesus the royal high priest.

In Hebrews 8:6, Jesus is presented as high priest who is a mediator of a better covenant, a covenant based upon God's promises to Jeremiah. The term "mediator" (μεσίτης) signifies a "neutral" person "between contestants or parties" "to remove a disagreement or to reach a common goal." He or she is an arbitrator that both sides can trust and one who can negotiate peace (cf. *TDNT* 4:599; BAGD 506d; BDAG 634b; *TLNT* 2:465–68). For instance, Caesar Augustus was the "neutral" person who negotiated peace between Herod the Great and his sons, Alexander and Aristobulus, those whom Herod had accused of treason (Josephus, *Ant.* 16.118–19;

cp. 16.24–26). Although the term occurs only once in the LXX (Job 9:33), in other Jewish literature, angelic beings (*T. Dan.* 6:2; Philo, *Somn.* 1:142–143) and Moses (*T. Mos.* 1:14; 3:12; Philo, *Mos.* 2:166 [Exod 32:31–32]; Gal 3:19–20) are described as mediators. In Heb 8:6, Jesus is the person, or more specifically, the regal priest (8:1), who is a mediator. What he mediates is a "better covenant" (8:6), which is based entirely upon what God promised through Jeremiah (Jer 38 LXX [31]:31–34, cp. Heb 8:8). Thus Jesus' mediation in Hebrews is *always* in relation to what God has initiated and implemented. God governs the covenant through Jesus, his appointed royal priest. The reason why Jesus is the mediator of the covenant is found in Hebrews 9.

In Hebrews 9:15, the author provides the reason (δια τουτο, *dia touto*) why Jesus is the mediator of God's covenant. Jesus, as high priest and sacrifice (9:11–12), is the prerequisite for, or the factor, that provides inner cleansing (9:13–14; cp. 1 Tim 2:5–6). Unlike the previous covenant and the priests who performed daily sacrifices of external rite or ritual purity (9:13; 10:1–3, 11), the effectiveness of Jesus' better sacrifice guarantees the effectiveness of God's better covenant promised in Jeremiah 31:31–34. Jesus is the mediator of the better or new covenant because God has declared Jesus' sacrifice to be more effective than those offered during the previous era of Mosaic law. Chart 70 has its roots in Hagner's *Encountering the Book of Hebrews* (2002), 101, 104.

72 Biblical Covenants of God's Program

Any theological understanding of Hebrews must begin with the Hebrew Scriptures where the theme of promise is introduced (Gen 1:1–2). **Chart 72** traces God's covenants as they were made and finally fulfilled in Jesus. The assumption of the chart is that God has a strategic program: *to reestablish his kingdom* on earth and *to redeem a people* to enter into that kingdom. This divine strategy seems evident in the opening and closing chapters of the Bible—Genesis introduces God's creation of all things, Revelation looks forward to God's creation of a new heaven and a new earth. Thus, there is a linear movement in Scripture in which God is advancing from an old created order (Gen 1–2; cp. Isa 66:22–23) to a new one (Rev 21:1–7; 22:1–4; cp. Rom 8:18–24; 2 Pet 3:13). God, however, does not reveal the details of his kingdom-redemptive program all at once. Each promise through the stages of human history incrementally reveals God's strategy. We can identify at least two stages/time periods/dispensations in the Hebrew Scriptures: Pre-Mosaic and Mosaic. God inaugurates the fulfillment of the Abrahamic, Davidic and new covenants during the life of Jesus. In fact, God's kingdom-redemption program is anchored in the life, death, and resurrection of Jesus. Like the era of promise, the era of fulfillment has two stages/time periods/dispensations: the church period where God's promises are inaugurated and the millennial period where God's promises are consummated and may, in fact, continue into the eternal state. God initiated his kingdom-redemptive program in the historical events of Jesus (Heb 1:2; 1 Pet 1:20). Jesus is the one through whom God has spoken (Heb 1:2a; 12:25), and the one whom God sent into the world to carry out God's plan (Heb 3:1b; 1 Pet 1:20; 1 John 4:9–10, 14; cf. Acts 3:18–21). See Bateman, "The Theology of the General Letters."

73 "Once for All" in Hebrews

Chart 73 quotes five pronouncements in Hebrews about the superiority of Jesus' sacrifice compared to all the others offered beforehand. "One of the striking affirmations in Hebrews," according to Hagner, "is the stress upon the 'once for all' character of Christ's sacrifices of the Levitical priesthood" (Hagner's *Encountering the Book of Hebrews* [2002], 105).

Although **Chart 73** merely lists five occurrences of the two words meaning "once for all" (ἅπαξ, ἐφάπαξ), the term "once" (ἅπαξ) occurs fourteen times in Hebrews (see Chart 102). The noun is first introduced in Heb 6:4: "Those who have once been enlightened." It is particularly important in 9:24-28, where the use of ἅπαξ in vv. 26, 27 and 28 drives home the uniqueness of Christ's sacrifice—a "once for all" event so efficacious that it rendered the Mosaic system obsolete. Verse 26 contrasts the absurd idea that Jesus' self-sacrifice would need continual repetition ("many times"; vv. 25–26a) with the reality of his one-time sacrifice. Then the author uses a proverbial wisdom statement: people are "appointed to die once" (9:27) to reinforce his point. Together, these verses speak of Christ's death and exaltation (cp. 1 Pet 3:18; Rom 6:10; 1 Cor 15:3–4; Attridge, *Hebrews*, 264). Here the author drives home his message with a passage from the Old Testament, saying, "Christ was offered once *to bear the sins of many*" (Isa 53:12). The life Jesus lived was unique and his unique sacrifice was so effective "he put away sin" (1:3b; 10:12; cp. 8:1).

In contrast to Hebrews 9:26, Hebrews 10:2 underscores the ineffectiveness of previous sacrifices. The imperfection of the Mosaic system of sacrifice is a theme the author continues to repeat (7:11, 18–19; 8:7; 9:9; 10:8–9, 11). Up until this point in time, no "once for all" purification existed in Judaism. Worshippers under the old covenant needed repeated sacrifices for ritual, *outward* purity (9:13), whereas worshippers under the new covenant receive *inner* purification (10:10, 14–18, 22) due to the unique and unrepeatable sacrifice of Jesus (9:26; cp. 10:10). Thus the point of 10:2 is that under the old covenant, Judaism lacked an effective sacrifice, but Jesus' "once for all" sacrifice was unique and definitive (cp. 7:27, 9:12).

74–76 Inheritance, Perfection and Other Concepts in Hebrews

This series of charts highlights themes of inheritance, perfection, glory, hope, heir, oath, promise, and word. These charts present "already-not yet" aspects of a believer's salvation. **Chart 74** discloses the future inheritance of a believer, the "not yet" aspects of our salvation. Although the concept of perfection is a vexing challenge in Hebrews, **Chart 75** traces this difficult theme of perfection that runs throughout the book. The chart surveys terms associated with perfection, then moves to identify the perfection of Jesus, who is the Christ, as well as the perfection of believers. **Chart 76** deals with several other theological themes that appear in Hebrews—glory, hope, heir, oath, promise, and word—as they are applicable to both Jesus and believers throughout the book of Hebrews. Charles Martin created Chart 75. Several sources proved helpful for Charts 74–75; two stand out: deSilva's *Perseverance in Gratitude*, 194–205; and Hagner's *Encountering the Book of Hebrews* (2002), 57, 136. One work proved extremely helpful for Chart 74: O'Brien, *The Letter to the Hebrews* (2010), 175, 194, 270, 399.

Of particular significance is the ***concept*** of "oath," about which two points must be made. On the one hand, God makes and then confirms his oath by appealing to himself ("he swore to himself") since he is without a superior (Heb 6:13–20). Unlike people who take oaths, "there is nothing amiss," according to Philo's comments on Gen 22:16, "in God bearing witness to himself. For who else would be capable of bearing witness to him? He alone shall affirm anything regarding himself, since he alone has unerringly exact knowledge of his own nature. God alone therefore is the strongest security first for himself, and in the next place for his deeds also, so that he naturally swore by himself when giving assurance regarding himself, a thing impossible for anyone else" (*Leg.* 3.205–07). God makes such an oath so that Abraham's "mind might be established more securely and firmly even than it was before" (Philo, *Abr.* 273). God's oath points to his unequivocal capability in and of himself to uphold his promise (Heb 6:17–18; cf. Ps 89:35), and thereby the oath serves as his bond. Thus the point is this: God's spoken bond of promise not only provided security to Abraham (cp. 6:15 with 11:12, 17–19), it also provides encouragement to Abraham's heirs of promise. On the other hand, the word "oath" occurs only in Hebrews (7:20, 21 [twice], 28). Yet it does appear in extrabiblical material. It was a "sworn affirmation" or "a confirmed oath" by Caesar Augustus, along with his council, that allowed the Jews to follow their customs (Josephus, *Ant.* 16.163; cf. Ezek 17:18–19, 1 Esd 8:93). Few translations capture the truest sense of the term, namely "confirmed with an oath" (NRSV, ESV; cf. *TDNT* 5:463) or "a sworn affirmation" (NET). Nevertheless, God's oath in Heb 6:13–20 guarantees his promise to Abraham, so too, God's oath in 7:21 is a bond of confirmation of the royal Son's priesthood. An even stronger statement exists in 7:20a with the double negative, "not without an oath." This affirmation "came after the law" in that, historically, Ps 110:4 (Heb 7:21), which in context conceptually echoes God's promise to David concerning his son Solomon (2 Sam 7:8–16), is subsequent to the OT Mosaic law given at Sinai. Thus unlike the Levitical Aaronic/Zadokite priesthood ("without a sworn oath" Heb 7:20b), God's oath to Jesus via Psalm 110:4 confirms the Son's new and eternal royal priesthood (cp. Ps 89:35).

77 The Theme of Rest in Hebrews

Chart 77 addresses the Jewish concept of rest in Hebrews from a historical, eschatological, and philosophical perspective. The term "rest" occurs eleven times in Hebrews 3:11–4:11 (noun: 3:11, 18; 4:1, 3 [twice], 5, 10, 11; verb: 4:4, 8, 10) and indicates a theme of great theological import. While making use of the Old Testament rest tradition (3:11), the author of Hebrews explicates the physical place of rest to be entrance into God's place of rest in heaven where God holds his own Sabbath celebration in contrast to the earthly place of rest in Canaan (4:4). As God's promise spans the ages (4:7), the faithful community of believers will not only enter into God's resting place with him, they also will join in the Sabbath celebration of God with angelic beings at the day of their salvation. In Hebrews the term "to enter" speaks exclusively of entrance into a local reality (inner shrine behind the curtain, 6:19, 20; the holy place, 9:12, 25; the sanctuary, 9:24; the world 10:5). Second, "that rest" (RSV, NASB, NIV, ESV) refers to the combining of Psalm 95:11 and Genesis 2:2 in 4:3b–5, which speaks of entrance into a "place of rest" (NLT) in heaven. As in other Jewish literature, such a concept is not merely a state of mind but "resting places without number" and "dwelling places of the holy ones and their resting–places" (*1 En.* 39:4, 45:3; cp. *2 En.* 61:2–3 [J] with John 14:2; 2 Esd 7:36; 8:48–52; perhaps *Jos. Asen.* 15:7). Likewise, there exists a place of eternal torment for communities of people who reject God (2 Esd 7:26–44). Like his Jewish counterparts, the author concerns himself with "a place of rest" *prepared for the faithful community* (cp. 2 Esd 7:88–99). He, too, addresses an event that remains outstanding, namely, a community entrance into a future resting place, an entrance into that world to come, an event which has yet to be realized (cp. Rev 21:1–22:5). This future resting place stands alongside other future local realities in Hebrews: "the coming world" (2:5); the heavenly city (11:10, 16; 12:22; 13:14); the heavenly fatherland (11:14); and the unshakeable kingdom (12:28). Thus entrance into "that rest" in 4:11 is entrance into God's heavenly place of rest and Sabbath celebration (of the future world to come) where believers will join in the ongoing Sabbath celebration of God "at the day of their salvation" (cf. *EDNT* 2:266). See also Jon Laansma's *I Will Give You Rest.*

78 THE THEME OF ETERNALITY IN HEBREWS

Chart 78 focuses attention on eternality in Hebrews. The term "forever" (εἰς τὸν αἰῶνα / εἰς τοὺς αἰῶνας) occurs eleven times in Hebrews (1:8 [twice]; 5:6; 6:20; 7:17, 21, 24, 28; 13:8, 21 [twice]). Originally when used of a Davidic king in the Old Testament, it spoke of the temporal duration of the regal priest's ruling authority. "May the king live always" (of David at the end of his life, 1 Kgs 1:31; of Artaxerxes, Neh 2:3). Similarly, "I will sing forever" means "as long as I live" (Pss 52:9; 115:18; 145:1, 2). Thus in Psalm 45, "forever and ever" spoke of a ruling authority that would last throughout the monarch's life and be perpetuated through his descendants (Ps 45:17, cf. 2 Sam 7:11b–12, 14a, 16; 1 Chron 17:11–14; Ps 132:11–12). In Hebrews, this figurative Old Testament concept of "forever and ever" is no longer figurative for the temporal duration of a regal priest. "Forever" is elevated to speak quite literally and directly of the *eternal duration* of Jesus himself, his authority, his regal priesthood, and his accomplishments (salvation, redemption, covenant). Despite all of this preliminary work, the idea for this chart arose via Hagner's *Encountering the Book of Hebrews* (2002), 122.

79–82 EXAMPLES OF FAITH AND JEWISH ANCESTORS IN HEBREWS

This series of charts tackles the faithful ancestors listed in Hebrews 11. **Chart 79** begins the series with a detailed record of all things "unseen" by those who went before us. **Chart 80** continues the series with a list of those specifically named in Hebrews 11, a summary of the Old Testament event, the Old Testament reference, what Hebrews says and where Hebrews says it. **Chart 81** provides an explicit accounting of all those unnamed in Hebrews and offers suggestions as to who those unnamed individuals might have been, the possible Old Testament event and relevant verses. The series closes with **Chart 82**. It demonstrates that the author of Hebrews was not the first to produce a Jewish Hall of Fame of Faith. In fact, three antediluvian figures—Abel, Enoch, and Noah—attracted special attention in Judaism. Ben Sira, however, listed Enoch first in his praises of famous men of the Bible (Sir 44:1—50:24). Enoch's epitaph in Gen 5:21–24 is a record of his having been a person who had "walked with God" and then, after 365 years, the translations read "he was no more" or "God took him." Due to the many years spent in which he "pleased God," namely, that he believed God existed and lived by that belief (see Heb 11:6), Enoch was literally taken up and away to heaven (cp. Gen 5:24, Sir 44:16, Wis 4:10). Nevertheless, the parallel listing demonstrates the similarities and differences. A sister chart to these is Chart 92 "Examples of Chiasm in Hebrews 11." Charts 79–81 are revisions and expansions of charts that first appeared in Hagner's *Encountering the Book of Hebrews* (2002), 144, 146, 153.

Words of Exhortation in Hebrews

83–87 EXHORTATION AND WARNING IN HEBREWS

This series of charts identifies explicit exhortations throughout Hebrews and draws special attention to warnings. **Chart 83** identifies thirty-four exhortations that run throughout the Book of Hebrews. **Chart 85** more pointedly addresses the passive, active, and external dangers of apostasy in Hebrews. The term "believers" is used throughout the chart because of the frequent mentioning of "brothers and sisters" (generic use of ἀδελφοί in 2:11, 17; 3:1, 12; 10:19; 13:22) and their ability to "draw near" with "boldness" to God (4:16; 10:19, 22). The interpretive question then becomes whether these are genuine believers or not—a question this chart leaves the interpreter to ponder (cp. Charts 10, 83). **Chart 85** walks through each warning passage, identifying the exhortation, concern, historical precedent, dire consequence, and desired consequence. This chart builds upon, expands, and improves Bateman's initial charts presented in *The Warning Passages in Hebrews* (2006), 42–43, 71–73. **Chart 86** identifies the warning passages about apostasy as proposed by various commentators. **Chart 87** closes this series by providing the various positions commentators have taken as to whether the readers are "real Christians." Numerous works were used to create this series of charts. Nevertheless, a few sources warrant mention. Chart 81 is an expansion of two charts presented in these two works: Girdwood and Verkruyse's commentary *Hebrews* (1997), 15; and Hagner, *Encountering the Book of Hebrews* (2002), 134, 170. Chart 82 merely provides a visual for the information in Ellingworth's *The Epistle to the Hebrews* (1993), 78–79; and O'Brien's *The Letter to the Hebrews* (2010), 12.

As a sidebar, it is helpful to address ever so briefly the concept of apostasy in the LXX. Psalm 95:7–11, as it is quoted in Hebrews 3:7–10, reverberates with the heartbeat of the wilderness community. They *turned away* from God (Num 14:9, 32:9; cf. 13:1–14:45). Ezekiel parallels the wilderness community's *turning away* from God with that of the first temple (966 –586 B.C.E.) community's departure from the living God (Ezek 20:8, 38; cf. Jer 2:5; Dan 9:5, 9; Bar 3:8). Likewise, Second Temple (514 B.C.E. –70 C.E.) communities departed from God through "abandoning the religion of their fathers" (1 Macc 2:19) and through the actions "of the lawless who had rebelled against God" (1QpHab 8:11, 16; s.v. מרד, *TDOT* 9:1–5). To turn away from God, then, is deliberate rebellion against God: "Far be it from us that we should rebel (ἀποστραφῆναι, *apostraphenai*) against the LORD, and turn away (ἀποστῆναι, *apostenai*) this day from following the LORD …" (LXX Josh 22:29; cf. Wis 3:10). As is the case in Heb 3:12, one's "heart condition" frequents the discussions of forsaking the living God (Jer 17:5; Sir 10:12). Thus, the author cautions ("take care" or "see to it," βλέπετε, *blepete*) about having a hardened heart Heb 3:8, 15) or evil heart (3:12) that affects one's relationship with the living God.

Part 4: Exegetical Matters in Hebrews

Interpretive Issues in Hebrews

88–90 PENTATEUCH, PROPHETIC, POETIC CITATIONS COMPARED

These three charts are for those who wish to work first hand in the original languages. Whereas Chart 30 and Chart 31 merely listed Old Testament quotes so that a person might look them up on their own, these three charts provide the actual quotes from the Hebrew text, the Septuagint (Greek), and the Greek text of Hebrews. (The corresponding English Bible verse numbers are provided above each set of OT quotes.) **Chart 88** starts the series with a listing of citations from the Pentateuch. **Chart 89** lists four citations from the historical and prophetic books. **Chart 90** closes the series with eleven citations from the Psalms and the one and only citation from Proverbs 3:11–12. Naturally when using these charts, you will first examine the Hebrew text (translate it and note any significant Hebrew terms). Then translate the LXX and look for similarities and differences (addition of words or exclusion of words, or the Greek word used to translate significant Hebrew words, etc.). Finally, translate the text in Hebrews and once again look for similarities and differences; if there are any, ask why might the author have made such a change or how the change affects the author's point. For an example on how to use these charts for exegesis see Pss 2:7; 45:7–8; 102:26–28; 104:4; 110:1 and particularly Deut 32:43 in Bateman's *Early Jewish Hermeneutics and Hebrews 1:5–13* (1997), 125–47.

91 EXAMPLES OF JEWISH EXEGESIS IN HEBREWS

Chart 91 lists, defines, and provides examples of several forms of Jewish exegesis in Hebrews. When the author of Hebrews uses an Old Testament text, it is not unusual for a commentator to identify the usage in terms of Jewish exegesis. More frequently commentators will allude to *qal wahomer* and *gezerah shavah*, and less frequently to *kelal u-ferat, kayose bo bemaqom aher,* and *dabar halamed me-'inyano.* This chart helps to define each term and provide examples in Hebrews where this sort of Jewish exegesis might occur. Works that were foundational for this chart are Longenecker, *Biblical Exegesis in the Apostolic Period* (1999), 6–35 and Bateman, *Early Jewish Hermeneutics and Hebrews 1:5–13* (1997), 9–21, 217–37. For other uses of the Old Testament in Hebrews see Herbert W. Bateman IV, "Second Temple Exegetical Practices: Extra-biblical Examples of Exegesis Compared with Those in the Book of Hebrews" *SwJT* 53 (Fall 2010): 26–54.

Text Critical Issues in Hebrews

92–93 CHIASTIC STRUCTURES IN HEBREWS

This series of charts offers some suggestions about chiastic structures in Hebrews. Obviously, many more examples might be provided in this series, but we limit our examples to three: Hebrews 1:1–4, 5–13; 11:1–40. For other examples see Rhee's *Faith in Hebrews: Analysis within the Context of Christology, Eschatology, and Ethics* (2001). **Chart 92** suggests two chiastic structures for Hebrews 1. First, the focus of this chiastic structure in Hebrews 1:1–4 is 1:3a (letter "d"), and the focus of 1:5–13 is 1:8–9 (letter "c"). Second, the Son's designation as divine is not necessarily an ontological statement, but rather a statement of activities that identify him as God. **Chart 93** on Hebrews 11 is based upon Rhee's presentation in *Faith in Hebrews* (2001). The emphasis of the chiastic structure in **Chart 93** is as follows. First, the focus is Heb 11:13–16 (letter "H"). Second, Hebrews 11:13–16 contains the author's editorial insertion about faith. The "all these" (οὗτοι πάντες) in 11:13 appear to include all the exemplars of faith mentioned in 11:4–12 as well as subsequent exemplars in 11:17–38. Third, the aspect of faith in Hebrews 11:13–16 is both present and future oriented (the already and the not yet). The thrust of Hebrews as a whole has both a present and future orientation (e.g. 2:8; 10:13).

94–97 TEXT CRITICAL ISSUES IN HEBREWS

This series of charts provides information helpful to evaluate text critical problems in Hebrews. **Chart 94** begins this series of charts by listing, classifying, and dating every papyrus, uncial, and miniscule manuscript cited for Hebrews in the textual apparatus for the Nestle-Aland 27th edition of *Novum Testamentum Graece* and the 4th revised edition of *The Greek New Testament* published by the United Bible Societies. **Chart 95** lists the most consistently cited witnesses (44 total) for Hebrews. The chart identifies the character of the manuscript according to first and second order. Manuscripts charted in the first order are of high character or authority. **Chart 96** classifies manuscript evidence according to Alexandrian, Western, or Byzantine family. Once again, manuscripts are categorized within each family text type according to their importance. A select number of versions and Church fathers are also listed. The series closes with **Chart 97**, which isolates 42 significant text critical issues in Hebrews with variant options from the Nestle-Aland 27th edition and the United Bible Societies 4th edition. It identifies the significance of each option as it might relate to grammar, syntax, style, literature, exegesis, and theology; and it chooses and explains what option is best based upon an eclectic methodological approach that evaluates both external and internal evidence. Furthermore, it identifies whether some of our English translations follow those decisions, namely the ASV, ESV, KJV, NASB, NET, NIV, and the NRSV. Manuscripts marked with an * signify the reading of the original hand of the manuscript, though an alternative ("corrected") reading may exist above, below, or in the margin. Works that proved extremely helpful for this series of charts were Aland and Aland's *The Text of the New Testament* (1987); Metzger's *A Textual Commentary on the Greek New Testament* (1994) and Trotter's *Interpreting the Epistle to the Hebrews* (1997), 95–110. For commentaries that have similar information see Attridge's *Hebrews* (1989), 31–32; Ellingworth's *The Epistle to the Hebrews* (1993), 81–85; and Koester's *Hebrews* (2001), 129–31.

Figures of Speech in Hebrews

98–101 Figures of Speech in Hebrews

This series of charts isolates, identifies, and interprets the significant literary devices or figures of speech in Hebrews. **Chart 98** is a simple overview that names, distinguishes and defines figures of speech used in Hebrews, and provides references for example verses. Subsequent charts that treat each literary device—omission (**Chart 99**), addition (**Chart 100**), and change (**Chart 101**)—name, identify, and illustrate each figure using examples from Hebrews. The charts are meant to assist in identifying these literary features and then to offer some suggestions as to how to interpret them. Although numerous sources were of help here, the primary source was Bullinger's *Figures of Speech Used in the Bible* (1968). Another helpful source was Trotter's *Interpreting the Epistle to the Hebrews* (1997), 66–80, 163–177.

Important Words in Hebrews

102–104 Important Words in Hebrews

This series of charts lists and defines key words in Hebrews. **Chart 102** opens the series with a list of words that are most frequently used in Hebrews in comparison to their use elsewhere in the New Testament. This chart is based on one found in Andrew H. Trotter's *Interpreting the Epistle to the Hebrews* (1997), 137–38, and was compiled by searching for the Greek word rather than the English. The two subsequent charts list the lexical form of 143 Greek words unique to the Book of Hebrews. Of these, 121 words occur only once in Hebrews, while 22 words occur two or more times in Hebrews alone. The definition of each word is then provided according to eight English translations: ESV, KJV, NASB, NRSV, NIV, NET, NLT and TNIV. The Alphabetical Listing of Greek Words Unique to Hebrews (**Chart 103**) provides easy access for those interested in word studies or distinguishing features of the text. On the other hand, the Chapter Listing of Greek Words (**Chart 104**) is helpful for someone wishing to read Hebrews in Greek.

Bibliography

Part One: Introductory Considerations in Hebrews

Aland, Kurt and Barbara Aland. *The Text of the New Testament: An Introduction to the Critical Editions and to the Theory and Practice of Modern Textual Criticism.* Translated by Erroll F. Rhodes. Grand Rapids: Eerdmans, 1987.

Allen, David L. *Hebrews.* The New American Commentary: An Exegetical and Theological Exposition of Holy Scripture. Nashville: B & H Publishing Group, 2010.

_____. *Lukan Authorship of Hebrews.* Nashville: B & H Academic, 2010.

Anderson, C. P. "The Epistle to the Hebrews and the Pauline Letter Collection." *Harvard Theological Review* 59:4 (1966): 429–438.

_____. "Who Wrote 'the Epistle from Laodicea'?" *Journal of Biblical Literature* 85:4 (1966): 436–40.

_____. "Hebrews among the Letters of Paul." *Studies in Religion* 5 (1975–76): 258–66.

Apostolic Fathers. Translated by Bart Ehrman. 2 vols. Loeb Classical Library. Cambridge, MA: Harvard University Press, 2003.

Aquinas, Thomas. *Commentary on the Epistle to the Hebrews.* Translated by Chrysostom Baer. South Bend: St. Augustine's Press, 2006.

Aristotle. The Art of Rhetoric. Trans. John H. Freese. Loeb Classical Library. Cambridge, MA: Harvard University Press, 1926.

Arnold, Clinton E. "Colossae." Pp. 1089–90 in Vol. 1 of *The Anchor Bible Dictionary.* Edited by David Noel Freedman. 6 vols. New York: Doubleday, 1992.

Attridge, Harold W. *The Epistle to the Hebrews: A Commentary on the Epistle to the Hebrews.* Hermeneia. Philadelphia: Fortress, 1989.

Badcock, F. J. *The Pauline Epistles and the Epistle to the Hebrews in their Historical Setting.* New York: Macmillan, 1937.

Barclay, John M. G. *Jews in the Mediterranean Diaspora From Alexander to Trajan.* Edinburgh: T & T Clark, 1996. Rome: 282–319; Cyrenaica 232–58.

Barnabus, Epistle of. *Apostolic Fathers. vol. 2.* Translated by Bart Ehrman. Loeb Classical Library. Cambridge, MA: Harvard University Press, 2003.

Barrett, C. K. *A Critical and Exegetical Commentary on the Acts of the Apostles.* 2 vols. International Critical Commentary. Edinburgh: T&T Clark, 1994, 1998.

Bateman IV, Herbert W. *Early Jewish Hermeneutics and Hebrews 1:5–13: The Impact of Early Jewish Exegesis on the Interpretation of a Significant New Testament Passage.* American University Studies. New York: Peter Lang, 1997.

_____, ed. *Four Views on the Warning Passages in Hebrews.* Grand Rapids: Kregel, 2007.

_____. "The Genre of the General Letters" in *Interpreting the General Letters: An Exegetical Handbook.* Handbooks for New Testament Exegesis, vol 3. Edited by John D. Harvey. (Kregel, forthcoming).

_____. "The Theology of the General Letters" in *Interpreting the General Letters: An Exegetical Handbook.* Handbooks for New Testament Exegesis, vol 3. Edited by John D. Harvey. (Kregel, forthcoming).

Battifol, P. "De l;attribution de l'Épîtr aux Hébreux a saint Barnabé." Revue biblique 69 (1899): 278-96.

Black, C. Clifton, II. "The Rhetorical Form of the Hellenistic Jewish and Early Christian Sermon: A Response to Lawrence Wills." *Harvard Theological Review* 81:1 (1988): 1–18.

Black, David Alan. "Who Wrote Hebrews? Internal and External Evidence Reexamined." *Faith and Mission* 18:2 (2001): 3–26.

Bleek, Friedrich. Der Brief an die Hebräer, 3 vols. Berlin: Dümmler, 1828-40.

Boehme, Christian Friedrich. *Epistola ad Hebreaeos [Epistle to the Hebrews].* Leipzig: Barth, 1825.

Brown, J. V. "The Authorship and Circumstances of 'Hebrews'—Again," *Bibliotheca Sacra* 80 (1923): 505–38.

Brown, Raymond E. *An Introduction to the New Testament.* New York: Doubleday, 1997.

Bruce, F. F. *The Epistle to the Hebrews.* Rev. ed. The New International Commentary on the New Testament. Grand Rapids: Eerdmans, 1990.

Bullinger, Heinrich. *De testamento seu foedere Dei unico et aeterno. Zürich: Christoph Froschouer*, 1534.

Calvin, Jean. *The Epistle … to the Hebrews and the First and Second Epistles of St. Peter.* Calvin's Commentaries. Edinburgh: Oliver and Boyd, 1963.

Caméron, John. "As quaestiones in epistolam ad Hebraeos." *Praelectioni in selectiora quaedam Novi Testamenti loca Salmurii habitarum.* 3 vols. Salmurum: Girard and Lerpiner, 1626-28.

Carson, D. A. and Douglas J. Moo. *An Introduction to the New Testament.* 2nd ed. Grand Rapids: Zondervan, 2005.

Chapman, John. "Aristion, author of the Epistle to the Hebrews." *Revue bénédictine* 22 (1905): 50–64.

Childs, Brevard S. *The New Testament as Canon: An Introduction.* Philadelphia: Fortress Press, 1985, 413–15.

Clement of Rome. "Epistle to the Hebrews" in The Apostolic Fathers. Loeb Classical Library. vol. 1. Translated by Bart Ehrman. Cambridge, MA: Harvard University Press, 2003.

Cockerill, Gareth L. *Hebrews: A Bible Commentary in the Wesleyan Tradition.* Indianapolis: Wesleyan Publishing House, 1999.

_____. *The Epistle to the Hebrews.* The New International Commentary on the New Testament. Grand Rapids: Eerdmans, 2012.

Comfort, Philip W. and David P. Barrett, eds. *The Complete Text of the Earliest New Testament Manuscripts.* Grand Rapids: Baker Books, 1999.

Dibelius, F. Der Verfasser des Hebraerbriefes. Vërfasser des Hebräerbrief. Forschungen zur Religion und Literatur des Alten und Neun Testaments. Strasborg, 1910.

Dubarle, A. M. "Rédacteur et Destinaires de l'Epitre aux Hébreux." *Revue biblique* 48 (1939): 506–29.

Edmundson, George. The Church in Rome in the First Century. London: Longmans, Green and Company, 1913.

Ellingworth, Paul. *The Epistle to the Hebrews: A Commentary on the Greek Text.* New International Greek Testament Commentary. Grand Rapids: Eerdmans, 1993.

Eusebius. *Ecclesiastical History.* 2 vols. Translated by J. E. L. Oulton. Loeb Classical Library. New York: G. P. Putnam's Sons, 1932–36.

Feldman, Louis H. "General Index to Volumes 1–9" in Vol. 9 of *Josephus*. Loeb Classical Library. Cambridge, MA: Harvard University Press, 1965.

Fiensy, David A. *New Testament Introduction. The College Press NIV Commentary*. Joplin: College Press, 1994.

Ford, J. M. "The First Epistle to the Corinthians or the First Epistle to the Hebrews?" *Catholic Biblical Quarterly* 28:4 (1966): 402–16.

_____. "The Mother of Jesus and the Authorship of the Epistle to the Hebrews." *The Bible Today* 82 (1976): 683–94.

Forster, Charles.The Apostolical Authority of the Epistle to the Hebrews. London: James Duncan, 1838.

Frederic William Farrar. The Epistle of Paul the Apostle to the Hebrews. CGC. Cambridge, UK: University Press, 1881.

Geisler, Norman L., and William E. Nix. *A General Introduction to the Bible Revised and Expanded*. Chicago: Moody Press, 1986.

Girdwood, Jim and Peter Verkruyse. *Hebrews*. The College Press NIV Commentary. Joplin: College Press, 1997.

Gromacki, Robert G. *New Testament Survey*. Grand Rapids: Baker Book House, 1974.

Grotius, Hugo. *Christ's Passion: A Tragedie, with Annotations*. Translated by George Sandys, London: n.p., 1640.

Guilliaud, Claude. "Epistola beati Pauli as Hevraeos." Collatio omnes dive Pauli apostolic epistolas. Lyon: Sabastian Gryphius, 1543.

Guthrie, Donald. *The Letter to the Hebrews: An Introduction and Commentary*. Tyndale New Testament Commentaries. Grand Rapids: Eerdmans, 1983.

_____. *New Testament Introduction*. 4th rev. ed. The Master Reference Collection. Downers Grove: InterVarsity Press, 1990.

Guthrie, George H. "The Case for Apollos as the Author of Hebrews." *Faith and Mission* 18:2 (2001): 41–56.

_____. *Hebrews. The NIV Application Commentary*. Grand Rapids: Zondervan, 1998.

_____. *The Structure of Hebrews: A Text-Linguistic Analysis*. Supplements to Novum Testamentum, vol. 73. New York: Brill, 1994.

Hagen, Kenneth. *Hebrews Commenting from Erasmus to Bèze 1516–1598*. Tübingen: Mohr, 1981.

Hagner, Donald A. *Encountering the Book of Hebrews: An Exposition*. Encountering Biblical Studies. Grand Rapids: Baker Academic, 2002.

_____. *Hebrews*. New International Biblical Commentary, vol 14. Peabody: Hendrickson, 1990.

Harnack, Adolf von. "Probabilia über die Adresse und den Verfassere des Hebräerbriefs." *Zeitschrift für die Neutestamentliche Wissenschaft* 1 (1900): 16–41.

Hatch, William Henry Paine. *Facsimiles and Descriptions of Minuscule Manuscripts of the New Testament*. Cambridge, MA: Harvard University Press, 1951.

_____. "The Position of Hebrews in the New Testament Canon." *Harvard Theological Review* 29:2 (April 1936): 133–51.

Heen, Erik M. and Philip D. W. Krey, eds. *Hebrews*. Ancient Christian Commentary on Scripture: New Testament. Vol. 10. Downers Grove: InterVarsity Press, 2005.

Hewitt, Thomas. *The Epistle to the Hebrews: An Introduction and Commentary*. Tyndale New Testament Commentaries. Grand Rapids: Eerdmans, 1960.

Hoppin, Ruth. *Priscilla's Letter: Finding the Author of the Epistle to the Hebrews*. Fort Bragg: Lost Coast Press, 1997.

Hughes, Philip E. *A Commentary on the Epistle to the Hebrews*. Grand Rapids: Eerdmans, 1977.

Johnson, Luke Timothy. *Hebrews: A Commentary*. The New Testament Library. Louisville: Westminster John Knox Press, 2006.

Jurgens, William A. *The Faith of the Early Fathers*. 3 vols. Collegeville: Liturgical Press, 1970–79.

Keil, Carl Friedrich. *Commentar über den Brief an die Hebräer*. Leipzig: Dörffling und Franke, 1885.

Kirby, V.T. "The Authorship of the Epistle to the Hebrews." *Expository Times* 35 (1923): 375–77.

Kistemaker, Simon J. *New Testament Commentary: Exposition of the Epistle to the Hebrews*. Grand Rapids: Baker Book House, 1984.

Koester, Craig R. *Hebrews: A New Translation with Introduction and Commentary*. The Anchor Bible. Vol. 36. New York: Doubleday, 2001.

Kümmel, Werner Georg. *Introduction to the New Testament*. 14th rev. ed. Translated by A. J. Mattill, Jr. Nashville: Abingdon Press, 1966.

Lake, Helen and Kirsopp. *Codex Sinaiticvs*. Detroit: Brown & Thomas, 1982.

Lane, William L. *Hebrews 1–8*. Word Biblical Commentary. Vol. 47A. Dallas: Word, 1991.

_____. *Hebrews 9–13*. Word Biblical Commentary. Vol. 47B. Dallas: Word, 1991.

Legg, John D. "Our Brother Timothy, A Suggested Solution to the Problem of the Authorship of the Epistle to the Hebrews." *Evangelical Quarterly* 40 (1968): 220–23.

Lenski, R. C. H. The Interpretation of the Epistle to the Hebrews. Minneapolis, MN: Augsburg, 1961.

Leonard, William. *The Authorship of the Epistle to the Hebrews*. London: Oates and Washbourne, 1939.

Lindars, Barnabas. "The Rhetorical Structure of Hebrews." *New Testament Studies* 35 (1989): 382–406.

Linnemann, Eta. "A Call for a Retrial in the Case of the Epistle to the Hebrews." Translated by David E. Lanier. *Faith and Mission* 19:2 (2002): 19–59.

Luther, Martin. "Preface to the Epistle of Hebrews." In *Word and Sacrament I*. Luther's Works. Vol. 35. Translated, revised and edited by E. Theodore Bachmann. Philadelphia: Muhlenberg Press, 1960.

_____. *Lectures on Genesis, Chapters 45–50*. Luther's Works. Vol 8. Edited by Jaroslav Pelikan. Translated by Paul D. Pahl. St. Louis: Concordia, 1966.

Malherbe, Abraham J., trans. *Ancient Epistolary Theorists*. Sources for Biblical Study 19. Atlanta: Scholars Press, 1988.

Manson, T. W. "The Problem of the Epistle to the Hebrews." *Bulletin of the John Rylands Library* 32 (September 1949): 16–17.

Metzger, Bruce M. *A Textual Commentary on the Greek New Testament*. 2nd ed. New York: United Bible Societies, 1994.

Michaels, J. Ramsey. *Hebrews*. Cornerstone Biblical Commentary. Vol. 17. Carol Stream: Tyndale, 2009.

Migne, Jacques-Paul. Patrologiae cursus completus. Series latina. Parisiis, 1875-87.

Migne, Jacques-Paul. Patrologiae cursus completus. Series Graeca. Microfiche. Washington, Microcard Foundation, 1961.

Mitchell, Alan C. *Hebrews*. Sacra Pagina. Vol. 13. Edited by Daniel J. Harrington. Collegeville: Liturgical Press, 2007.

Moffatt, James. *Critical and Exegetical Commentary on the Epistle to the Hebrews*. International Critical

Commentary. Edinburgh: T&T Clark, 1948.

Norris, Fredrick W. "Antioch of Syria." Pp. 265–69 in Vol. 1 of *The Anchor Bible Dictionary*. New York: Doubleday, 1992.

O'Brien, Peter T. *The Letter to the Hebrews*. The Pillar New Testament Commentary. Grand Rapids: Eerdmans, 2010.

Owen, John. *Exercitation on the penman of the Epistle to Hebrews*. 4 vols. London: Robert White, for Nathaniel Ponder, 1668- 1684.

Peake, Arthur S. Hebrews: Introduction, authorized version, with notes and index. Edinburgh: T.C. & E.C. Jack, 1906.

Pfitzner, Victor C. *Hebrews*. Abingdon New Testament Commentaries. Nashville: Abingdon Press, 1997.

Pixner, Bargil. "The Jerusalem Essenes, Barnabas and the Letter to the Hebrews" in *Qumranica Mogilanensia*. Edited by Z. J. Kapera. Krakow: Enigman Press, 1992.

Pliny (the younger). Letters and Panegyricus. Trans. Betty Radice. Loeb Classical Library. 2 vols. Cambridge, MA: Harvard University Press, 1969.

Poster, Carol and Linda C. Mitchell, editors. *Letter-Writing Manuals and Instruction from Antiquity to the Present: Historical and Bibliographic Studies*. Columbia: University of South Carolina Press, 2007.

Ramsay, William Mitchell. *Luke, the Physician: And Other Studies in the History of Religion*. London: Hodder and Stoughton, 1908.

_____. "The Date and Authorship of the Epistle to the Hebrews." *The Expositor* 9 (1899): 401–22.

Robinson, John A. T. *Redating the New Testament*. Philadelphia: Westminster Press, 1976.

Rothschild, Clare K. *Hebrews as Psuedepigraphon*. Wissenschaftliche Unersuchungen zum Neuen Testament. Tübingen: Mohr Siebeck, 2009.

Salmon, George. A Historical Introduction to the New Testament. 3rd. ed. London: John Murray, 1888.

Schaff, Philip, ed. *A Select Library of the Nicene and Post-Nicene Fathers of the Christian Church*, First Series. 14 vols. New York: The Christian Literature Company, 1893; Reprinted Grand Rapids: Eerdmans, 1979.

_____. *A Select Library of the Nicene and Post-Nicene Fathers of the Christian Church*, Second Series. 14 vols. New York: The Christian Literature Company, 1893; Reprinted Grand Rapids: Eerdmans, 1979.

Seutonius. On the Twelve Caesars. Trans. Robert Graves. Harmondsworth: Penguin, 1957, revised by James B. Rives, 2007.

Spicq, Ceslas. Introduction to *L'Épître aux Hébreux*. Vol. 1. Paris: J. Gabalda, 1952–53.

Stedman, Ray C. *Hebrews*. The IVP New Testament Commentary Series. Downers Grove: InterVarsity Press, 1992.

Stowers, Stanley K. *Letter Writing in Greco–Roman Antiquity*. Literature of Early Christianity. Vol. 5. Philadelphia: Westminster Press, 1986.

Strabo. Geography. Loeb Classical Library. 8 vol. Cambridge, MA: Harvard University Press, 1917-1932.

Stuart, Moses. A Commentary on the Epistle to the Hebrews. 4th ed. rev. R. D. C. Robins. Andover: Warren F. Drapper, 1876.

Tacitcus. Annals. Loeb Classical Library. Cambridge, MA: Harvard University Press, 1937.

Tertullian. *Treatises on Penance: On Penitence and On Purity*. Ancient Christian Writers. Vol. 28. Translated and annotated by William P. Le Saint. New York: Newman Press, 1959.

Tertullian. Apology. Loeb Classical Library. Translated by T. R. Glover. Cambridge, MA: Harvard University Press, 1927.

Thompson, James W. *Hebrews*. Paideia Commentaries on the New Testament. Grand Rapids: Baker Academic, 2008.

Tyndale, William. "The Prologe to the Epistle of S. Paul to the Hebrues." In *The New Testament, translated by William Tyndale: A Reprint of the edition of 1534 with the translator's prefaces & notes and the variants of the edition of 1525*. Edited by N. Hardy Wallis. Cambridge, England: University Press, 1938.

Vanhoye, Albert. *Épître aux Hébreux: texte Grec structure*. Rome: Pontifical Biblical Institute, 1967.

_____. *A Structured Translation of the Epistle to the Hebrews*. Translated by James Swetnam. Rome: Pontifical Biblical Institute, 1964.

Villa, Lorenzo. Ad Hebreos, pages 241-50 in Collatio Novi Testment. ed. A. Perosa. Firenze: Sansoni, 1970.

Von Harnack, Adolf. "Probabilia über die Adresse und den Verfasser des Hebraerbriefs." *Zeitschrift für die neutestamentliche Wissenschaft and die Kunde der älteren Kirche* 1 (1900): 16–41.

Voulgaris, Christos Sp. "Hebrews: Paul's Fifth Epistle from Prison," *Greek Orthodox Theological Review* 44 (1999): 199–206.

Weiss, B. Der Brief an die Hebräer. KEK 13. Göttingen, Vandenhoeck & Ruprecht, 1888.

Welch, Adam. *The Authorship of the Epistle to the Hebrews and Other Papers*. Edinburgh: Oliphant, Anderson & Ferrier, 1898.

Westcott, Brooke Foss. *The Epistle to the Hebrews: The Greek Text with Notes and Essays*. 3rd ed. London: Macmillan, 1889.

Wills, Lawrence M. "The Form of the Sermon in Hellenistic Judaism and Early Christianity." *Harvard Theological Review* 77:3–4 (1984): 277–99.

Wilson, R. McLachlan. *Hebrews*. The New Century Bible Commentary. Grand Rapids: Eerdmans, 1987.

Wrede, William. Das literarische Rätsel des Hebräerbrief. FRLANT 8. Göttingen: Vandenboeck und Ruprecht, 1906.

Zahn, Theodor. *Introduction to the New Testament*. 3 vols. Translated from 3rd German ed. by J. M. Trout, et. al. 1917. Grand Rapids: Kregel reprint, 1953; Minneapolis: Klock & Klock reprint, 1977.

Part Two: Old Testament and Second Temple Influences in Hebrews

Aland, Kurt et al., eds. *The Greek New Testament*. 4th ed. Stüttgart: United Bible Societies, 1993.

Archer, Gleason. *A Survey of Old Testament Introduction*. Chicago: Moody Press, 1974.

Bateman IV, Herbert W. *Early Jewish Hermeneutics and Hebrews 1:5–13: The Impact of Early Jewish Exegesis on the Interpretation of a Significant New Testament Passage.* American University Studies. New York: Peter Lang, 1997.

_____. "Expectations of Israel's King." In *Jesus the Messiah: Tracing the Promises, Expectations, and Coming of Israel's King.* Grand Rapids: Kregel: 2012.

_____. "Psalm 45:6–7 and Its Christological Contributions to Hebrews." *Trinity Journal* 22NS:1 (2001): 3–21.

_____. "Response to Nathan Holsteen's 'The Trinity in the Letter to the Hebrews'" for the God and God Incarnate Study Group (Moderator: Douglas Blount), presented and discussed at the Annual National Meeting of the ETS (Nov 2009).

_____. "Two First Century Messianic Uses of the OT: Heb 1:5–13 and 4QFlor 1:1–19." *Journal of the Evangelical Theological Society* 38:1 (1995): 11–27.

Blau, Ludwig, and Kaufmann Kohler. "Angels." In *The Jewish Encyclopedia.* Vol. 1. New York: Funk & Wagnalls, 1901-06. Accessed 25 February 2011. Online: http://www.jewishencyclopedia.com/view.jsp?artid=1521&letter=A&search=Role%20of%20Angels#4346).

Davidson, Maxwell J. *Angels at Qumran: A Comparative Study of 1 Enoch 1–36, 72–103 and Sectarian Writings from Qumran.* Journal for the Study of the Pseudepigrapha Supplement Series 11. Sheffield: JSOT Press, 1992.

Dowley, Tim. *The Kregel Bible Atlas.* Grand Rapids: Kregel, 2003.

Ellingworth, Paul. *The Epistle to the Hebrews: A Commentary on the Greek Text.* New International Greek Testament Commentary. Grand Rapids: Eerdmans, 1993.

Evans, Louis H. *Hebrews.* The Communicator's Commentary. Vol. 10. Waco: Word Books, 1985.

Fitzmyer, Joseph A. "Further Light on Melchizedek from Qumran Cave 11." *Journal of Biblical Literature* 86:1 (1967): 25–41.

Girdwood, Jim and Peter Verkruyse. *Hebrews.* The College Press NIV Commentary. Joplin: College Press, 1997. Pp. 281, 286–87; 341–42.

Gottlieb, Isaac B. "Hillel." In *The Oxford Dictionary of the Jewish Religion.* New York: Oxford University Press, 1997.

Hagner, Donald A. *Encountering the Book of Hebrews: An Exposition.* Encountering Biblical Studies. Grand Rapids: Baker Academic, 2002. Pp. 98, 144, 153.

Isaac, E. "1 (Ethiopic Apocalypse of) Enoch" In *Apocalyptic Literature and Testaments.* Vol. 1 of *The Old Testament Pseudepigrapha.* Edited by James H. Charlesworth. Garden City: Doubleday, 1983.

Josephus. *Josephus, The Essential Writings: A Condensation of Jewish Antiquities and the Jewish War.* Edited and translated by Paul Maier. Grand Rapids: Kregel, 1988.

Koester, Craig R. *Hebrews: A New Translation with Introduction and Commentary.* The Anchor Bible. Vol. 36. New York: Doubleday, 2001.

Lane, William L. *Hebrews 1–8.* Word Biblical Commentary. Vol. 47A. Dallas: Word, 1991.

_____. *Hebrews 9–13.* Word Biblical Commentary. Vol. 47B. Dallas: Word, 1991.

Longenecker, Richard N. *Biblical Exegesis in the Apostolic Period*. 2nd ed. Grand Rapids: Eerdmans, 1999. Pp. 147–48.

Mach, Michael. "Angels." In *Encyclopedia of the Dead Sea Scrolls*. Edited by Lawrence H. Schiffmann and James C. VanderKam. New York: Oxford University Press, 2000.

Machiela, Daniel A. *The Dead Sea Genesis Apocryphon: A New Text and Translation with Introduction and Special Treatment of Columns 13–17*. Studies on the Texts of the Desert of Judah. Vol. 79. Leiden: Brill, 2009.

Martínez, Florentino García, and Eibert J. C. Tigchelaar, eds. *The Dead Sea Scrolls Study Edition*. 2 vols. Grand Rapids: Eerdmans, 2000.

Nickelsburg, George W. E. *1 Enoch 1: A Commentary on the Book of 1 Enoch*. Hermeneia. Minneapolis: Fortress, 2001.

O'Brien, Peter T. *The Letter to the Hebrews*. The Pillar New Testament Commentary. Grand Rapids: Eerdmans, 2010.

Philo. *The Works of Philo: Complete and Unabridged*. New Updated Edition. Translated by C. D. Yonge. Peabody: Hendrickson, 1993.

Porten, Bezale. The Elephantine Papri in English. Cocuments et Monumenta Orientis Antiqui 22. Leiden: Brill, 1996.

Schwerdtfeger, Patricia Jean. "Portraits of Melchizedek: Tracing the Development from the Old Testament to 11Q13 to Hebrews." ThM Thesis, Southwestern Baptist Theological Seminary, 2010.

VanderKam, James C. *From Joshua to Caiaphas: High Priests After the Exile*. Minneapolis: Fortress Press, 2005.

Wintermute, O. S. "Jubilees." In *The Old Testament Pseudepigrapha*. Vol. 2. Edited by James H. Charlesworth. Garden City: Doubleday, 1985.

Part Three: Theology in Hebrews

Allen, David L. *Hebrews*. The New American Commentary: An Exegetical and Theological Exposition of Holy Scripture. Nashville: B & H Publishing Group, 2010.

Attridge, Harold W. *The Epistle to the Hebrews: A Commentary on the Epistle to the Hebrews*. Hermeneia. Philadelphia: Fortress, 1989.

Bateman IV, Herbert W. "Defining the Titles 'Christ' and 'Son of God' in Mark's Narrative Presentation of Jesus," *Journal of the Evangelical Theological Society* 50:3 (2007): 537–59.

———, ed. *Four Views on the Warning Passages in Hebrews*. Grand Rapids: Kregel, 2007.

———. "Hebrews One Commentary." In *Early Jewish Hermeneutics and Hebrews 1:5–13: The Impact of Early Jewish Exegesis on the Interpretation of a Significant New Testament Passage*. American University Studies. New York: Peter Lang, 1997.

_____. "Psalm 45:6–7 and Its Christological Contributions to Hebrews," *Trinity Journal* 22NS:1 (2001): 3–21.

_____. "Psalm 110: A Royal Psalm of Assurance in the Midst of Change." In *Interpreting the Psalms for Teaching and Preaching*. Edited by Herbert W. Bateman IV and D. Brent Sandy. St. Louis: Chalice Press, 2010.

_____. "Response to Nathan Holsteen's 'The Trinity in the Letter to the Hebrews'" for the God and God Incarnate Study Group (Moderator: Douglas Blount) at the Annual National Meeting of the ETS (Nov 2009).

_____. "Psalm 110:1 and the New Testament," *Bibliotheca Sacra* 149:596 (1992): 438–53.

Bock, Darrell L. "Coming of Israel's King." In *Jesus the Messiah: Tracing the Promises, Expectations, and Coming of Israel's King*. Grand Rapids: Kregel: 2012.

Bruce, F. F. *The Epistle to the Hebrews*. Rev. ed. The New International Commentary on the New Testament. Grand Rapids: Eerdmans, 1990.

Cockerill, Gareth. "A Wesleyan Arminian View." In *Four Views on the Warning Passages in Hebrews*. Edited by Herbert W. Bateman IV. Grand Rapids: Kregel, 2007.

deSilva, David A. *Perseverance in Gratitude: A Socio-Rhetorical Commentary on the Epistle "to the Hebrews."* Grand Rapids: Eerdmans, 2000.

Dunn, James D. G. *Christology in the Making: A New Testament Inquiry into the Origins of the Doctrine of the Incarnation*. Philadelphia: Westminster, 1980.

Ellingworth, Paul. *The Epistle to the Hebrews: A Commentary on the Greek Text*. New International Greek Testament Commentary. Grand Rapids: Eerdmans, 1993.

Fanning, Buist M. "A Classical Reformed View." In *Four Views on the Warning Passages in Hebrews*. Edited by Herbert W. Bateman IV. Grand Rapids: Kregel, 2007.

Girdwood, Jim and Peter Verkruyse. *Hebrews*. The College Press NIV Commentary. Joplin: College Press, 1997.

Gleason, Randall C. "A Moderate Reformed View." In *Four Views on the Warning Passages in Hebrews*. Edited by Herbert W. Bateman IV. Grand Rapids: Kregel, 2007.

Guthrie, George H. *Hebrews*. The NIV Application Commentary. Grand Rapids: Zondervan, 1998.

_____. *The Structure of Hebrews: A Text-Linguistic Analysis*. Supplements to Novum Testamentum. Vol. 73. New York: Brill, 1994.

Hagner, Donald A. *Encountering the Book of Hebrews: An Exposition*. Encountering Biblical Studies. Grand Rapids: Baker Academic, 2002.

Hamerton-Kelly, Robert G. *Pre-Existence, Wisdom and the Son of Man: A Study of the Idea of Pre-Existence in the New Testament*. Cambridge, England: Cambridge University Press, 1973.

Hewett, Thomas. *The Epistle to the Hebrews: An Introduction and Commentary*. Tyndale New Testament Commentaries. Grand Rapids: Eerdmans, 1960.

Hodges, Zane. "Hebrews." In *Bible Knowledge Commentary: An Exposition of the Scriptures*. Vol. 2. Edited by John F. Walvoord and Roy B. Zuck. Wheaton: Victor Books, 1983.

Holmén, Tom. *Jesus & Jewish Covenant Theology*. Leiden: Brill, 2001.

Hughes, Philip E. *A Commentary on the Epistle to the Hebrews*. Grand Rapids: Eerdmans, 1977.

Kittel, G., and G. Friedrich, eds. *Theological Dictionary of New Testament*. Translated by G. W. Bromiley. 10 vols. Grand Rapids: Eerdmans, 1983.

Koester, Craig R. *Hebrews: A New Translation with Introduction and Commentary*. The Anchor Bible. Vol. 36. New York: Doubleday, 2001.

Laansma, Jon. *"I Will Give You Rest": The "Rest" Motif in the New Testament with Special Reference to Mt 11 and Heb 3–4*. Wissenschaftliche Untersuchungen zum Neuen Testament. Tübingen: Mohr Siebeck, 1997.

Lane, William L. *Hebrews 1–8*. Word Biblical Commentary. Vol. 47A. Dallas: Word, 1991.

———. *Hebrews 9–13*. Word Biblical Commentary. Vol. 47B. Dallas: Word, 1991.

Marshall, I. Howard. *Kept by the Power of God: A Study of Perseverance and Falling Away*. Minneapolis: Bethany Fellowship, 1969.

McKnight, Scot. "The Warning Passages of Hebrews: A Formal Analysis and Theological Conclusions." *Trinity Journal* NS 13:1 (1992): 21–59.

O'Brien, Peter T. *The Letter to the Hebrews*. The Pillar New Testament Commentary. Grand Rapids: Eerdmans, 2010.

Osborne, Grant. "A Classical Arminian View." In *Four Views on the Warning Passages in Hebrews*. Edited by Herbert W. Bateman IV. Grand Rapids: Kregel, 2007.

Peterson, David W. *Hebrews and Perfection: An Examination of the Concept of Perfection in the "Epistle to the Hebrews."* Society for New Testament Studies Monograph Series. Vol. 47. New York: Cambridge University Press, 1982.

Phillips, John. *Exploring Hebrews: An Expository Commentary*. John Phillips Commentary Series. Grand Rapids: Kregel, 1988.

Rhee, Victor (Sung-Yul). *Faith in Hebrews: Analysis within the Context of Christology, Eschatology, and Ethics*. Studies in Biblical Literature. Vol. 19. New York: Peter Lang, 2001.

Sappington, Thomas J. *Revelation and Redemption at Colossae*. Journal for the Study of the New Testament. Supplement Series. Vol. 53. Sheffield: JSOT Press, 1991.

Silva, Moises. "Perfection and Eschatology in Hebrews." *Westminster Theological Journal*, 39:1 (1976): 60–71.

Wray, Judith Hoch. *Rest as a Theological Metaphor in the Epistle to the Hebrews and the Gospel of Truth: Early Christian Homiletics of Rest*. SBL Dissertation Series 166. Atlanta: Scholars Press, 1998.

Part Four: Exegetical Matters in Hebrews

Aland, Kurt et al., eds. *The Greek New Testament*. 4th ed. Stüttgart: United Bible Societies, 1993.

Aland, Kurt and Barbara Aland. *The Text of the New Testament: An Introduction to the Critical Editions and to the Theory and Practice of Modern Textual Criticism*. Translated by Erroll F. Rhodes. Grand Rapids: Eerdmans, 1987.

Attridge, Harold W. *The Epistle to the Hebrews: A Commentary on the Epistle to the Hebrews*. Hermeneia. Philadelphia: Fortress, 1989. Pp. 31–32.

Bateman IV, Herbert W. *Early Jewish Hermeneutics and Hebrews 1:5–13: The Impact of Early Jewish Exegesis on the Interpretation of a Significant New Testament Passage.* American University Studies. New York: Peter Lang, 1997.

_____. "Expectations of Israel's King." In *Jesus the Messiah: Tracing the Promises, Expectations, and Coming of Israel's King.* Grand Rapids: Kregel: 2012.

_____. "Psalm 45:6–7 and Its Christological Contributions to Hebrews," *Trinity Journal* 22NS:1 (2001): 3–21.

_____. "Response to Nathan Holsteen's 'The Trinity in the Letter to the Hebrews'" for the God and God Incarnate Study Group (Moderator: Douglas Blount), presented and discussed at the Annual National Meeting of the ETS (Nov 2009).

_____. "Second Temple Exegetical Practices: Extra-biblical Examples of Exegesis Compared with Those in the Book of Hebrews." *Southwestern Journal of Theology* 53:1 (2010): 26–54.

_____. "Two First Century Messianic Uses of the OT: Heb 1:5–13 and 4QFlor 1:1–19." *Journal of the Evangelical Theological Society* 38 (1995): 11–27.

Bullinger, E. W. *Figures of Speech Used in the Bible, Explained and Illustrated.* London: Messrs. Eyre and Spotiswoode, 1898. Reprint Grand Rapids: Baker Book House, 1968.

deSilva, David A. *Perseverance in Gratitude: A Socio-Rhetorical Commentary on the Epistle "to the Hebrews."* Grand Rapids: Eerdmans, 2000.

Ellingworth, Paul. *The Epistle to the Hebrews: A Commentary on the Greek Text.* New International Greek Testament Commentary. Grand Rapids: Eerdmans, 1993.

Greenlee, J. Harold. *Introduction to New Testament Textual Criticism.* Grand Rapids: Eerdmans, 1989.

Heen, Erik M. and Philip D. W. Krey, eds. *Hebrews.* Ancient Christian Commentary on Scripture: New Testament. Vol. 10. Downers Grove: InterVarsity Press, 2005.

Koester, Craig R. *Hebrews: A New Translation with Introduction and Commentary.* The Anchor Bible. Vol. 36. New York: Doubleday, 2001.

Lane, William L. *Hebrews 1–8.* Word Biblical Commentary. Vol. 47A. Dallas: Word, 1991.

_____. *Hebrews 9–13.* Word Biblical Commentary. Vol. 47B. Dallas: Word, 1991.

Longenecker, Richard N. *Biblical Exegesis in the Apostolic Period.* 2nd ed. Grand Rapids: Eerdmans, 1999.

_____. *The Christology of Early Jewish Christianity.* Studies in Biblical Theology 17. London: SCM Press, 1970.

Metzger, Bruce M. *The Text of the New Testament: Its Transmission, Corruption, and Restoration.* 3rd enl. ed. New York: Oxford University Press, 1992.

_____. *A Textual Commentary on the Greek New Testament.* 2nd ed. New York: United Bible Societies, 1994.

Moffatt, James. *Critical and Exegetical Commentary on the Epistle to the Hebrews.* International Critical Commentary. Edinburgh: T&T Clark, 1948.

Nestle–Aland 27th edition of *Novum Testamentum Graece* and the 4th revised edition of *The Greek New Testament* published by the United Bible Society. New York: United Bible Societies, 1994.

Rhee, Victor (Sung-Yul). *Faith in Hebrews: Analysis within the Context of Christology, Eschatology, and Ethics.* Studies in Biblical Literature. Vol. 19. New York: Peter Lang, 2001.

Trotter, Andrew H. *Interpreting the Epistle to the Hebrews.* Guides to New Testament Exegesis. Grand Rapids: Baker Books, 1997.